Commenda

CW00403333

This book takes an honest look at the gende
extraordinary impact of that imbalance on so
asks real questions that we need to face, calli........
different ministries and areas of church life – especially to look at our evangelism and
discipleship of men.
**Dr Rachel Jordan-Wolf, National Mission and Evangelism Advisor to the
Church of England**

This book is so practical, theological and pragmatic in its approach that it would
enhance any church ministry in the totality of church being family. It is also prepared
to base a lot of its findings on research, which I found enlightening, and its abundantly
practical approach to the issues the church family faces is so exciting. It is inspiring to
see how the church could look different in the future.
Roy Crowne, Executive Director, HOPE

This book not only articulates a compelling vision – that our churches have a healthy
view of Christian singleness, dating and marriage – but also sets out the practical
steps we need to take in order to see that vision become a reality. With informed
contributions from those who are experts in their fields it addresses not just the 'what'
but the 'how'. All churches will benefit from the wisdom in this book. Read it for a
wake-up call to action alongside some clear strategies to implement that will make a
difference to our churches in every generation.
Katharine Hill, UK Director, Care for the Family

What a vital subject and a key resource to provoke thousands of conversations.
I'm convinced as a church community, we are just not talking enough about our
gender imbalance, singleness, 'going out' (dating) or commitment (marriage). My
encouragement to church leaders would be: share it around the team, discuss it with
those who are single in your church and see if you can agree a way forward.
Steve Clifford, General Director, Evangelical Alliance

This is a great book with an important message. It deserves to be widely read. The
authors bring relevant theological insight and psychological expertise, and draw on
deep wells of practical experience and spiritual wisdom. Readers will grow in their
understanding of the key issues and be inspired to work together with others for the
emergence of a gender balanced church that gives time and attention to teaching
about healthy Christian singleness, dating and marriage. As the current Principal
of Ridley Hall, I'm thrilled that this college hosted the conference that led to the

EDITED BY ANNABEL CLARKE & NATHAN BLACKABY

7

REASONS

YOUR

CHURCH

NEEDS

MORE

MEN

How to lead a gender balanced
church supporting healthy singleness,
dating, marriage & youth

Some notes of thanks

Thank you to Helene Felter and everyone who has helped with the production of this book.

Thank you to the chapter authors for donating the royalties from the book to the work of The Engage Network.

First edition.

To the best of our knowledge, all facts in this book are correct at the time of publication. If you believe there to be any inaccuracies, please contact us via our website (www.engage-mcmp.org.uk) so that issues can be addressed as appropriate in the next edition.

Unless otherwise indicated, all Scripture references are from the Holy Bible: New International Version (NIV), copyright © 1973, 1978, 1984, 2011 by Biblica.

A catalogue record for this book is available from the British Library.

Cover design and typesetting by Beth Evans.

ISBN: 9781973447016

Independently published by The Engage Network.
Email: info@engage-mcmp.org.uk
Website: www.engage-mcmp.org.uk

Editors

Annabel Clarke

Annabel Clarke is a Chartered Psychologist, an Associate Fellow of the British Psychological Society, and works as a Senior Specialist Educational Psychologist for a large Local Authority. She has over 20 years' experience supporting children, young people, adults, families and organisations, at work and through ministry in local churches. She is Co-Founder and Co-Chair of The Engage Network, facilitating collaboration between national Christian organisations and churches to help 'make Christian marriage possible'.

Nathan Blackaby

Nathan Blackaby is CEO of Christian Vision for Men (CVM). Following 10 years of supporting work in Brazil, including as a Chaplain for Teen Challenge (Christian drug rehabilitation centre), Nathan and his wife returned to the UK in 2011. After pastoring a church with Rural Ministries he became involved with CVM. He has many years' experience of effectively equipping and engaging the church and individuals to boldly step out, share their faith, and see a revival of men coming to faith in Jesus Christ. Nathan is Co-Chair of The Engage Network.

Authors

Harry Benson
Research Director, Marriage Foundation. Chapter 3.

Nathan Blackaby
CEO of Christian Vision for Men and Co-Chair of The Engage Network. Chapters 6 and 12.

Revd Dr Adrian Chatfield
Fellow of Ridley Hall, Cambridge and Co-Founder of The Engage Network. Chapter 2.

Annabel Clarke
Chartered Psychologist, Co-Founder and Co-Chair of The Engage Network. Chapters 1, 4, 5 and 8.

Laura Hancock
Director of Resources, British Youth for Christ. Chapter 11.

David and Liz Percival
Directors of 2-in-2-1. Chapter 9.

Paula Pridham
Executive Director of Care for the Family. Chapter 10.

Revd Kate Wharton
Vicar of St. Bart's Church, Roby and Assistant National Leader for New Wine. Chapter 7.

Contributors

We would like to thank the many people who contributed to the consultation sessions which form the basis of much of this book. Groups of experts from across the UK gathered to share ideas for a vision of 'what it would look like if things were working well in the church' for their ministry field. They included:

- Mark Chester, Founder, Who Let The Dads Out? (men's ministry).
- David King, England and Wales Single Adult Ministry Coordinator, New Testament Church of God (singleness).
- Revd Will van der Hart, Pastoral Chaplain Holy Trinity Brompton, The Dating Course & The Singleness Conversations HTB (dating).
- Fiona Banes, Executive Director, Time for Marriage (marriage).
- Katharine Hill, UK Director, Care for the Family (marriage).
- Richard and Maria Kane, Marriage Week International (marriage).
- Revd Nicky and Sila Lee, Associate Vicar Holy Trinity Brompton and Founders of The Marriage and Parenting Courses, HTB and Alpha International (marriage).
- Jason Royce, Director, The Souster Youth Trust (young people).
- Sarah Smith, CEO, acet UK (young people, parenting).

Foreword

We, like the Israelites in exile in Babylon, live in an alien culture in the UK — a culture in which long-term commitment is under-valued; a society with the highest level of family instability in the Western world; an environment in which marriage is too often delayed and sometimes avoided altogether. And the church is inevitably affected, sometimes obviously, sometimes more subtly, by the values of this culture in which we live.

We are called as God's people to discern his word to us today in order to march to a different tune, to build communities of Christians who seek to live by God's ways for us, and to influence the world around us with the love and truth we ourselves experience.

This is the work of Engage, and this book is the fruit of many hours of praying and planning, of listening to one another and discussing the way forward, of seeking to engage the church more nationally on a topic of supreme importance for us all and of acute pain for many within the body of Christ.

"Marry and have sons and daughters; find wives for your sons and give your daughters in marriage, so that they too may have sons and daughters. Increase in number there; do not decrease," was God's word to his people. Some Christians know they are called to singleness, and the writers of this book affirm that gift as much as the gift of marriage. But many others who are currently single would love to be married in order to fulfil what they believe to be God's plans and purposes for their lives. Every reader, whether single or married, whether or not a church leader, can play a part in helping to make that desire a reality.

You may come across an idea in the following pages that you feel is a way you could make a difference. When you do, pray about it, discuss it with others and take the first brave steps to put it into action. As Adrian Chatfield writes in his fascinating and compelling chapter on the theological foundations for this work: "a major thrust of this book is that as Christians we need to be much more proactive in making the possibility and privilege of Christian marriage a realistic one."

Changing a culture involves many people, requires many initiatives and can take a long time. But, as the Chinese proverb goes, a long journey starts with the first step. God raised up Jeremiah to encourage his people in Babylon that they could make a difference to their situation then. He has raised up Annabel, Nathan and the other contributors of this book to be his mouthpiece around the topics addressed here that together we might make a difference today.

Nicky and Sila Lee
Founders of The Marriage Course

Contents

CHAPTER 1

What is The Engage Network and why is it needed?

Annabel Clarke

During a haircut, two men in their twenties were recently in conversation:

Barber: How's it going then?
Client: Yeah, not bad thanks. How about you – you still seeing that girl?
Barber: No, we split up.
Client: Oh, sorry about that.
Barber: Well, that's life. You had a busy weekend?
Client: Well actually I went to a wedding on Saturday.
Barber: Oh right?
Client: Yeah, it was a Christian wedding. My friend is like, you know, properly Christian. It was really good actually.
Barber (sounding surprised): Really?
Client: Yeah, lots of people there. Lots of girls...(suddenly thinks)...Mate! You should go to church! There are loads of hot women there!

Across the other side of the salon, I was getting my hair cut too. You might think I shouldn't have been listening to their conversation, but since I was the only other person there, it was a bit hard not to. Yes, we might prefer a guy to go to church for reasons other than the women, but still, I couldn't help thinking – the hairdresser's isn't usually the place you expect to hear a fairly accurate analysis of the statistical church gender imbalance. If it's that clear to a non-Christian visitor, how come so many in the church have yet to understand the problem or do anything about it?

The whole topic was something I first came across in 2007. I found a page of data on the internet that showed there were nearly twice as many women as men in the church. The ratio really struck me, as did the implications for men, women and children. Where were all the men? What about the women who won't be able to marry a Christian man, or get married at all? What about spiritual fatherlessness for children of the next generation? And what about the children who won't even be born because of the imbalance?

Over the next few years, I started to hear about ministries and people that seemed relevant to the situation of the church gender imbalance, but who weren't necessarily jointly working on the issues. They included ministries around men, singleness, dating, marriage, young people and others. It seemed like it would be useful to get them together and join the dots.

I'm absolutely not a 36-visions-before-breakfast sort of person at all, but one night in 2010 I had a very powerful 'God' dream. I had an extraordinary sense of his presence, in a way that I'd never had before (or since). All I knew was that in the dream, a friend from church was praying for me and we were at 'a small conference at Ridley'. Ridley Hall Theological College in Cambridge was a place I'd lived close to for 15 years, but had never visited. Suddenly, less than a week after the dream, I was invited to a seminar there, went along, and met one of the senior tutors (Adrian Chatfield). Adrian understood the issues, and in 2012, we got together some key ministry leaders and held our first Symposium. And so it was that we found ourselves at 'a small conference at Ridley', as the dream had indicated.

From these beginnings, The Engage Network has become a growing group of national Christian organisations and churches in the UK, with interest from other countries too. We have a steering group whose members are from different relevant ministry fields. Our vision is this:

> *"To make singleness or marriage a genuine choice for*
> *all Christian women and men, through a church which*
> *is gender balanced and teaches about healthy Christian*
> *singleness, dating and marriage."*

We hold events for Christian ministry and church leaders and we have a resource website (www.engage-mcmp.org.uk). We facilitate joint work between different partners, which has ranged from research projects to connecting speakers for national conferences. We run sessions for theological colleges or groups of ministers. And very often, it's about promoting all the great work that other people are doing.

7 reasons your church needs more men

To give an overview, here are the reasons your church needs more men:
- For men.
- For women.
- For children and young people.

- For singleness.
- For dating and relationships.
- For marriage.
- For parenting.

These reasons will be threaded through this book. It will firstly explore some of the issues that the church is experiencing because of the lack of men, and show how these really do constitute a crisis situation. Later, it will consider how to lead church in ways that can resolve the problems. This chapter will look at why the Engage vision and work is needed.

Could I suggest that as you read the book, you stay aware of how you feel? You may respond differently depending on your age or gender, whether you're single or married, and whether you have children or not. Sometimes the authors might talk about things that are outside your own personal experience. Hopefully, though, that will be useful, because part of the value of Engage has been to bring different people together, so that everyone can share and learn from each other's experience and expertise.

Before going further, I'd like to outline a few points that underpin the work of Engage.

- We're keen for what we do to be biblically-based and research-based. Adrian Chatfield gives a theological perspective on our work in chapter 2, and relevant research is referred to throughout the book.
- The Great Commission is central. Jesus said, "Go and make disciples of all nations, baptising them in the name of the Father and of the Son and of the Holy Spirit, and teaching them to obey everything I have commanded you" (Matthew 28:19-20). Engage is about people having the opportunity to hear and respond to the gospel, and experience effective discipleship.
- Relationship with Jesus, spiritual and emotional flourishing, and relationships of all kinds are key discipleship issues for everyone, requiring regular teaching from churches.
- The Bible values singleness and marriage. Single people are equally valuable and competent as married people. At the same time, God's design from the start has been for marriage to reflect his covenant relationship with the church, to be foundational to society, and to be personally experienced by most people.
- Engage is about 'making Christian marriage possible' (not compulsory!). By this, we mean marriage between Christians. Because the context of the church gender imbalance is core to our work, our focus is on relationships between men and women, including making it possible for a single Christian woman to marry a single Christian man, making

it possible for any emotional barriers to marriage to be resolved, making it possible for a non-Christian spouse to come to faith, making it possible for marriages to be all they can potentially be when God is at their centre, and making it possible for the church's children to marry a Christian when they grow up. In the context of Engage, we use the phrase 'gender balanced' to mean an equal number of men and women.

- Engage is about working together so that everyone benefits. It's about men and women equally supporting each other. It involves organisations and churches collaborating because we see the overall 'big picture'.

Now more than ever, it seems that the church needs to articulate a clear vision of what healthy Christian singleness, dating and relationships and marriage can involve. Christians need to speak this out, live it, and model it to the next generation and the rest of society as a witness to God's grace and love. Engage therefore set up a series of consultation events which were attended by relevant experts from across the UK. We wanted to co-create a positive vision of what things could look like if they were working well in the church in each of the ministry areas involved in Engage. The idea being this: if the church can clearly articulate where it wants to get to, it's more likely to get there. We used a structured framework, which helped us come up with a series of 'consultation vision grids', which form the basis of chapters 6-11. You'll see these later in the book, each at the end of the appropriate chapter. We then asked one person from each of the ministry areas to develop key points from their group's vision grid into a chapter, to explain things further.

Before we look at these solutions and ways forward, however, we need to understand the problems and issues that we're facing.

Background

A YouGov survey in 2014 showed that in Great Britain, a third of adults in church are single.[1] The largest ever survey of its kind of over 3000 single adult Christians (*Singleness in the UK Church*, Pullinger, 2014) showed that most of them (57%) could not see they would ever marry a non-Christian, while 31% said they might, but the person would need to be sympathetic to their faith.[2] In addition to this preference indicated by single people, we can probably assume that Christians who are married to a non-Christian would want their spouses to come to share their love for Jesus. Research by the Evangelical Alliance has also found that over 90% of Christian couples expressed happiness with their marriage, compared to 66% of those in a mixed marriage (a Christian married to a non-Christian).[3]

Sometimes, of course, neither of the spouses are Christians when they marry, and one of them later comes to faith. But most Christians would probably say that it's best for someone who is already a Christian to be married to someone who shares their faith. They might refer to Paul's teaching in 1 Corinthians 7:39 that "A woman is bound to her husband as long as he lives. But if her husband dies, she is free to marry anyone she wishes, but he must belong to the Lord." Paul also writes in 2 Corinthians 6:14, "Do not be yoked together with unbelievers. For what do righteousness and wickedness have in common? Or what fellowship can light have with darkness?" (For a more in-depth theological perspective on this, please see Dr David Instone-Brewer's article on the Engage website.[4])

However, while Christians might want to be married to someone who is also a Christian, how often can that aspiration become a reality?

Barriers to Christian marriage

At the moment, there seem to be three main barriers to Christian marriage.

The church gender imbalance
Current figures suggest that there is a gender imbalance ratio in the church of about 40% men to 60% women overall (we'll look at the relevant research in more detail in chapter 4).

This means:
- Men aren't being given equal opportunity as women to respond to the gospel and grow in faith – current church approaches are not as effective for them as for women.
- Christian women don't have equal opportunity as Christian men to get married to a Christian and have children.

Lack of teaching in the church
In the church as a whole, there's a significant lack of teaching about marriage, about restoring the gender balance, or about relationships in general. In chapter 3, Harry Benson explains some of the present wider societal context around marriage. It's really important that we're aware of what 'real life' is like, so that we can effectively support those in church and our communities. Churches very rarely get teaching on healthy Christian singleness. You do sometimes get teaching on marriage (e.g. marriage preparation/marriage

courses), but usually only if you've already found someone to marry, and perhaps that's leaving it a bit late? You hardly ever get teaching on how to get from A to B in a godly way (i.e. via dating and relationships). Each of these aspects of teaching, however, is vital.

Lack of awareness of the situation

Many Christians are unaware of the church gender imbalance and its impact, and therefore there's a general lack of action. Even for those who are conscious of it, we've often heard church leaders say things like "I know it's an issue, but what can you do?" To help us be informed, we'll consider current research on the numbers of men in church in chapter 4 and possible reasons for the imbalance in chapter 5.

Consequences

There are many consequences of these three barriers. Some of the key ones are outlined next, and I'll cover a bit more on singleness, dating and relationships, because these are usually discussed less often in the church.

Consequences for men

Church is failing to reach men, and there's a massive need for more effective evangelism and discipleship for them. Fewer men in church means fewer opportunities for them to develop close friendships with other Christian men. Supporting each other in life and growth, including in their singleness, dating and relationships, marriage and parenting is then more difficult. For example, how often do Christian men intentionally disciple, support, and challenge other men about their relationships with women? In chapter 6, Nathan Blackaby will explore how the church can reach and disciple men more effectively. It is important to note that this book focuses more on men and church, because we want to address the impact of the church gender imbalance. However, women's evangelism, discipleship and ministry are equally important!

Consequences for singleness

A third of adult church members are single, as we saw earlier. For every couple, there is a single person. There are a range of reasons why Christians might be single. Some have never married, some have been married before. Some may have made a conscious choice to be and stay single (either temporarily or long-term), but most probably won't have done so.

YouGov research (2014) found that overall, there are up to double the number of single women than single men in church.[5] Evangelical Alliance research (2012) found that among the over 55s, the imbalance rises to three single women to one single man, and 61% of adult Christians under 35 are single.[6] This is a very high proportion, and much higher than in previous generations. There are various reasons for this situation, which include:

- The limited number of available single men.
- Less expectation from general society that people will get married – more couples cohabit now, but this isn't so common among Christians.
- More people experiencing their parents splitting up, meaning some people avoid marriage because they are afraid of being hurt, or of failing, or of repeating mistakes they have seen others make.
- 'FOMO' (Fear Of Missing Out – a very prevalent modern phenomenon) if they commit to one person.
- Protracted singleness due to unresolved spiritual and emotional issues for some people.
- The lack of teaching and ministry around healthy singleness and dating and relationships and marriage.

There is often a 'spiritual re-framing' (whether uninformed or unintentional) of the unprecedented rate of singleness in our present-day church, which is simply often deemed 'a God-given gift' for individuals – whether it's wanted or unwanted, and whether it's healthy or unhealthy. No further questions about the contemporary setting are asked. This approach, though, is a mistake.

Christians often refer to 1 Corinthians 7, where Paul writes about singleness and marriage. Paul tells us that the historical context at the time in Corinth is one of "much immorality" (v1) and in "present crisis" (v26). Biblical commentators note that it's a situation of particular suffering, persecution and distress.

In chapter 7 verse 2, Paul addresses the issue they've put to him – "It is good for a man not to marry" – by saying, "But since there is so much immorality, each man should have his own wife, and each woman her own husband." (He notes how they belong to each other and should avoid sexual temptation from outside the marriage.) In verse 6, however, he explains, "I say this as a concession, not as a command"; marriage is desirable and part of God's plan, but not mandatory, especially under the difficult circumstances in Corinth. Verse 7 continues: "I wish that all men were as I am. But each man has his own gift from God; one has this gift, another has that." As The Message version puts it, "Sometimes I wish everyone were single like me – a simpler life in many ways! But celibacy is not for everyone any more than marriage is. God gives the gift of the single life to some, the gift of the married life to others." Paul describes singleness as a gift, but also acknowledges that a life of celibacy isn't for everyone.

The conclusion often drawn from this verse is that if someone is single, then they have 'the gift of singleness', and if someone is married, then they have the 'gift of marriage'. Their current status is simply equated with a 'gift'. The words 'calling' and 'vocation' are sometimes used by Christians instead of 'gift' in the same sort of way in relation to singleness.

Spiritual gifts are described in various Bible passages such as Romans 12:6-8, 1 Corinthians 12:8-10 and 28-31, Ephesians 4:11-13 and 1 Peter 4:9-11. What is the purpose of these gifts that God gives? These passages tell us that they're about building up and strengthening the health of the body of Christ (the church), to prepare us for works of service, and for the praise of God. In today's 'present crisis' of the church gender imbalance and lack of appropriate teaching, however, singleness is not just a 'gift' in the biblical sense, in that it's given as a special grace to some, and it builds up and strengthens the health of the body of Christ. Certainly, some people may feel they have a gift of singleness or a particular calling or vocation to be single, and the church must support them. But this is completely different from enforced singleness, experienced by up to half of all single Christian women, due to the church gender imbalance. In addition, there are at least half a million more women than men in the GB church[7] – if these women stayed single and childless instead of marrying a non-Christian and having a couple of children each, this could mean potentially a million babies whose births are prevented because of the church gender imbalance. This makes the issue an intergenerational one.

Simply to say that all this is due to a God-given 'gift' for every single person is just not appropriate. Unfortunately, it is largely due to the church not addressing the issues we've been discussing. Some might also say that the situation sounds rather like part of an enemy strategy to weaken the church and people's relationships.

Back in 1 Corinthians 7:8-9, Paul continues, "To the unmarried and the widows I say: It is good for them to stay unmarried, as I am. But if they cannot control themselves, they should marry, for it is better to marry than to burn with passion." In other words, it's good for them to stay unmarried, but if they want to get married, then they should. Later he specifically says in verse 25 that the reason his view is that it is good for the single women "to remain as you are" and the unmarried (men) not to look for a wife is because "of the present crisis." This is a teaching for the specific context of Corinth at the time. Elsewhere (e.g. Ephesians 5:22-23; Colossians 3:18-19; 1 Timothy 3:2, 12; 5:14), Paul speaks very much in favour of the married state.

What are the overall messages of this passage that we can actually apply to single men and women in our own context today? These seem to be:

- If you want to stay single, that's good.
- If you want to get married, that's good.

In the culture of those times, when in general, everyone was expected to get married, the fact that Paul taught that if people want to stay single, then that's good, would have been radically liberating. If Paul was to preach to us now in our modern 'present crisis' however, would he perhaps actually teach that many more single people should be getting married (like most of them want to do), and the church should be making much more of an effort in appropriate ways to help them do so? Balanced teaching for everyone about healthy singleness and healthy dating and relationships and healthy marriage is an essential part of this.

We need people to know that it's possible to live a fulfilled life as a single person. At the same time, it's important to acknowledge that it's possible for some single mature Christians to be flourishing in every aspect of life, but dealing with hidden grief about not having a spouse and children – these aspects (and the consequences) are the only ones in which they aren't fulfilled. There are a lot of deep issues here which we need to acknowledge, hold together, and sensitively consider. In chapter 7, Kate Wharton will explore in more depth how churches can be understanding of single Christians and the issues they face, and help them thrive as they are included in community.

Consequences for women: the single sacrifice

I recently met up for coffee with Emma, a fabulous friend of mine who's 22. She's godly, fun, intelligent and single. She told me there are virtually no single men in her church. I explained the national gender imbalance, and she immediately said, "But it means that half the Christian women have to choose between marrying a non-Christian and staying single and childless for the rest of your life – and that's no choice at all!"

If women are genuinely and honestly content with their singleness, then of course that is good. But as we've already indicated, Emma is describing how many single Christian women feel. It's a stance that non-Christians (and some Christians) may find completely incomprehensible or completely wrong. In one sense, of course, all Christian single people have a choice about whether or not to get married. They can marry a Christian or a non-Christian. In another sense though, many Christian women don't have a choice, if they want to marry a Christian man who shares their faith and/or believe the Bible teaches that this is what they should do. If a church also teaches this but is doing nothing about the gender imbalance in their congregation (if there is one), and is doing nothing to support women in finding suitable marriage partners, then there's a significant disconnect between its words and actions.

After a session which Engage ran for all the students at one theological college, a single female ordinand told me, "It's excruciating – and no one ever talks about it." Many women have to reconcile their suffering, resulting from faithful sacrifice, with a God who loves them. One respondent from the biggest ever national survey of single Christians summarised what it's like for many women who are choosing to be single instead of marry a non-Christian:

> "It has made me count the cost of following Christ more than any other single thing."[8]

Consequences for women: church causing childlessness

It is important that assumptions are not made about why a woman does not have children, or how they feel about their situation. Some women may not want children and some may feel content about not having children, and it is important that this is acknowledged and understood. But for many, that's not the case.

Andrea is a godly woman I know who was single until her late thirties. She then got married. She worked with children and had always longed to have her own, but she and her husband struggled with infertility for several years. Despite her grief and heartache, she told me, "At least now I'm better off in four ways than when I was single and childless. I've got a husband, so at least I can have sex and try and get pregnant. I've got a life partner to share and process the pain with. We can try IVF. We can consider adoption together."

Most Christians are empathetic towards childless couples they know who would like a family. Even so, 70% of respondents in an Evangelical Alliance survey didn't agree that their church offers good pastoral support for couples in this situation.[9] More prevalent, but much less recognised, however, is the situation of single Christian women who would like to have children, but aren't able to because they can't find a suitable marriage partner.

Many single women who can't have children have told me their experiences, and it's worth noting that they're all mature Christian women, who are involved in leadership of some sort in their local churches:

> "Nobody ever stops to think what it might be like for me when they're all talking about their children." (Louise, 42)
> "The biological time bomb makes you constantly feel like your body's about to explode." (Susie, 39)
> "You spend 10 years slowly watching your children die." (Nina, 48)
> "All my friends are talking about their grandchildren, but I can't – and my niece has just had a baby." (Claire, 62)

"The enemy is stealing a generation of children, but no one is seeing it." (Laura, 65)

To investigate this area a bit more I carried out a survey of over 300 single Christian women over the age of 35, who don't have children (biological, fostered or adopted).[10] What was interesting, firstly, was how many of the respondents specifically said they appreciated being asked their views on these issues; "Thank you so much for doing this, it's very necessary," "It's the first time I've ever formally been asked to talk about this subject, and yet it occupies so much of my brain and heart space!"

When asked if they agreed that their church offers good pastoral support for single Christian women who are childless but would like a family, 32% strongly disagreed, 33% disagreed, and 27% weren't sure. Some women felt that overall, not having children had made their faith stronger (24%), most reported a neutral impact (60%), and 16% said that it had made their faith weaker. Nearly half (45%) reported that not having children has had a negative impact on their emotional wellbeing and social relationships. When asked to describe in one word how they felt about not having children, some highlighted that they felt 'OK' and noted the freedom that their situation could bring. However, most used negative descriptions, as shown in Figure 1, and nearly half (46%) reported that they are dealing with grief and loss around not having children.

Figure 1. Single Christian women's feelings about not having children.

The main reasons attributed for them not having children were 'There aren't enough single Christian men in the church', 'I want to get married before I have children and I'm not married yet', 'I haven't met the right man yet' and 'I didn't meet the right man in time'. Looking ahead to the future, 55% said that they had considered fostering or adopting a child/children, 18% had considered having their eggs frozen, and 13% had considered using a sperm donor.

They reported that some of the least helpful things people had said with regards to them not having children included:

"Well, you should have got married, shouldn't you!"

"At least you don't have to get up early/change nappies/always deal with children etc."

"It's God's will."

"Just get a dog."

Some of the things people had said which they found most helpful included:

"I know it doesn't take away the pain but we are so grateful for the input you have with our children."

"This must be hard and it's OK to grieve this. How can I help?"

"We will keep on praying."

"My nephew said he'd look after me when I'm old."

Here are key things the women reported that church could helpfully do to support them:

"Provide a community where everyone is included, encouraged and celebrated."

"Address the issue of the lack of men in our congregations!"

"Recognise our grief and talk to us about our experiences."

"Invite us into your family life, but recognise that that won't be helpful for everyone."

Another practical point noted was that it's usually best to ask someone a general question such as "Do you have family nearby?" rather than directly "Do you have children?" This way you won't potentially risk highlighting what might be the most painful aspect of their life, and the conversation can continue more easily.

Some women find Gateway Women[11] (run by non-Christians) or Saltwater and Honey[12] (run by Christians) helpful in dealing with involuntary childlessness (whether married or single). But for church leaders, as a minister once told me, "If it matters to my flock, it matters to me. If more men need to hear the gospel, and women are suffering and can't find Christian husbands and have children, it's my pastoral responsibility to do something about it and help change the situation." Let us pray for more ministers to take the same approach.

Consequences for psycho-social dynamics

Sometimes there are healthy relationships between single men and women, however overall, the church gender imbalance has had a significant adverse effect on the psycho-social dynamics between them. In summary, there is now a power imbalance in men's favour, which is in turn impacting on Christian singleness, dating, relationships and marriage. Such inter-personal patterns were reported in *Singleness in the UK Church* research survey.[13] Maybe you often see these things too, or maybe you're not aware they're happening. They include:

- Competition between women for men.
- Men feel 'pounced on', or are passive/picky.
- Women are often like 'bees round a honey pot' (a man).
- Men get a better deal (e.g. women who are more spiritually mature, more educated, better looking).
- Women pro-actively pursue men.
- Men are indecisive/play the large field without always sufficiently valuing women.
- It's hard to make friends without everyone thinking this initiates a relationship.
- Men keep waiting for someone better to come along, wonder why they cannot find someone, wonder if there's something wrong with them, or say finding compatible women is difficult.
- Women give up and date non-Christians, whom they report pay them more attention.
- Older men pursue women 10 or 20 years younger with whom to have children.
- Older women are left silently dealing with lifelong childlessness.

These dynamics were again corroborated by a survey focused on a large UK church with over 1000 members, involving 200 surveys from singles aged 18-40 (Verbi, 2017).[14] The report describes how:

- A dyadic power is very present and influential within the gender imbalanced dating market of the church.
- A significant over-supply of women in the dating market results in a very low level of exclusive dating commitment from men, but relatively high level of emotional and sometimes physical intimacy given by women. To gain access to the resources offered by women, church men do not need to put in the same level of effort or the same level of commitment as they would in a balanced dating market.
- Women continue to give to men emotionally, despite not only poor levels of initiation and commitment, but also a general lack of respect

(men can literally 'afford' to treat women with less honour).

- Women are more than twice as likely to be asked on a date by a non-Christian than a Christian because of a much more balanced level of supply and demand ("I've had more lovely/respectful dates on [Tinder and Happn] in the past 6 months than in 3 years at church"; "[Non-Christian men] don't have as many options as [men] in the church, they have to make more of an effort. And they actually have to treat someone well").
- Men perceive that they can achieve a 'super model' girlfriend, who fits some very specific criteria, whilst women would almost always say yes to any date.
- 70% of the women want men to 'man-up' and ask them out.

Clearly not all dynamics between all single men and women are unhealthy, but this overview shows our current, very sobering reality, which is more widespread than many realise. Unless we address this culture, any teaching about dating and relationships will inevitably have limited positive impact.

Another important element in this mix is the wider spiritual context. Ephesians 6:12 tells us "For our struggle is not against flesh and blood, but against the rulers, against the authorities, against the powers of this dark world and against the spiritual forces of evil in the heavenly realms." Lin Button, leader of the Healing Prayer School ministry, has made the following observation, based on many years of extensive pastoral experience:

"My big picture thinking on the shortage of available Christian men is that they are being held captive by the enemy. We have had two World Wars which physically killed or severely emotionally damaged two/three generations of men and now we are in an invisible spiritual war whereby the enemy has got men in captivity. Some he has so blinded and deafened that they have never become Christians. Others are converted but emotionally damaged.

The emotional damage I can see from several different angles. In some families there have been generations of silent fathers, thus leaving their sons ill-equipped for the modern world where women expect more from men in terms of emotional support and spiritual intimacy. Very frightening for some men. Secondly, they have bonded together to make the prison more comfortable. This means that whenever one of the tribe finds a woman, for these men there is, at a deep unrecognised level, a mixture of betrayal and jealousy. This results in the woman not really being welcomed into the friendship group and then the guy wondering if she is really 'his type socially'. The whole relationship is then sabotaged. Thirdly, these men seem to have experienced some sort of arrested development. When they come to their senses in their mid-to-late forties they then want someone (younger) who can have children. I am not sure if this is naive but genuine, or another defence mechanism, as the sort of women they then want a relationship with are never going to say 'Yes'. Some men are too imprisoned to be free to enter into a woman's world."[15]

We urgently need to call out and address these dynamics and needs, and equalise the church gender balance. Otherwise, we will continue to prevent the growth of healthy Christian men, women, singleness and marriage, both now and in the future.

Consequences for dating and relationships

As a result of what we've outlined so far, we are now in a situation where the dating and relationships culture in the church is pretty paralysed. Research has shown that 54% of single Christian adults said that they haven't dated for at least a year, or, it is many years since they last went on a date.[16]

To counteract secular dating attitudes that damaged and devalued people, a young American church pastor (Joshua Harris) taught Christians to reject dating in his 1997 book *I Kissed Dating Goodbye*.[17] This hugely influenced the dating scene in the US, UK and other countries, but actually contributed to a much more 'high stakes' pressurised culture, where a single man just meeting up with a single woman already implied very serious intentions. (Harris now says he regrets this and has changed his views.)

To counteract the difficulties caused, Henry Cloud (an American Psychologist, well known for co-authoring the *Boundaries* series with John Townsend), wrote a book called *How to Get a Date Worth Keeping*. His stated aim was to teach Christians to date more widely in a godly and honouring way, and to de-pressurise dating without de-valuing people, whilst learning more about themselves, others and relationships in the process.

Based on years of observing the Christian dating culture in the UK, I would encourage church leaders to clarify for people that (in the UK at least), there are two very distinct stages to navigate before engagement. Firstly, 'dating', and secondly 'relationships'. The days of it being possible to 'just get to know someone at church then start an exclusive relationship' are long gone for most people unless they go to a large church with lots of single people to choose from.

In today's world, I would suggest that 'dating' in the UK can be accurately and practically defined as "getting to know someone with a view to seeing whether or not we want to be in a relationship", i.e. meeting up with someone between once and a few times. People need to be what I call 'intentional but not intense' about dating. Dating these days includes using online approaches to meet a wider range of people.

A 'relationship' (or 'going out' in the UK) can be defined as "getting to know someone with a view to seeing whether or not we want to get engaged", i.e. an exclusive, romantic relationship. It's not suggested that teenagers in relationships should be thinking about engagement, but in adulthood, this is applicable. In the UK at least, conflating the term 'dating' with the term 'a relationship' can cause a lot of misunderstanding and confusion, and perpetuate our current, unhelpful 'high stakes' culture, where people aren't sure if a date might automatically mean we're thinking about marriage.

People need to have a clear understanding and overview of both stages, which is why the consultation vision grid and chapter about Dating and Relationships is structured into separate sections for Dating and Relationships. Within each of these, it is also helpful to consider and analyse what needs to happen at the beginning, middle and end. This isn't because we want Christians to follow some sort of set formula and abandon all enjoyment and spontaneity! But because psychologically, it is helpful for people to have a 'mental map' they can explicitly know, talk about openly with friends and church members, and follow. This way, they can feel more confident, and they are more likely to reach the right destination wisely and safely – whether this is breaking up or moving on to the next stage. If this sort of 'map' was widely understood, we could really set more Christians free to date and form relationships in a godly way. In chapter 8, I'll describe more about how the church can develop a much healthier culture around dating and relationships.

Consequences for marriage

The church has been working to support healthy marriage for many years. Lots of helpful resources have been produced that are appropriate for Christians, non-Christians or both.

For the purposes of Engage, we want to focus some more on what is uniquely possible in marriages where both spouses are Christians. We want to make it possible for such marriages to be all they can potentially be, when God the Father, Son and Holy Spirit are at their centre.

This isn't necessarily something which is talked about openly in churches very often.

We also want to highlight the challenges of 'mixed' marriages, where one spouse is a Christian and the other isn't. Some people become Christians after they get married, but many marry someone who doesn't share their faith – often as a direct result of the church gender imbalance. It's worth stopping to count for a moment: how many 'mixed' marriages are there in your congregation? How often have those involved had a chance to talk about their experiences of the spiritual mismatch, in an appropriate and supportive context with someone at church?

Research indicates:

- Overall, women are more often the Christian partner where there's a Christian married to a non-Christian (not really a surprise, considering the church gender imbalance).
- 13% of Christian men married a woman who was not a Christian at the time of their marriage, whereas 23% of Christian women married a non-Christian man. In other words, Christian women were nearly twice as likely to marry a non-Christian than men, which perhaps reflects the finding that there are up to twice as many single women as men in the church.
- Over 90% of Christian couples expressed happiness with their marriage, while only 66% of those in a mixed marriage did so.[18]

For Christians whose spouses are not yet Christians, or who have drifted from their faith, there is often no recognition or support, and sometimes just judgment from the church. Every church has significant numbers of mixed marriages, and needs to intentionally support those involved. Some have suggested that it may be helpful to set up local or national prayer and support networks. In chapter 9, David and Liz Percival explore further how we can help marriages flourish where either one or both spouses are Christians.

Consequences for parenting and young people

In one sense we'd like to be able to discuss everything to do with encouraging and parenting the spiritual, social and emotional development of children and young people, because it's all so important. But that's far beyond our scope, and there are plenty of other resources which cover those issues.

Two of the key reasons that the church needs more men are for the sake of children and young people, and for parenting. Spiritual fatherlessness is widespread due to the lack of Christian men around. Children and young people need male support and role-models, but not all of them will have a father present in the home, let alone a Christian father. Many have had to deal with their parents separating. This has huge implications for all aspects of their life and development, including for their relationships. The massive challenge of spiritual fatherlessness and spiritual parenting (for many adults too, not just children and young people) is one that churches need to take into account when looking to grow a healthy congregation.

In this book we are going to focus on the theme of young people's dating and relationships. Right from the start, children are learning from those around them about themselves, Jesus, relationships and marriage, whether consciously or unconsciously. All experience carries forward into their relationships (of all kinds) as they grow older, and also into any later romantic relationships and marriage.

Engage is very keen to encourage churches to recognise the intergenerational nature of the issues we're addressing. We all know that many adults experience difficulties in their relationships and marriages, and so we also need to think of what we can do 'further upstream', in terms of formative and preventative work to help young people make wise decisions. It has often been the case that young people in church have received more teaching and support about self-identity, relationships and sex than the adults have. But there's still not enough input on these themes, perhaps because they are some of the most challenging to cover. Paula Pridham (in chapter 10) and Laura Hancock (in chapter 11) will show us how the roles of parents, families, churches and youth workers are all essential for discipleship in these areas.

Consequences for Christian marriage in the future

It is crucial that we're paying explicit attention to present-day trends in the factors affecting Christian marriage, but also are fully conscious of where we're heading, longer-term.

In summary, there are fewer children now born to Christians in the first place (more Christian women are not having children because they remain single). Fewer children are now able to grow up in a Christian family with two Christian parents (because of the church gender imbalance). The biological replacement rate of committed Christians has been found to be just over 50%, i.e. only half of the children of committed Christians later become committed Christians themselves.[19] More organisations are now producing resources to address this.

We therefore estimate that only about 16% of today's church's grandchildren will have two Christian parents, if current trends continue.

- The average church gender imbalance found in research (see chapter 4 for details) is 40% men, 60% women.
- This means that only 80% of Christians will be able to get married to a Christian (i.e. in theory, statistically, all of the men can, only two thirds of the women can).
- Add into this the 50% biological replacement rate of committed Christians.
- The resulting percentages of today's church's descendants who will be able to have two Christian parents can be seen in Figure 2 to be decreasing at a very fast rate.

Figure 2. Consequences of the church gender imbalance for Christian marriage in the future.

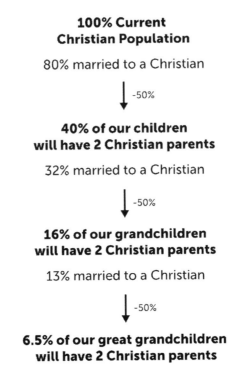

**100% Current
Christian Population**

80% married to a Christian

↓ -50%

**40% of our children
will have 2 Christian parents**

32% married to a Christian

↓ -50%

**16% of our grandchildren
will have 2 Christian parents**

13% married to a Christian

↓ -50%

**6.5% of our great grandchildren
will have 2 Christian parents**

5% married to a Christian

Because of this, there will be even less opportunity for Christian marriage to be modelled to those in the church and in our communities in the future. The negative intergenerational consequences of today's church gender imbalance will be exacerbated unless we act to change things.

Solutions

These are massive issues which we're raising. It is unfortunately not an exaggeration to say that they constitute a crisis situation for the church. Thankfully, God's power to change things is greater than we can ever imagine! And we all need to work together on implementing solutions.

Spiritually, the first thing for us all to do is pray. We each need to pray that God will act to bring change, and ask him what part he wants us to play in the process. Practically, there are actions we can take to improve the situation, which are described throughout the rest of this book. Psychologically, there are a few perspectives that can help us, and which inform the work of Engage.

We have to see issues and individuals in context. The psychologist Urie Bronfenbrenner first introduced what has become a famous and influential model, foundational to how many psychologists now examine people's functioning and interaction with their environments.[20] He described how a person is influenced by contexts immediately around them (e.g. family) and also wider contexts (e.g. societal influences). He called the contexts 'eco-systems', and showed how they interact. It is a type of this 'eco-systemic interactionist' approach that we use for Engage to show how all the elements of our work are related, as Figure 3 illustrates.

Figure 3. The Engage Network 'eco-systemic interactionist' approach.

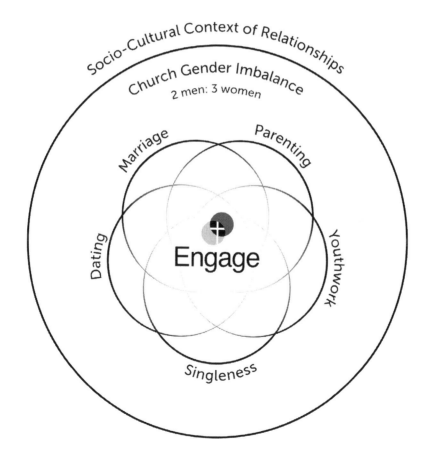

It's important to note that not everyone has to 'go round the circles' in the middle, but that these reflect life stages experienced by most people. Some of you might be wondering where students fit into this, and although we have not specifically talked about them as a separate group in this book, we hope that what is written for adults will be helpful for them too.

As The Engage Network got going, it seemed that lots of people were doing great work in the ministry areas in the diagram, but not really linking up when it could be helpful to do so. Every one of these ministries is affected by the others, and promoting the effectiveness of one will positively impact on the others too. The intergenerational issues affect everybody. Although it might seem rather complex (we're not just focusing on one thing), it's vital that we see the metaperspective or helicopter view of all these elements together.

Along with this, it's useful to draw on approaches from Positive Psychology (the scientific study of human flourishing) and Solution Focused Psychology, which focuses on what people want to achieve. These perspectives inform our consultation vision grids and chapters, which are structured around three 'systemic' levels (or contexts); the individual, the local church, and the national church. These are intentionally given in parallel (columns) in the grids, because in order to support a healthy church, we need to move forward on these different fronts at the same time. The chapter authors have written sequentially about individuals, local churches, and the national church. That's not because our thinking should start at the individual level, but because you can't really write a whole chapter in columns! Strategically, of course, if leaders are working first to bring culture change at national and local church levels, this will maximise the impact on individuals.

We are very grateful to all our chapter authors for collaborating on this book – it's very much a team effort. They all have different backgrounds, perspectives and personal situations and that's why we've asked them to contribute. They may have different views, and you may have different views, but we can learn from each other. And just to note, any names they've written have been changed to protect identities.

The format of the book

Having now explained Bronfenbrenner and our Engage diagram, the chapter order of this book will hopefully make more sense.

Firstly:

- The theological and spiritual context which permeates everything (chapter 2).

- The socio-cultural trends in relationships of wider society that we're all living in (chapter 3).
- The church context, with its gender imbalance (chapters 4-5).

Then "What would it look like if things were working well in the church?" (based on our consultations, and written by one of the participants) for each of the following:

- Men's ministry (chapter 6).
- Singleness (chapter 7).
- Dating and relationships (chapter 8).
- Marriage (chapter 9).
- Parenting and discipleship around young people's dating and relationships (chapter 10).
- Youth work and discipleship around young people's dating and relationships (chapter 11).

It is our hope and prayer that this book will contribute to the church becoming gender balanced, and to supporting healthy Christian singleness, dating and marriage both now and in the future.

> *"Now to him who is able to do immeasurably more than all we ask or imagine, according to his power that is at work within us, to him be glory in the church and in Christ Jesus throughout all generations, for ever and ever! Amen."*
> (Ephesians 3:20)

CHAPTER 2

Theological foundations

Adrian Chatfield

Introduction

One of our neighbours, with whom we are on good and honest terms, has told us recently that after a failed eight year informal partnership, she has gone through a string of unsatisfactory associations, all of which have diminished or demeaned her in some way. So we have been surprised that after an internet exploration, she has joined up with yet another man and committed herself to him in a quick and intense way.

Perhaps we shouldn't have been surprised. This is the 'new normal', except that we belong to a culture in which the very idea of normality is rejected. There are no norms except those we choose for our own particular circumstances. The idea of absolutes, values or healthy patterns of behaviour is met with derision or worse.

Dim echoes of an old world remain. My – and my wife's – immediate family, siblings and their children, are all married, and though there have been many rocky roads, all the marriages remain intact, some in working-class and others in middle-class settings. This too is surprising, because few of them inhabit a Christian world, in which a God-given order is offered as normative, wholesome and hope-filled. It is the principles underlying that God-given order to which this chapter will speak, in the hope that it will provide a pattern for reflection on following chapters of the book.

To this end, we offer four themes. The first is a brief cultural reflection, as the background against which the Kingdom of God is unfolding. Then we move on to examine the corporate nature of our createdness in the image of God: to be human is in many senses to be in community. The next step is to examine the biblical idea of covenant as inherent in the very idea of marriage, and finally, we will consider the fact that marriage is a vocation, one among many, but a key vocation for the mission of God.

Culture and chaos

In 2016, I addressed an Engage conference on the toxic cocktail of our current social mores. This ranged widely, to show how Christian norms have been underplayed, undermined and overthrown over a long period of time. My own home region of the Caribbean has endured a 'crisis of the West Indian family' ever since slavery actively split up communities, refused to allow formal marriage and objectified the people in its thrall. Similarly, the mining culture of South Africa, by dislocating workers from their home regions, led to plural relationships, bigamous marriages, heterosexual and homosexual prostitution as well as child rape. The story is well-documented, but nonetheless gruelling in the telling.

For us in the United Kingdom, the active questioning of the gift of marriage and the social fragmentation that it has caused, have a theological and philosophical background in the Enlightenment. Since the 18th century, we have celebrated human reason as the means towards a glorious end: self-assured and self-determined civilisation. Modernity's thesis was that we could create an alternative order and pattern to life, determined without reference to God. Increasingly, religion was sidelined and privatised. The Romantic reaction of the early 19th century added the key element of individualism. Though there was a backlash in the 20th century, as two World Wars led many to question our ability to build a world of peace and prosperity, there was no return to faith. Rather, even if God was not blamed for it all, all structures were found wanting, all systems were questioned.

This in the course of the century emerged in academic discourse as postmodernity, and accompanying philosophical positions lumped together as postmodernism. As a cultural mood, it was characterised by suspicion of all frames of reference, a rejection of all formal belief, and an assumption that everything was relative. There were no more standards or absolutes. Above all, no one had the right to speak on behalf of another or to speak with authority for a higher power, human or otherwise. The image I hold in my mind is that of quicksand, which looks stable, supports nothing and sucks in without mercy those who dare approach.

This has led to the emergence and gradual dominance of a so-called 'liberal society' in which anything goes as long as it doesn't hurt anyone (the vainest of all vain wishes). The word 'liberal' is both deceptive and slippery, but in our cultural setting it suggests three things:
- An unregulated society, in which we form our own regulations, patterns of behaviour and life choices.
- An illiberal society, which is ironically liberal only towards those who

hold the same postmodern position, and is increasingly fierce towards those who question it.

- A 'slippery-slope' society, in which there is only one mode of social development and transformation, towards ever greater divergence, experimentation and questioning. This is evident in the fields of euthanasia, abortion, sexual morality, but even more worryingly in the emergence of transhumanist and artificial intelligence debates.

Created for community

The theological starting point for this discussion is the act of creation and the fact of our creatureliness. Most remarkable is that we have been created in the image and likeness of God. To be human is to be divinely imaged, and even the fall does not deprive us of that image. There are many opinions as to the nature of that imaging: the ability to reason has been most often proposed. However, given that the God who has created us is the Three-in-One, the Holy Trinity, the emphasis should not be placed on my individual humanity, or on any aspect of my biological or psychological makeup. To be created in the image and likeness of God is rather to be created as an interdependent community of persons, a society of diverse, unique but interconnected individuals.

To put it simply, relatedness is of the essence of the divine image which is embedded and imprinted in us. Genesis 1:26-27 has to be read in the plural. The consequence of the sin of Adam and Eve is not only to be distanced from God, but to be distanced from one another. Solitude may be balm for our souls in times of stress, but isolation will drive us mad. We know that solitary confinement dehumanises those on whom it is inflicted, but it also dehumanises those who inflict it. When we separate humans from each other and undermine relatedness, we mar the likeness of God in us.

On the positive side, which is where we need to move now, all relationships are natural responses to God's creative intent. This is as true of groups and communities like church congregations as it is of one-to-one relationships. In one-to-one contexts, it is as true of collegiality or friendship as it is of marriage, and it is important neither to understate nor to overstate the significance of marriage in this regard. Marriage is a particular, a unique and a distinct marker of the fact that we are created for community, but it is not a cause of boasting. Above all, it is not 'the ideal human state'. I say this early in the chapter not because I want to diminish the importance of marriage, but because marriage is not merely a legal status. Later on we will see that it is a gift, vocation and privilege, but never grounds for pride.

Having cleared the ground a little, we can focus on the particular sign that marriage is of God's image and likeness embedded in a couple who enter it. There are five points worth making here. The first is the obvious one, so easily missed, that marriage is procreative, an invitation by God to continue in his creative work of bringing life into being. In a medically-sophisticated age, this comes about in a multiplicity of ways, some of which we might struggle with ethically, but we must not lose sight of the creative impulse which is inherent in the marriage relationship.

Following this, marriage is family-building. While our experiences of family life and shared experience are often mixed, they too are a sign within marriage of the nature of the Holy Trinity. Sadly, many families close in on themselves to the exclusion of others, but the family is at its truest and best when its borders are porous, open to the outside. That openness includes all sorts of inclusions: visitors, fostered and adopted children, travellers, the wounded and the broken, but at its heart is the hospitality of the family, reflecting the hospitality of God.

The 15th century icon by Michael Rublev of the three persons of the Holy Trinity sitting round a Eucharistic table teases us with this vision of hospitality, of incorporation into the divine meal. Here too, the boundary of the divine family is broken down: the fourth place at the table is empty, and the reversed perspective of the icon draws the viewer in with a simple 'Come and sit with us. Join in the family'.

Building on this, we can say that marriage is inherently hospitable, inclusive rather than exclusive. Of course this is not in the mistaken and bizarre sense of the 'open marriage' in which other sexual relationships are possible, but in the proper sense that two together reflect the nature of God and can make others feel fully at home.

Thirdly, marriage reflects the diversity, complementarity and mutuality of the Godhead. The coat of arms of my home diocese of Trinidad and Tobago visualises this well, drawing on the medieval iconography of the *Scutum Fidei* or Shield of Faith (see Figure 4). While all three of the persons of the Trinity are equally God, neither is the same as the other. Without getting into tangled early church debates, each person of the Trinity has its distinct and unique place in the community that is the one God.

Figure 4. The Shield of Faith.

Similarly, each person in a marriage has her or his distinct and unique place, a distinctiveness which is different from the spouse, complementary to him or her and mutually beneficial. Here I must issue a caveat! In using the word 'complementary', I am not smuggling in a particular view of marriage often described as complementarian, in which particular and specific roles are ascribed to men and women, and women are (usually) put in their place 'under' the authority of men. My use of the idea of complementarity is softer, suggesting simply that each contributes in a distinct way which enriches and builds up both. What that is in each marriage is to be worked out by the couple together, and not imposed from outside.

Fourthly, marriage is a particular kind of friendship, which is another way of saying that it is a kind of one-to-one relationship. My reason for including it here is that there is a clear theology of friendship in the scriptures (including in what Jesus says about his followers) but little effort in the church over the past two thousand years to build on that. If Jesus longs for friendship with his companions, and longs for his companions to be sociably united to God, it follows that he longs for us to be in friendship with one another. There isn't space here to expand on the theology of friendship, but part of what it means to be married is to be good friends, perhaps often best friends.

Finally and fundamentally, marriage is a formal sign of the relationship between God and his people, between Christ and his Church. In both Testaments of the Bible, we learn that God has a forward intention in creating us for community, and that intention is to be a revelation of his character and his will towards us. Through this forward intention we learn that:

- As unfaithfulness in marriage leads inexorably to crisis, a sense of betrayal and rejection, because the gifted intimacy of marriage is an exclusive one, so God is passionately jealous of his love towards his people Israel (Hosea).

- As the lover and the beloved in the Song of Songs celebrate their journey of relationship ecstatically, so God pursues us relentlessly with love, lavishes that love on us, and delights eternally in our relationship with him (Song of Songs and Jesus' parables of the Wedding Feast).
- As a husband gives himself sacrificially to his wife, and she responds in equal measure, so God gives himself sacrificially to his people, the Church (Ephesians 5).
- And in Revelation 19-22, the metaphor is dissolved into the reality, that both marriage and life with God are beginning and end, promise and completion, consummation and eternal joy.

Sealed in a covenant

The new Church of England marriage service, along with many others, says in its introduction that "for Christians, marriage is...an invitation to share life together in the spirit of Jesus Christ. It is based upon a solemn, public and lifelong covenant between a man and a woman, declared and celebrated in the presence of God and before witnesses." This builds on the language of the old prayer book, where the minister prays "so these persons may surely perform and keep the vow and covenant betwixt them made, whereof this ring given and received is a token and pledge" immediately after the putting on of the ring.

Formal and ceremonial liturgical language is not carelessly chosen. Rather, it aims to embed the principles of biblical theology in the performance and practice to which the rite points. That is, covenant theology.

Covenants are agreements. They occur repeatedly in the scriptures, as simple agreements, as binding legal contracts, and most significantly as the formal description of the way in which God relates to his people, both in creation and in redemption. The key features of a covenant are:

- A pledge, a promise or a commitment.
- The sealing of that commitment, sworn or written.
- The terms.
- The underlying conditions.
- The blessings or rewards or intended outcomes.

Some biblical covenants are invalidated when the conditions are broken. We see this in Deuteronomy, where obedience is rewarded with blessing, disobedience with an attendant curse. Others are not invalidated, though they may be hindered or stinted. What holds all covenants together is the fact that they formalise a relationship, are mutually binding and mutually beneficial.

Covenants are the way in which God formalises and expresses his relationship with us. Human relationships, which mirror God's covenants, are formalised in the same way, and the key to understanding a biblical theology of marriage is to recognise the covenantal character that is built into it. It would be tedious, in making each point, to say that 'this reflects God's use of covenant in relating to us', so in reading what follows, you need to read it into the text.

- Marriage is a pledge, a promise and a commitment. It is both legally and morally binding, not just in the eyes of the law or the society which adopts those laws, but in the eyes of God. We do not, or should not slide into marriage. We decide to get married, and that decision includes a refusal to consider the opposite. It is, of course, a tragedy when a marriage fails, and we are often puzzled as to why. There is no doubt, however, that some marriages fail because it is easier to make a partial promise, a half-hearted pledge, a commitment with fingers crossed. There is a proper positive pastoral and theological response to be made when marriages fail, but the key premise is an abiding promise: 'Till death us do part'.

- The act of marriage is the sealing of that commitment. Again, in my own Anglican practice, I love binding the hands of the couple with a stole and saying – especially in the resonant 16th century words – "Those whom God hath joined together, let no one (*originally* no man) put asunder." Roman Catholic theology speaks of the indissolubility of the marriage vows, which has a complex history and some difficulties, but the power of the language of indissolubility proclaims the solemnity and the strength of what is being done. It is good also to note that there are witnesses, as in any legal transaction: in this case, two human witnesses, and God! Even in our lax and liberal society, to 'un-marry' is a very complicated and often painful legal process.

- And so we come to the terms and conditions. Marriage, like God's relationship with us, is intended to be for the duration, in this life so far as marriage is concerned, eternally with respect to God. There are no circumstances which can invalidate it, and there are echoes here of Paul's song of praise in Romans 8:35, "Who will separate us from the love of Christ?" The covenant does not admit of any circumstances which are grounds for annulment, making clear that this is 'for better, for worse' and so on. If there are 'conditions', they are implicit in the liturgical language of self-giving and uncompromising love shown in affection, in service, in forgiveness. In reality, of course, marriages do break up (and so do Christian marriages), and grace means that those whose marriages fail are able under God to move forward. This does not, however, take away from the core theological emphasis, that marriage is intended to be lifelong and indissoluble.

- The attendant blessings are the fulfilment of our humanity in mutuality and intimacy, the fulfilment of our character in being able to give and receive, and the fulfilment of our obedience to God through social and moral responsibility.

All this is why, though the words 'covenant' and 'contract' imply much the same, it is far better for Christians to talk of marriage as a covenant, with its relational overtones, rather than in the bald, somewhat mechanical language of contract. If getting the language right in the liturgy is key, getting the language of our conversation about marriage right in the public forum is equally important. In an age which thinks little about God and less about lifelong commitment, we need to gossip the gospel of marriage confidently without defensiveness or stridency.

Before we move on to the final section, we should tease out some of the implications of a covenant understanding of marriage. The first of these is that all human covenants flow out of the great covenant that God has made with his people. In the same way as God initiates the covenants he has with us, he is a key participant in human covenants, and a Christian marriage has a triangular character to it. It is important not to think of God as standing at a distance from a marriage relationship, overseeing it and demanding obedience. Rather, God is fully involved and shares in the dynamic of self-giving love and commitment.

This begs the question whether a marriage between two people who do not acknowledge the presence or even the existence of God has the same character to it. The answer is Yes and No. Yes, in that marriage is a creation ordinance or sacrament (depending on your theology) and God is active in it with or without recognition. The No arises from the fact that two of the three participants are negligent of the original divine intention, and are unlikely to act in ways that build on that dynamic.

There is an additional complicating scenario which arises when a Christian marries a non-Christian. The classic text in 2 Corinthians 6:14 "Do not be mismatched with unbelievers" (New Revised Standard Version) is taken by many to refer to such 'mixed marriages', though not all scholars agree. What is clear is that significant difficulties arise in many such marriages because the underlying spiritual vision is inevitably disparate. This is precisely why the work of Engage, and the subject matter of this book, is so crucial to the wellbeing of the church and the mission of God's kingdom today. If there are fewer men than women in our churches, there is significant pressure on those Christian women who desire marriage to look outside the church for a spouse. While many of us know of such situations where there is a good 'working agreement', it cannot be transformed into a norm or an ideal.

The second implication of all this is that as God constantly takes the first step in any covenant, creating us out of nothing, redeeming us 'while we were still sinners', so too God takes the first step in a marriage, making it a divine gift. This does not mean that God chooses my spouse. Many Christians have got tangled up with the false assumption that God makes those decisions. Rather, as I make the choice (hopefully in prayer and with thought and careful reflection) God gifts me and my spouse with the possibility and the privilege of marriage. Indeed, a major thrust of this book is that as Christians we need to be much more proactive in making the possibility and privilege of Christian marriage a realistic one.

Thirdly, God's covenant with his people always demands some kind of response. Gratitude, obviously, but also needs the willingness to work at that which has been given freely. Our salvation is a gift, but Paul enjoins us in Philippians to 'work out our own salvation with fear and trembling' (Philippians 2:12). Similarly, marriage is a gift with which we may be graced, but it involves much graft and the investment of the whole of myself. That for me is what the words of the vow imply, for example: "all that I am I give to you, and all that I have I share with you."

Finally, harking back to biblical passages referred to in the first section of this chapter, Christian marriage has a prophetic function, pointing out the way in which God relates to his people Israel and to the new Israel which is the church. This is not an invitation for those of us who are married to draw attention to ourselves and say 'Look at us and see God at work'. Rather, we are invited by the gospel to look at our own marriages and the marriages of other Christians, and in them see strong signs of the way in which God works more generally in the world. And where we don't see that in our own marriages, that is a call for a couple to repent and realign themselves with the will of God for their marriage as a symbol of covenant love.

Given as a vocation

There's a negative aspect of the idea of vocation that needs to be cleared out of the way before we can make the main point. That is, that Christian discourse often applies the concept of vocation particularly to the single life, as if it made singleness special. One of the reasons for the existence of Engage is that many single people do not feel themselves called by God or anyone else to the single life, but it seems to be the default that the church is offering them. As a wise Benedictine oblate puts it, "Some single people have satisfying social, religious and professional lives, while others feel a social and emotional disconnect and often experience loneliness."[1]

Of course, it is true that there has been, and will always be a specific calling to celibacy, not least in the monastic life, but that is worlds apart from the fact of singleness in today's church. Just because a Christian is single, does not mean that this is their God-given call and vocation. So in what follows, the emphasis must be on that which is both the call of God and a freely-chosen acceptance of that call.

What then are the special characteristics of the vocation of marriage? The first characteristic is that we receive it as gift, not so much the gift of a spouse as the gift of the state of 'being married'. It is an act of God's grace, and demands gratitude as a response. If it is truly a vocation, we can never take it for granted. It may seem tedious – and not a little irritating – to say 'thank you for marrying me' too often, but it is of paramount importance that we thank God for calling us into this lifelong relationship, accept it as a gift, and celebrate it.

This leads us to the second point, that a gift is not given because it is deserved. It is given and received out of sheer love. Christians receive their marriages from God and from each other without an underlying nervousness about the possibility that it might be taken away. We do not say, 'this is too good to be true'. Rather, those called to be married (and who are able to find a suitable marriage partner) are called to inhabit a solid, reliable and permanent relationship that does not need to question itself all the time, a relationship so secure that it opens freely towards 'the other' without holding back in any way. At its heart, we find a spirit of acceptance: this is who and what we have been called to be and do together, for God, for each other and for the kingdom.

Thankfulness and acceptance are closely followed by generosity in this trinity of 'vocation values'. If it is our call to be married, we are not just married by the will of God and for each other, we are also married 'towards the world'. Marriage is missional. It is missional in its open-spiritedness towards others, the hospitality of the home; it is missional in its servant-spiritedness towards the world; and it echoes the sacrificial love of Christ on the cross through a generosity that does not fear running out of steam.

Like all other vocations, the vocation of marriage is characterised by change. It is a relationship of journey, marked by discovery, responses to unforeseen circumstances, unexpected twists and turns and all the times and seasons of life. So while a couple know themselves to be given to each other fully, completely and forever in this life, they cannot know what adaptations will be demanded of them as time goes on. In this proper sense, marriage has to be worked at, re-evaluated, renewed and refreshed. In our own marriage, there was a season of sharing our home with others, many of whom had been scarred by life, so that we referred to our home as 'Hotel Chatfield'! When that season passed, we missed it but were also relieved to have the pressure lifted off us. The practical outworking of the vocation changed; the vocation itself remained, and remains.

What of the future? On the one hand, the stability and lifelong continuity of marriage offers a relationship so rich that it foreshadows eternity. On the other hand, Jesus has told us that "For when they rise from the dead, they neither marry nor are given in marriage, but are like angels in heaven" (Mark 12:25). On more than one occasion, I have been asked anxiously by a couple whether it is fair of God to deprive them of their life partner in heaven. Surely, they imply, heaven will be the less for the rupture or divine divorce forced on them. My stock answer here is that there will be no diminution of relationship, but that all relationships will reflect the completeness which they have experienced towards each other in this life. If this is true, of course, it means that marriage really is a sign of the fact that we are created to be in community, given to each other in covenants blessed and sealed by God, and called to live not for ourselves alone but for the greater and nobler cause that is the heavenly vision, the new Jerusalem of God.

Pointing (to) the way forward

The work of Engage is crucial at a theological and spiritual level because marriage is rooted in the character of God, and the consequent way in which God relates to humankind; it is a sign of the presence of God embedded in all of creation and of the redemptive love and grace of God restoring us to him and to each other. As a result, the erosion of our understanding of marriage, its value and its values is a reflection of a serious social disruption that impacts on all of us. A crisis in marriage is a crisis for the whole of society, and we are already reaping the fruit of that far beyond the family and the home. When the church is almost as confused as the wider society about the nature and the function of marriage, it loses its prophetic edge and part of its ability to witness to the nature and mission of God.

This brings us to the heart of the issues that gave birth to Engage. In the present context, the troubling gender imbalance in the church means that even where there is a will to foster and nurture healthy Christian marriages, it is plainly not possible for many Christian women. With the best will in the world, preaching that marriage is a spiritual act, a social blessing and a sign of the Kingdom accomplishes little unless we find creative ways of 'making Christian marriage possible'.

This book is a key contribution towards discerning those creative ways, but I'd like to end the chapter by making two appeals:

- First, we are calling on those who carry the vision of particular churches and church groups, inviting them to recognise that a failure in the area of Christian marriage is not just a failure of pastoral care or of social wellbeing. It contains the seeds of a theological failure, and obscures key aspects of God's nature and purposes in this world. If this is so, then there is a clear call for the whole church, with its leaders, theologians and ministry educators to collaborate in re-envisioning Christian marriage as a core gospel sign, and to invest in its restoration 'while there is yet time'.
- Secondly, there is a challenge to those in every ministry field. Part of the trouble with Christian ministry in our churches and with the Practical Theology disciplines in our training institutions is that they are fragmented and over-boundaried. To put it crudely, those who work with children, or married couples, easily feel detached from 'ministry to singles'. Women's ministries are kept at arm's length from men's evangelism, and so on. Everybody needs to see the 'big picture' and work together. Subject-specific Practical Theology builds long lists of 'things that we mustn't omit' and proceeds to leave out 'the things there isn't time for'. Yet on the ground, in churches, in colleges and on courses, stories abound of how difficult it is to be single in an environment which privileges marriage, a Christian man in a setting where the norm is a Christian woman, chaste in a church where the use of pornography is as rife as in the society at large.

The crisis situation that this book will go on to describe in significant detail is not one that can be consigned to a 'men's worker', or a 'singles group'. It is a crisis in understanding, in envisioning and strategising, which the mission of the whole church and its attendant institutions must address.

CHAPTER 3

The wider context: current marriage trends

Harry Benson

The search for reliable love

It is not good for man to be alone, God tells Adam in the Garden of Eden.[1] And most of us seem to agree.

Even if it's relatively easy to find adult men and women who live on their own – roughly a quarter do so in most age groups – as people get older it becomes increasingly rare to find those who have *never* lived with anybody else in an intimate relationship.[2]

This is the current picture in Britain:

- Among adults in their early thirties, 74% of women and 68% of men already live with a partner. Two out of three of these couples are married. Of the remainder who live alone, most have not married, leaving 21% of women and 30% of men still single, unattached and never married.
- By the time adults are in their late forties, those who stay single are already becoming a lot harder to find. Whereas 81% of women and 76% of men have ever been married by then – not all of whom successfully of course – just 13% of women and 12% of men live alone, not cohabiting and not yet married.
- Once in their early sixties, just 6% of women and 9% of men have remained single throughout their adult life, not cohabiting with anyone and having never married.

Paul tells us (in the context of 1 Corinthians 7) that to stay single and not to marry is 'good' or even 'better'.[3] Yet only a small minority of today's general population goes down that route, whether through choice or not. For almost all of us, it's therefore fair to say that we're looking for reliable love. The question is how we find it.

Family breakdown and the trend away from marriage

In the last 40 or so years, the game of love has changed and we are not playing it at all well. A report published in early 2017 by the Social Trends Institute, a US think tank, found that Britain has the highest rate of family instability in the entire developed world.[4] Three out of five children born to unmarried parents experience family breakdown before they reach their teenage years. That's worse than in America where the equivalent figure is just under half. It's worse than anywhere in Europe. In Belgium, for example, the figure is one in six. In Spain, it's one in 16.

Our own research at Marriage Foundation mirrors these findings. Using big national surveys, we showed that just under half of all British teenagers are not living with both natural parents.[5] The reason that figure is less than the 'three out of five' above is because children born to married families do so much better and bring the average down.

In another study we showed that whether your parents are married or not when you are born has a huge effect on whether they will still be together when you take your GCSEs at age 16.[6]

- Among parents who were married when their child was born, 24% had split up by the time their child was aged 16.
- Among parents who got married, but only after their child was born, 56% split up.
- Among parents who lived together as a couple when their child was born, but never married, 69% split up.

This is pretty astonishing.

We hear a great deal about high divorce rates, rising divorce rates, skyrocketing divorce rates. The figure of 40% is often cited, and it is indeed about right for all marriages with or without children.[7] But when marriage begins to involve children, the figure is far lower. Some marriages fail - even Jesus acknowledged that.[8] The 24% divorce rate among parents is still high, but it's not that high.

Yet what we rarely hear about is the wholesale collapse of unmarried families with children. The break-up rate of 69% among parents who don't marry is nearly three times the rate of those who do. It may also seem odd that getting married after having a child doesn't seem to help stability as much as you might think, reducing the risk from 69% to 56%. These are parents who love each other enough to have a baby, love each other enough to say "let's get married," and yet still more than half split up.

What's going on? The likely answer lies in how commitment works.

Does marriage work?

So why is it that so many unmarried couples are breaking up? Some researchers – and plenty of politicians – have convinced themselves that the explanation is all down to 'selection'. The kind of people who marry, they argue, are the same kind of people who also tend to commit and stay together. Better educated people, older people, happier people, healthier people, richer people, all 'select' into marriage and do better. For example, 90% of parents in the top income quintile (which is anyone paying a higher rate of income tax) are married if they have children under five. Compare that to 25% of parents of young children in the lowest income quintile who are married.[9] This rich-poor marriage gap also happens in the US and all across Europe, including Scandinavia. But the richer ones were going to do better anyway, goes the argument. So it's not marriage that makes couples more stable, or not being married that makes them less stable, it's all these background factors, they claim. Apart from disregarding the possibility that there may be some practical merit in getting married, this argument falls short on both evidence and theory.

Although it makes sense that relative wealth and poverty are likely to have an impact on relationships, the reverse is also the case. Getting married can make people better off and splitting up can make people poorer. Because it's difficult to disentangle these interactions, most studies – like ours – prefer to take into account the effect of mother's education rather than income (because education usually happens long before people marry or cohabit or divorce) to see if being married makes a difference. Any social scientist worth his or her salt includes background factors when trying to infer any kind of link between factors and outcomes. As well as a legion of studies in academic journals which do exactly that, our own studies at Marriage Foundation show that even after taking into account the age, education, ethnicity and relationship happiness of the mother, and whether the birth was planned or not, whether the parents were married or not when their child was born remains one of the top influences on whether they stay together as a couple or not in both short and long term.[10] While it's true that 'correlation' doesn't imply 'causation', it's equally true that neither should you rule out causation as a possibility.

Birth control has changed the game

To understand what's going on here, let's go back to the introduction of the contraceptive pill. In fact let's go back a lot further. Since 1845, the Office for National Statistics has produced records on the number of births each year and all sorts of details about mothers, including how many were married rather than unmarried. From that time until the early 1970s, the proportion of births to unmarried parents stayed both remarkably low and remarkably consistent.

In any one year, at least 95% of all births were to married mums and thus fewer than 5% – one in 20 births – to mums who were not married. There were a couple of small blips that coincided with the First and Second World Wars, when the unmarried rate went up a bit, but only a bit. Within a year or two, it was back to the old familiar level of 5% or thereabouts.[11] In short, almost all babies were born to parents who were married. There's no reason to suspect that this hasn't always been true throughout history. Understanding why this is the case is pretty straightforward. It also gives a huge clue as to why marriage tends to work so much better than unmarriage.

Imagine two young adults who fall in love. As normal healthy human beings, they desperately want to sleep together. But they can't and they don't. Because they know that if they do, there is a risk that the woman will get pregnant. It seems likely that at least some of those births to married parents would have involved 'shotgun weddings'. If you haven't heard the expression, it means the father of a pregnant daughter pointing his shotgun at the man responsible and ordering him to 'marry her'! But that's exactly the point. It wasn't just the couple who knew that they couldn't sleep together. Families knew it. Society knew it. Governments knew it.

The main purpose of marriage has always been to ensure that a man makes a long-term commitment to a woman before he gets her pregnant. The motivation for this changes from culture to culture. But the rationale is the same. You got married, you had children. Near enough everybody did. Rich and poor alike. Marriage has therefore always been primarily about providing the stability necessary to help a couple stay together while bringing up their children. This has been true since the time of Genesis where the writer talks about a man and a woman coming together as 'one flesh'. 'One flesh' by definition includes sexual union, and therefore pregnancy, and therefore children.

Now fast forward to the 1970s when birth control – 'the pill' – became widely available. Until then, unmarried cohabitation was both frowned upon and rare. In the 40-50 years since, we have gradually come to accept cohabitation as a new norm. Today, 47% of births are to unmarried parents. But in the grand sweep of history and in the context of human nature, unmarried cohabitation is anything but normal. It breaks up the natural link between sex, commitment, children and marriage, with the following consequences:

- It is almost certainly the cause of the highest family breakdown rates in human history.
- It brings about a situation where a huge number of children are being raised by single parents, with fewer parental resources of time and money, with less parental input from both father as well as mother, and with ever more children experiencing family dysfunction and transitions.
- It contributes to high levels of teenage mental health problems. Family breakdown is the number one predictor of mental health, contrary to government policy papers that wrongly attribute it to the mercifully rare parental conflict.[12]

The two sides of commitment

So if it is marriage that makes the difference, and not the kind of people who marry, what's the magic ingredient? The answer boils down to the clarity, and removal of any lingering ambiguity that comes from making a mutually-agreed decision about the future. In this way the ties that bind are a good thing and not a trap. This is the norm for married couples but only the exception for cohabitees.

To understand this better, it helps to understand how commitment works.[13] If you can 'get' commitment, you'll 'get' marriage. When two people meet one another and fall in love, they begin to establish a new identity as a couple. Instead of just 'you' and 'me', there is now an 'us'. Imagine this new identity begins to surround them like a bubble, so that when they look at one another, they don't just see another person – 'you' or 'me' – they see the bubble of 'us' that surrounds them. This is how most of us think about commitment. It's the strength and importance of the new identity as a couple. Researchers call this inner bond between two people 'dedication'. Christians will recognise it as 'covenant' or 'one flesh', the Old Testament ceremony where two people exchange their old identities for one new one.[14]

There are really three ingredients to 'dedication':

- **Couple:** The extent to which each person sees themselves as part of the bigger picture of 'us'. They are a couple. They start talking about themselves as a couple. They insert the words 'we' or 'us' into their conversation.
- **Future:** The extent to which they look forwards and plan their lives accordingly.

- **Decision:** The extent to which each person decides that this is what they want. They have bought into their future as a couple. It's not a 'sliding' thing. It's a 'deciding' thing. It's deliberate, intentional.

The ultimate expression of commitment, dedication, is when two people agree to spend the rest of their lives together. In other words, they **decide** to be a **couple** with a permanent **future.**

Marriage is the ultimate step of dedication. It reflects and represents a mutually agreed plan to spend a life together. And in taking this step, any lingering doubts, uncertainties, anxieties, and ambiguities are laid to rest. At least that's the general idea.

But there's another side to commitment that we don't think about much. The outer bonds that treat two people as one couple, that see one bubble more than two individuals, are called 'constraints'. Constraints can include anything from friends and family knowing you're a couple, to living together as a couple, to having children as a couple, to getting legally married as a couple. All of these things stand on the outside pressing in, affirming the new identity as couple. The flip side is that constraints restrict our choices and make it harder to leave, should we wish to do so.

Marriage versus cohabitation

Think about two people who want to grow a garden together in an imaginary and boundless field. They want to let friends and family know that they are growing a garden together. So they stake it out and put a fence around it. Friends and family can look on admiringly and see that they have established a garden together. At first the happy couple just plants a few flowers. The fence makes them feel safe in their fledgling garden. It wouldn't be hard to escape if things didn't work out. But the existence of the fence encourages them to do a little more gardening together. One day they decide that they want to dig flower beds together. They enjoy this very much and the garden starts to look beautiful. So they decide they want to go all out and plant trees. This is going to be a fabulous garden that lasts forever. But to do this they feel they need to make the fence taller and stronger. The taller fence gives them extra peace of mind but it also helps reinforce to their friends on the outside that they are serious.

I hope you can see where I'm going with this. The order of things matters. It's best to plan and grow the garden before you build the fence. The trick to growing a really good garden together is therefore to do it slowly, to do it together, and to plan it together. In that way, if things are going to work out, couples can decide together to put up a bigger fence that affirms and protects them. Building the fence before developing the garden can end up trapping the couple in a garden that should never have really got going in the first place. This is the story of marriage versus cohabitation.

Marriage is all about building dedication – a mutual decision to be a couple with a permanent future that affirms your commitment to one another – before adding all the constraints of a shared abode. Marriage establishes the garden plan before putting a fence around it. In contrast, cohabitation tends to begin with the constraint of living together before a couple has necessarily clarified their commitment to a shared future together. Alas the very act of building the fence introduces inertia, reducing choices, making the temptation greater to stick with a garden that may be less than ideal.

Sliders

Commitment theory explains a great deal about what we see in terms of couple outcomes.[15] Dedication and constraints are the structure. But we need to consider the process. Every time a couple passes through a relationship transition, they can either **'decide'** or **'slide'.**

- **Deciding** is good. It's deliberate. It establishes clarity. It sends a signal. It's intentional. It resolves any lingering ambiguity. It means you are committed and it tells your spouse you are serious, dedicated.
- **Sliding** is bad. It's ambiguous. It leaves questions unanswered. It presumes. It leads to doubts and insecurity. It tells you nothing about dedication.

Either way, whether you slide or decide into being 'in a relationship', cohabiting together, getting married, or having a baby, you are adding constraints. Whether you planned it or not, each of these transitions increases the size of the fence. It limits your options.

Consider the couple who haven't been in a relationship long but move in together. Their relationship feels good but much has yet to be discussed. Over time, an unspoken air of uncertainty grows. One partner thinks they are heading for marriage. The other is comfortable with the status quo. Out of nervousness, neither partner raises the topic of marriage, or even about the future, because it's a tricky subject. The future, even planning ahead, becomes a no-go zone which leads to frustrations on both sides. If marriage isn't yet on the table, maybe having a baby will sort things out. Lots of people think like this. But as any parent knows, having a baby is an exhausting business. Relationships struggle when couples are tired. Misunderstandings, assumptions and niggles creep in. And all too soon the prospect of bringing up a child together for many years becomes too hard. The arrival of the baby turns out to be a fence too far. One or both partners feel trapped. They split up. This is the story of family breakdown in the UK. Half of our teens are not living with both natural parents. But half of all those will have seen – or not seen – their parents split during pregnancy or before their second birthday. The overwhelming majority of this early breakdown comes from unmarried couples.[16]

Deciders

The big question for stability is whether couples decide or slide. Where break-up rates are high, it's likely that there are more sliders than deciders. Where stability is high, more couples have bought in. Earlier, I pointed out the apparent paradox that couples who marry after their child is born also have very high break-up rates. How can this be?

You might think that people getting married are all deciders. After all, marriage requires a big decision. Yet many people still go to the altar or register office feeling pressured in some way. That's the most plausible explanation here. It's likely that many couples who marry after their baby is born are doing it for the children, or because it's the right thing, or because it's what she wants, or because it's what the family wants. In short, they don't get married for themselves but for others. They are sliders and not deciders.

A similar explanation accounts for the collapse in early divorce rates. After rising through the 70s, 80s and 90s, divorce rates in the early years of marriage have fallen steadily. Given the rising acceptance of cohabitation, it seems likely that those who do now get married really mean it. In another Marriage Foundation study, we found that pretty well all of the fall in divorce happens in the early years and among divorces granted to wives.[17] In other words, today's newlywed men are the ones doing better. They are deciders and not sliders.

Breaking the cycle

Now that the trend away from relatively stable marriage and towards relatively unstable cohabitation has become established, producing record levels of breakdown, what hope is there that the cycle can be broken? For me, one of the first steps is to acknowledge that the birth control genie is well and truly out of the bottle. It's no good telling people that cohabitation is risky for relationships and that few unmarried relationships tend to last. Young couples are going to sleep together and move in together because they can. Cohabitation is here to stay. What doesn't have to be here to stay is the incredibly high break-up rate among cohabiting couples. Not all cohabitees do badly. One in three unmarried parents do manage to bring up their children and stay together throughout.[18] But most don't. Living together has become more or less inevitable, and 21% of new parents who identified as Christians in the year 2000/1 were unmarried cohabitees.[19] It's not the ideal. But we need to work with it.[20]

I think the answer to strengthening families and reducing family breakdown lies in finding ways to encourage commitment and get things in the right order. So couples need to be a lot clearer about their plans for the future before moving in together. Ironically, people who say they are moving in to 'test their relationship' tend to have the worst outcomes – more negative communication, more aggression, less confidence, more insecurity – almost as if they already knew![21] Most millennials want to get married some day. Various surveys confirm this.[22] The trouble is that on present trends, only just over half will actually achieve their ambition.[23] As to why, cohabitation has changed the game. Couples tend to move in together early on in their relationship, thus building a fence around them before working out their plans for the garden. Without an explicit promise of a life together, the relationship can easily drift in a state of ambiguity and insecurity until some trigger, such as a baby or cheating, exacerbates their problems enough to make them leave. Then they have to start again, older and hurt. We need to help our children to choose well and, when the time is right, to commit fully or split.

Rules for romance

I have some guidelines that I have used to discuss this with my own teenage and young adult children. To my great delight, they even apply these ideas!

My 'rules for romance' are:

- **Take it slow.** Get to know each other properly – don't rush through society's usual stages of being an official couple, moving in together, getting pregnant and getting married. These all raise the height of the fence and reduce your options before you've settled on a plan.
- **Is he or she marriageable?** You don't have to marry them just yet but nor do you want to waste time on somebody with whom you could never plan a future. 'Marriageable' can mean whatever you like. But

it probably covers things like future potential, kindness, generosity, wisdom, love, not being selfish, and not being manipulative.

- One for the girls. **Does he fight for you?** Boyfriends must be willing to go out of their way for you. Willingness to sacrifice is one of the strongest indicators of men's commitment.[24] This is less true for women whose sacrifice tells you less about their commitment.
- Also for the girls. **Can he make decisions?** Again, this applies more to men than women.[25] If he can't decide, he'll never commit.
- For the boys, **be that man.** Be the man who is marriageable, who puts himself out for women, and who makes decisions.
- And, again for the boys, **choose wisely.** If you're a man of God, choose a woman of God. And look for character. As Proverbs points out three times, watch out for a quarrelsome wife![26]
- Finally, think about a **'two year rule'.** An ambiguous relationship that drifts on without a clear plan tends to suit men more than women. Many women get stuck in a relationship that is going nowhere. Five years later they are still there. So don't waste time on a directionless relationship. Once you're past your early twenties, two years or so should be enough to figure out if this is the right one. How long do you need to find out? Either commit or split.

Action points for church leaders

What can church leaders do to help change the trends in their own congregation?

- **Read some of the empirical research findings** that support the case for marriage, such as via the Marriage Foundation website. Married families tend to be more stable and produce better outcomes for children. Some relationships are bound to fail. But marriage maximises the potential and minimises the risk.
- Recognise that we need to **talk about the importance of marriage.** It's not offensive to single people, lone parents or those divorced or widowed if it's done sensitively. After all, marriage is supposed to model the relationship between Jesus and me, as outlined by Paul in Ephesians chapter 5. In a world of family breakdown and patriarchy, what better way to challenge negative stereotypes about marriage and build confidence that the real biblical model is so liberating, healing and life-giving! Not talking about marriage means ignoring this uplifting context and thus amounts to a surrender to spiritual warfare.

- Really **understand why cohabitation without clear commitment is so destructive** and unhelpful. Cohabitation puts a barrier around a relationship that makes it harder to leave before a plan for the future has been established. It limits choice before the choice has been made. So encourage couples to go slow and have clear unambiguous conversations about their commitment before even thinking about moving in together.
- **Run a marriage course** for those married and a marriage preparation course for those getting married. Courses are off-the-shelf and can be done with videos. No expertise is needed and so there is no excuse for not doing it! Courses can and should be open to cohabitees of course.
- **Rules for romance!** Talk about how to choose well. Most of the practical skills taught on marriage and relationship courses happen automatically if couples have chosen well. Character – such as the 'fruit of the Spirit' (Galatians 5:22-23) – plays a crucial role in how any of us get on with one another. Minimise the scope for ambiguity in relationships by encouraging teens and young adults to have conversations about their plans for the future with their partner. It's only by talking about the shared future that couples can ever be clear about each other's commitment at each stage of the relationship.

CHAPTER 4

Men and church: the 'What?' questions

Annabel Clarke

*Acknowledgements: we would like to thank
Dr Peter Brierley (www.BrierleyConsultancy.com) for his
kind help with sourcing data included in this chapter.*

About the chapter

A few months ago, it was a sunny morning and I was re-painting my garage door. A neighbour who was fairly new to the street came by and we got talking. It turned out that he's a retired church pastor. He and his wife have decades of experience doing fantastic ministry work. The conversation continued, and when I briefly mentioned Engage, he immediately asked some really good questions about men in church – all of which I've often been asked by others. It seems that lots of people are interested in common themes.

This chapter is designed to be a summary, indicating answers to some of the most Frequently Asked Questions (FAQs) which I've heard regarding information about men and church. It will review the available data on the gender imbalance in today's church, how it has changed over the years, whether it varies with age group and marital status, how far it affects different denominations and churchmanships and whether there is a link to the gender of ministers. It isn't intended to be a comprehensive review of all the research available relating to males and females, Christianity and church. It is also beyond the scope of this chapter to offer explanations for all the results and trends. I've just highlighted some key issues which are hopefully a starting point for Christian leaders to consider what we already know and to find out more about what we don't yet know.

I realise most people are busy and might not have time to read in-depth research findings, so I've kept things fairly concise. If you'd like to investigate the questions and research further, I'd suggest that you look at the data sources given for more information.

One thing is certain: there's a clear need for ongoing research to help us answer these questions more fully and effectively. The church urgently needs to understand the gender imbalance it has created, in order to change it.

About the research

We need to bear in mind that direct comparison between different studies outlined in this chapter is difficult for various reasons, such as their use of:

- Different populations/population samples (e.g. data might be for either Great Britain, the United Kingdom, England, Ireland, Scotland, Wales, England and Wales, or a sample within the countries).
- Different definitions of religion or Christianity, or no particular definition.
- Different research methodology (e.g. surveys of the general population, surveys of Christians).
- Different data analysis approaches.
- Different ways of presenting and reporting the data.

Despite these issues, we can look at relevant information and any overall trends to help answer the questions which lots of people seem to be asking.

Is there a gender imbalance in the general UK population?

Only a very slight one overall. The percentage of men varies a little depending on the age group, and overall has gone up a bit over the last 25 years, with more men living longer.

- 0-19 years: There are very slightly more males than females born in the UK. The normal birth ratio of gender is about 106 male: 100 female.
- 30-44 years: This is the age band where the percentage of men first drops a bit below that of women.
- 65 years+: More men are living longer, but more women are still living longer than men.

Table 1. Percentage of males and females born in the UK by age, 2016.[1]

Age group	2016 % of UK population male	% of UK population female
0-19	51	49
20-29	51	49
30-44	50	50
45-64	49	51

Age group	2016	
	% of UK population male	% of UK population female
65-74	48	52
75-84	45	55
85+	35	65
Average	48	52

In the research, is 'church attendance' the same as 'Christian'?

No. Different research studies and different people use 'church attender', 'Christian' and other terms in different ways. This is important because when varying research methodologies and terminology are used, comparison between sets of results becomes difficult. In this chapter we'll focus more on Christians who attend church regularly.

Self-identification

In some research, such as a census, people are asked which religion, if any, they identify with. The 2011 Population Census for England and Wales asked people to tick a box to indicate which religion they self-identified with, or if they had no religion.[2] The religion question was the only voluntary question, and 7.2% of people didn't answer it. It's important to remember that it was only asking about religious affiliation (how we connect or identify with a religion). There are other aspects of religion such as religious belief, religious practice or belonging which are not covered by the analysis in this census. In census terminology, 'Christian' usually therefore includes Nominal or Notional Christian, or a Christian Adherent, as well as Practising Christian.

Going to church may not necessarily mean that someone is a Christian

People who self-identify as 'Christian' may vary in what they understand by the term. People who go to church (even regularly) may not necessarily hold Christian beliefs that most would consider orthodox (not meaning the Orthodox denomination), or consider themselves Practising Christians.

Some Christians don't go to church

In his book The Invisible Church, Steve Aisthorpe highlights research that shows there is a growing number of people who hold orthodox Christian beliefs, but who no longer go to church, for various reasons.[3] He very helpfully explores the myths and stereotypes of churchless Christians and how the church can effectively engage with them.

'Church attendance'

Church attendance can be measured in different ways. One way is to literally count (as it were) 'bottoms on pews'. The English[4] and Scottish[5] Church Censuses do this for example, as they survey who was actually in church, across the denominations, on a certain day (the last ones being 2005 in England, and 2016 in Scotland). Another way is to gather attendance data based on sample surveys. However, this needs to be "treated with caution given well-established concerns over the 'aspirational' reporting of attendance by respondents involving exaggeration of how often they actually visit places of worship."[6] 'Regular' church attendance is generally considered in research terms to be at least once per month. This takes into account that people may not attend every week, or may take part in other church activities during the week or month (and not just go on Sundays).

'Membership'

Some Christian denominations have certain criteria for 'membership'. This generally implies a more committed relationship to a church than 'self-identification' or 'attendance', but variation in the criteria mean that it's difficult to use the term to directly compare churches or denominations.

Issues with measuring 'Christianity'

Most research asks people whether they are 'Christian' without defining the term using doctrinal statements of belief. Some research asks people to describe how much their faith impacts their life, and about how often they do certain activities such as prayer, reading the Bible and going to church, which may indicate the strength of a person's devotion to God. There are some scales and sets of questions that investigate the nature of people's faith in more detail. However, lots of research doesn't incorporate these. Different research may give different figures as to how many 'Christians' there are in a certain population, due to different definitions being used. Sometimes even the way a question is worded (e.g. "Do you regard yourself as belonging to any particular religion?" instead of "What is your religion?") can lead to variations in results in how many people say they are 'Christian'. And ultimately, only God knows where a person is in relationship to him.

Are there gender imbalances in religions worldwide?

It seems to depend on the religion and the country's religious majority. Information from The Pew Research Centre[7] notes that among Muslims and Orthodox Jews, men attend religious services more often, whereas among Christians, women do; "higher levels of weekly attendance among Muslim and Jewish men are due in large part to religious norms that prioritise men's participation in worship services." For example, in most Islamic societies "Muslim men are expected to attend communal Friday midday prayers in the mosque, while women can fulfil this obligation individually, either inside or outside the mosque." Reflecting all this, "the gender gap in worship service attendance differs between Muslim-majority and Christian-majority countries. Men attend more often in predominantly Muslim countries and Israel, but women attend more often than men in predominantly Christian countries."

The Pew Research Centre notes that across religions it has been found that:

- Generally, more women than men pray daily.
- Religion is equally or more important to women than to men.
- Women and men are about equally likely to believe in heaven, hell and angels.

Do other religions have a gender imbalance in the UK?

Not as much as Christianity does, according to the 2011 Population Census for England and Wales[8] and Scotland's Census 2011.[9]

Christianity seems to have the largest gender imbalance, with 46% male and 54% female in this data. We need to remember that the voluntary question on religion in the 2011 Census was intended to capture people's religious affiliation and identification at the time of the Census, irrespective of whether they practised or believed in that religion or how important it was in their lives. If a person had no religion then the first of a series of tick boxes could be selected. This means that the proportions of men and women in this data may not match the proportions in other data (e.g. church attendance data), but at least it's information which allows some comparison with other religions.

In summary:

- There are more male Muslims, Hindus and Sikhs than there are females for each of those religions.
- There are fewer male Christians, Buddhists and Jews than there are females for each of those religions.

- The biggest gender imbalanced groups are 'Other religion', where there are fewest men (44%), and 'No religion' where there are most men (55%).
- Overall, men are generally less likely to self-identify with a religion.

The percentage of male and female for different religions is given in Table 2, from the 2011 Population Census for England and Wales. The gender imbalance trends are comparable and in the same direction for the UK as a whole and so aren't all given in detail for ease of reading and comparison.

Table 2. Percentage of males and females by religion in England and Wales, 2011.[10]

Religion	% Male	% Female
Other religion	44	56
Christian	46	54
Buddhist	47	53
Jewish	49	51
Sikh	51	49
Religion not stated	51	49
Hindu	52	48
Muslim	52	48
No religion	55	45

Some other interesting comparison points from the 2011 Population Census for England and Wales are these.

Table 3. Some trends in religion by age and ethnic background, 2011 Population Census for England and Wales.

	Christian	Muslim	No religion
Change in last 10 years	4.1 million fewer. Decrease equally split between men and women.	1.2 million more. Increases for both men and women.	5.8 million more. Increase to 13.1 million.
Age trends	Male 35 to 39 age group decreased the most with 47% reporting as Christian in 2011 compared to 66% in 2001.	Increases for every age group.	Increases for every age group.

	Christian	Muslim	No religion
Ethnic background and country of birth	89% Christians born in the UK. 11% born outside the UK, 25% of these from EU accession countries (including Poland).	47% Muslims born in the UK. 53% born outside the UK.	93% born in the UK. 7% born outside the UK.

To give the wider context, the number and proportions of people answering the 2011 Population Census question about religion across the UK were as follows.

Table 4. Number and proportion of people in the UK by religion, 2011.[11]

	Christian	Muslim	All other religions	No religion	Not Stated	Total
England						
Total	31,479,876	2,660,116	1,954,128	13,114,232	3,804,104	53,012,456
% of population	59	5	4	25	7	100
Wales						
Total	1,763,299	45,950	37,282	982,997	233,928	3,063,456
% of population	58	1	1	32	8	100
Scotland						
Total	2,850,199	76,737	59,312	1,941,116	368,039	5,295,403
% of population	54	1	1	37	7	100
Northern Ireland						
Total	1,490,588	In 'All other Religions'	14,859	183,164	122,252	1,810,863
% of population	82	In 'All other Religions'	1	10	7	100
Whole UK						
Total	37,583,962	2,782,853	2,065,581	16,221,509	4,528,323	63,182,178
% of population	60	4	3	26	7	100

Is there definitely a gender imbalance in today's church?

Yes, there's a definite gender imbalance in today's national church. Overall, the church leaders we've been working with are very conscious of the problem and want to do something about it. Some church leaders have told us they think the gender imbalance isn't too bad in their church. However, when asked, they usually admit that they've never actually counted the numbers of men, women, boys and girls, and so their perception isn't really evidence-based. One church leader told me that his congregation had "loads of men." I happened to be visiting his church just after that, so I counted. It was 87% women. Perhaps as a man he more easily saw the men? Could it be that a bit of 'confirmation bias' was at play here? Perhaps he was keen to confirm and convey that he didn't have a problem?

How much of a gender imbalance is there in the church?

The answer to this question varies, depending on what research we look at and how it was carried out. Table 5 gives a summary of findings from some key relevant research.

Table 5. Surveys reporting the numbers of men and women in the national church.

Research	Methodology	Men	Women
2005 English Church Census[12]	Surveyed who was actually in church (total 3.2 million), across the denominations, on a certain day.	43%	57%
2016 Scottish Church Census[13]	Surveyed who was actually in church (total 390,000), across the denominations, on a certain day.	40%	60%
2007 Tearfund report "Churchgoing in the UK"[14]	A representative poll of 7000 adults in the UK which asked about typical churchgoing habits and experiences of all adult respondents except those of other religions.	47% of men said they were "Christians". 35% of "Regular churchgoers" (attend at least monthly). 7% attend church weekly.	60% of women said they were "Christians". 65% of "Regular churchgoers" (attend at least monthly). 13% attend church weekly.

Research	Methodology	Men	Women
2014 YouGov for Christian Vision for Men and Single Christians report "Men practising Christian worship"[15]	YouGov representative survey of 7212 GB adults aged 16+. An invited panel of internet users completed an online survey. Responses weighted in line with demographic information.	13.9% identified as Practising Christians. 8.6% Practising Christians going to worship at least once a year. 4.4% Practising Christians going to worship at least once a month. 3.0% Practising Christians going to worship at least once a week.	16.7% identified as Practising Christians. 10.6% Practising Christians going to worship at least once a year. 5.2% Practising Christians going to worship at least once a month. 3.5% Practising Christians going to worship at least once a week.
2011 National Census for England and Wales[16]	Self-identification of type of religious affiliation: Christian.	46%	54%
2011 Scotland's National Census[17]		48%	52%

Although it is not possible to directly compare results between surveys using different methodologies, it is interesting to note that the average proportions of men and women across the different surveys described here are as follows for monthly church attendance.

Table 6. Average proportions of male and female monthly church attenders in four national surveys.

Survey	Monthly church attenders	
	Male	Female
English Church Census (2005)	43%	57%
Scottish Church Census (2016)	40%	60%
Tearfund UK (2007)	35%	65%
YouGov GB (2014)	45%	55%
Average	40%	60%

It is therefore suggested that for ease of communication about the current church gender imbalance overall, the summary average figures of '40% male: 60% female' or '2 men: 3 women' could be considered appropriate.

Some other key points from the information for this section are as follows:

- 2005 English Church Census data shows a gender imbalance of 43% males, 57% females. **This equates to 444,900 more women than men.**
- 2016 Scottish Church Census data shows a gender imbalance of 40% males, 60% females. **This equates to 80,130 more women than men.**
- YouGov (2014), for Christian Vision for Men and Single Christians found 4.4% of GB men attending church at least monthly and 5.2% women doing so. **This equates to half a million more women than men.**
- Tearfund (2007) found 35% of regular churchgoers (at least monthly) to be men, and 65% to be women. **This equates to about 2.3 million more women than men.**
- 2011 National Census data tells us who affiliates with Christianity or self-identifies as Christian, which includes nominal and non-practising Christians. For England and Wales the imbalance is 46% male, 56% female. **This equates to 2.65 million more women than men.** For Scotland, the imbalance is 48% male, 52% female. **This equates to 160,515 more women than men.**
- Overall, these national research findings indicate, depending on methodology, a huge gender imbalance amongst Christians and in the church, of **between half a million and about 2 ½ million more women than men.**
- This clearly has massive implications that must be addressed for men, women, children and young people, those outside the church and church leaders.

How has the proportion of men and women in church changed over time in the UK?

The 2001 England and Wales Census was the first to ask a question about religious belief – and famously also recorded that 390,000 residents said they were of the Jedi 'faith'.[18]

In order to consider information over a longer (and perhaps more reliable) time frame, we can look at the Church Census data for England and Scotland (actual church attendance recorded on a specific day). This indicates that overall, the proportion of men has gone down in England, and the proportion of women has gone up. In contrast, the proportion of men has gone up in Scotland, and the proportion of women has gone down.

English Church Census

This data is taken from the English Church Census Data for 1979, 1989, 1998 and 2005 (and extrapolated forwards for 2010 and 2020). Instead of showing just people who report that they are 'Christian' (like the National Population Census), this surveys who was actually in church, across the denominations, on a certain day. And it shows a bigger gender imbalance than the 2011 Population Census for England and Wales.

It also shows that the proportion of males attending church has declined over time, with current proportions in the church estimated to be about 41% male, 59% female. The number of additional females has remained remarkably even, given the overall declining numbers.

Table 7. Change in proportion of males and females attending church in England, 1980-2020.[19]

	Total	% Male	% Female	Number of additional females
1980	4,477,700	45	55	474,900
1990	4,070,500	44	56	478,700
2000	3,454,000	43	57	487,200
2010	3,068,300	42	58	474,700
2020	2,786,300	41	59	467,300

Scottish Church Census 2016

Whilst it might sound like a good thing that the proportion of men in church in Scotland is increasing, this is in the context of a very big decline in numbers overall of people attending church, and at least partly due to the large numbers of women also leaving the church (see also the answer to the next question). The number of additional females has decreased over time.

Table 8. Change in proportion of males and females attending church in Scotland, 1984-2025.[20]

	Total	% Male	% Female	Number of additional females
1984	853,700	37	63	221,960
1994	691,120	39	61	152,040
2002	570,130	40	60	118,030

	Total	% Male	% Female	Number of additional females
2016	389,510	40	60	80,130
2025 predicted	294,500	40	60	59,500

Are men and women joining or leaving church at the same rate?

It's very useful to consider the proportions of males and females in the church. However, if we just looked at the proportion data alone, it could be misleading. What if the proportion of males is going up in some church congregations just because there are lots more females leaving? Looking at the Church Census data over time, it seems that this is actually the case in Scotland, but not in England. In England, more males have left the church than females. In Scotland, more females have left the church than males.

It should be noted that English data was last collected in 2005 and later years are extrapolated, whereas Scottish data is more recent. The available timeframes don't exactly match and so comparisons can't be exact, but they are still interesting.

Table 9. Percentage average annual change in church attendance in England (1980-2020) and Scotland (1984-2016).[21]

	England % AAC*		Scotland % AAC*	
	1980-2020		1984-2016	
	Male	Female	Male	Female
Overall	-1.4%	-1.0%	-1.6%	-2%

*%AAC = Percentage Average Annual Change

Do different age groups in church show a different gender balance?

Again, we can look at the English and Scottish Church Census data. It is important to note two factors about death and birth when looking at any gender imbalance by different age groups, which will impact overall summary proportion figures across all age groups. Firstly, one of the reasons for there being more women than men in the church overall is that women live longer than men. This affects the '65 & over' patterns in Tables 10 and 11. However, the church gender imbalance in older age groups is not just due to normal demographic differences, as we will see. Secondly, the gender birth ratio in Great Britain is currently about 106 boys for every 100 girls. Ideally, we should therefore see slightly more boys than girls in church. However, in this, as in other demographic characteristics, the church does not proportionally reflect general society.

English Church Census 2005
Overall, this data indicates there are currently more females than males in all age groups, except for those aged 15-19. Over time, the proportion of males attending church has gone down in most age groups (under 15, 20-29, 45-64), stayed the same in a couple of age groups (30-44, 65 & over), and gone up in one age group (15-19). There are more women than men in the over-65 age group, but this is not simply due to normal demographic differences. In the general population of England in 2005 there were 1.31 women for every man aged 65 or over; in the churches there were 1.56.

Table 10. Percentage of males and females attending church in England, 1980-2020, by age group.[22]

	Under 15		15-19		20-29		30-44		45-64		65 & over	
	%M	%F	%M	%F	%M	%F	%M	%F	%M	%F	%M	%F
1980	50	50	44	46	45	55	44	56	45	55	38	62
1990	50	50	46	44	44	56	43	57	43	57	38	62
2000	47	53	49	51	44	56	43	57	42	58	39	61
2010	46	54	50	50	44	56	43	57	41	59	39	61
2020	45	55	50	50	44	56	44	56	40	60	39	61

Scottish Church Census 2016
This data shows that there are more females than males in all age groups. The overall proportion of males was 40% compared to 60% females. There are almost twice as many women as men in the over-65 age group but this is not simply due to normal demographic differences. In the general population of Scotland in 2016 there were 1.25 women for every man aged 65 or over; in the churches there were 1.76. It's interesting to see that over time, the proportion of males has gone up across all age groups.

Table 11. Percentage of males and females attending church in Scotland, 1984-2016, by age group.[23]

	Under 15		15-19		20-29		30-44		45-64		65 & over	
	%M	%F	%M	%F	%M	%F	%M	%F	%M	%F	%M	%F
1984	44	56	40	60	33	67	33	67	37	63	32	68
1994	48	52	46	54	38	62	35	65	37	63	36	64
2002	44	56	48	52	47	53	38	62	40	60	35	65
2016	46	54	45	55	44	56	42	58	40	60	36	64

Does the church gender imbalance differ with marital status?

Yes, the gender imbalance (fewer men) is bigger among single/unpartnered people than among married/partnered people.

YouGov (2014) undertook a survey of adults in Great Britain for Christian Vision for Men and Single Christians Ltd.[24] For this, 'Partnered' included Married, Civil Partnership, Living together as married and Separated. 'Unpartnered' included Never Married, Divorced and Widowed. It was found that:

- Overall, there are more unpartnered women (18%) than men (14%) attending church at least once a year (and a similar order was found for those attending at least once a month).
- Amongst the middle class, there are double the number of unpartnered women than unpartnered men (see also the next question).
- Both men and women are less likely to attend church regularly (at least once a month) if they are unpartnered, than if they are partnered.
- Unpartnered men are the least likely to go to church regularly.
- There are lots more partnered people in church (68%) than unpartnered (32%).
- There are more partnered women than men in church (where are their husbands?).
- There are more partnered and fewer unpartnered people in church than in wider society.

The Evangelical Alliance (2012) carried out an online survey of adult evangelical Christians (1219 volunteers).[25] This found:

- There were 1.7 single females to each single man, although there was about the same number of men and women completing the survey.
- Among the single people over-55, the imbalance rose to 1 man: 3 women (this will be somewhat, but not entirely due to women living longer).

Points stated by the report included the following:

- There are significant numbers of single people – especially women – who would like to be married but can't find a Christian partner, or have gone into relationships or marriages with non-Christians, in some cases with unhappy results.
- Around 22% of respondents were single, with 37% of them living alone. Around 61% of the under-35s said they were single, compared to 7.5% of the over-55s.
- 80% of the male respondents were married, compared to 58% of the women – who were almost twice as likely as the men to be single, widowed or living in a relationship other than married.
- 87% of men had married a woman who was a Christian at the time they got married, 23% of women had married a non-Christian man. This probably reflects more than anything else the comparative absence of eligible men in churches.
- Having a Christian spouse is a significant factor for a happy marriage. Over 90% of Christian couples expressed happiness with their marriage, while only 66% of those in a mixed marriage did so.

The following conclusions were also highlighted, all of which are relevant to the partners of Engage, and this book.

"If these patterns are in any way typical of the population of evangelical Christians in British churches there are some serious questions as to the scarcity of unmarried men.

- Are men in general less likely to have found faith, or do they feel uncomfortable in church unless they are part of a couple or family?
- Or is church culture simply reflecting broader social patterns and becoming increasingly feminised or emasculated?"

All this information on singleness and marriage gives a very clear wake-up call to the church.

Does the church gender imbalance vary depending on socio-economic status?

Yes. The definition of social grades is used and maintained by the Market Research Society. The grades are often grouped into ABC1 and C2DE and these are usually taken to equate to middle class and working class respectively.

YouGov (2014) for Christian Vision for Men and Single Christians Ltd found that:

- Overall, 62% of regular church attendees are middle class (ABC1) and

only 38% working class (C2DE).
- There was less of a gender imbalance among partnered ABC1 men and women (23% and 26% respectively), and partnered C2DE (working class) men and women (18% and 20% respectively).
- There are twice as many unpartnered middle-class women than unpartnered middle-class men.
- The only group that did not show a gender imbalance was unpartnered C2DE (working class) people.[26]

This is based on data about people who said they attended church at least once a year, although results were reported to be similar for people who said they attended regularly (at least once a month).

Does the gender imbalance vary depending on where you live?

Not really. The English Church Census (2005) found that there was very little variation in the percentages of men who attended church in the following environments: city centre, inner city, council estate, suburban, separate towns, other built up, commuter rural, remoter rural.[27]

Is the gender imbalance the same across different types of churches?

No, it varies. We can look at this in two ways, either by denomination or by churchmanship. Overall, data suggests that the extent of the gender imbalance has more to do with churchmanship than denomination.

Denomination

The following table shows the percentages of male and female data from the English Church Census 2005, given in order of the most gender balanced denominations first. The numbers of older people (and women living longer) will be a factor affecting these figures to some extent.

Table 12. Percentage of males and females attending church in England by denomination, 2005.[28]

Denomination	% Male	% Female	% Fewer males than females
New Churches	50	50	0
Pentecostal	49	51	-2

Denomination	% Male	% Female	% Fewer males than females
Independent	48	52	-4
Roman Catholic	45	55	-10
Orthodox	45	55	-10
Smaller Denominations	42	58	-16
Baptist	41	59	-18
Anglican	40	60	-20
Methodist	36	64	-28
URC	35	65	-30

If we look at figures over time, these show that some denominations have seen a decreasing proportion of males.

Table 13. Changes in percentage of male church attenders in England by denomination, 1989-2005.[29]

Denomination	% Male		Become more balanced over time?
	1989	2005	
New Churches	N/A	50	N/A
Pentecostal	43	49	Yes
Independent	49	48	No
Roman Catholic	45	45	No
Orthodox	44	45	Yes
Smaller Denominations	41	42	Yes
Baptist	40	41	Yes
Anglican	39	40	Yes
Methodist	37	36	No
URC	37	35	No

Female attendance figures are the percentages given for males taken away from 100.

Churchmanship

The overall context of churchmanship attendance is that Evangelical churches are the largest proportion and growing, whereas Liberal/Broad churches are declining.[30] With the most gender balanced churchmanship given first, the overall percentage of males and females (again from the English Church Census 2005) are as follows.

Table 14. Percentage of males and females attending church in England by churchmanship, 2005.[31]

Churchmanship	% Male	% Female	% Fewer males than females
Catholic	46	54	-8
Charismatic Evangelical	46	54	-8
Mainstream Evangelical	43	57	-14
Others	42	58	-16
Anglo-Catholic	41	59	-18
Broad Evangelical	41	59	-18
Broad	40	60	-20
Liberal	39	61	-22
Low Church	37	67	-30

Most types of churchmanship have seen a slightly increasing proportion of males over time. This seems like good news, considering that, as we've seen, the overall picture for England is not one of more women than men leaving the church. However, as the answers to our other questions show, there is still a very long way to go in creating a gender balanced church across all types of churchmanship.

Table 15. Changes in percentage of male church attenders in England by churchmanship, 1989-2005.[32]

Churchmanship	% Male		Become more balanced over time?
	1989	2005	
Catholic	44	46	Yes
Charismatic Evangelical	42	46	Yes
Mainstream Evangelical	41	43	Yes
Others	41	42	Yes
Anglo-Catholic	40	41	Yes
Broad Evangelical	40	41	Yes
Broad	39	40	Yes
Liberal	39	39	No
Low Church	37	37	No

Female attendance figures are the percentages given taken away from 100.

Implications

This information suggests that what's needed is for all churches, regardless of their denomination or churchmanship, to gather demographics data (including gender, anonymously) for their congregations. If this was done at local church and national levels more regularly, it could then helpfully inform positive action to redress the gender imbalance. When one of my friends heard that some of the most recently collected relevant data we have available is from 2005, he commented "But that's nearly half a generation ago!"

Has the increased number of women ministers led to the decreased numbers of men in church?

Data does not indicate that this is the case. Sometimes when people ask this question, they are thinking that the gender of a church's minister is the only factor affecting the gender balance of the congregation, although this is very unlikely. However, we can look at figures for denomination, churchmanship, proportion of female ministers and the extent of the church gender imbalance.

Context

The proportion of female ministers in the UK has risen from 9% in 1995 to 16% in 2017, and will rise to 17% by 2030 if present trends continue.[33]

The most recent data available regarding the congregational gender balance for different denominations is from the English Church Census 2005. This is given below, along with data for the total number of ministers and percentage of female ministers in 2005 in the UK. Clearly this is putting data for England alongside data for the whole of the UK, and so direct and accurate comparisons cannot be drawn. Another issue is that unfortunately, while the number of minsters and female minsters in the UK for 2017 is available, recent congregational gender balance data is not available. This does highlight the need for regular data collection. The following is nevertheless included in case it is of interest.

Denominations

Table 16. Proportion of female ministers by UK denomination.[34]

Denomination	2005			2017	
	Total no. of ministers, UK	% Female ministers, UK	% Fewer males than females in the English Church Census	Total no. of ministers, UK	% Female ministers, UK
Catholic	5316	0%	-10	4889	0%
Orthodox	297	0%	-10	359	0%
Independent	1959	2%	-4	2267	5%
New churches	2583	14%	0	3433	17%
Baptist	2894	10%	-18	2761	13%
Pentecostal	5514	15%	-2	8814	14%
Anglican	10,350	16%	-20	8558	28%
Smaller Denominations	1808	46%	-16	5098	10%
Methodist	2290	29%	-28	2140	39%
Presbyterian	2323	18%	-30	1949	18%
Total	35,334			40,268	

Despite it not being possible to compare 'like-with-like' data here, some observations can be made. From denominational data, if the gender imbalance in the church was solely caused by the increasing numbers of female ministers, we might expect to see, for example:

- Denominations that don't have any women ministers to be gender balanced – but they're not (Catholic and Orthodox churches).
- All the denominations that have a small gender imbalance to have a smaller proportion of female minsters – but they don't necessarily (Pentecostal churches).
- Denominations that have a similar proportion of female minsters to have a similar gender imbalance – but they don't (Baptist and Pentecostal churches).

So it seems we can't simply conclude that the extent of the gender imbalance in a church or a denomination is just due to the number of female ministers. The picture is clearly more complex than that – there must be other factors involved.

Churchmanship

If the gender imbalance in the church was solely due to numbers of female ministers, we might also expect to see a straightforward pattern in the churchmanship data of those with fewer female ministers being more gender balanced. However, this isn't the case. As with the figures for denominations, the picture is mixed, indicating that other factors are involved.

Table 17. Proportion of female ministers by churchmanship in the UK, 2005.[35]

Churchmanship	Total number of UK ministers, 2005	% Female ministers UK, 2005	% Fewer males than females in church, 2005
Catholic	730	5%[36]	-8
Charismatic Evangelical	347	6%	-8
Mainstream Evangelical	458	9%	-14
Others	1556	17%	-16
Anglo-Catholic	412	7%	-18
Broad Evangelical	912	8%	-18
Broad	1682	10%	-20
Liberal	2143	18%	-22
Low Church	422	15%	-30
Total	8662		

Is church growth due to having a male minister?

Denominations

If church growth was solely due to having a male minister, we might expect to see, for example:

- Denominations that only have male ministers to be growing faster over time – but they're not necessarily (Catholic churches).
- Denominations that have proportionally more women minsters to be growing more slowly or declining faster over time – but they're not necessarily (Pentecostal and New Churches).

The picture is therefore mixed, and it seems that church growth or decline cannot simply be attributed to the gender of its minister.

Table 18. Change in numbers of attenders (2012-2017), and proportion of female and male ministers (2017) in the UK by denomination.[37]

Denomination	Total UK numbers 2017	% Change in numbers 2012-2017	% Female ministers, UK 2017	% Male ministers, UK 2017
Catholic	1,300,703	-12	0%	100%
Orthodox	514,095	+17	0%	100%
Independent Churches	233,487	+6	5%	95%
Smaller Denominations	289,071	+9	10%	90%
Baptist	179,611	-6	13%	87%
Pentecostal	399,504	+11	14%	86%
New Churches	209,906	+13	17%	83%
Anglican	1,167,201	-18	28%	72%
Methodist	198,120	-15	39%	61%
Total	**4,491,698**			

Churchmanship

Currently available data for this is less recent (2005) and so can't be directly compared to figures just given about denominations (2017). However, it still does not suggest that church growth is solely due to the gender of the minister. Differences must involve other factors.

Table 19. Change in numbers of attenders (2000-2005), and proportion of female and male ministers (2005) in the UK by churchmanship.[38]

Churchmanship	Total UK numbers 2005	% Change in numbers 2000-2005	% Female ministers, UK 2005	% Male ministers, UK 2005
Catholic	874,300	-10%	5%	95%
Charismatic Evangelical	505,800	-3%	6%	94%
Mainstream Evangelical	597,600	-6%	9%	91%
Others	104,900	-7%	17%	83%
Anglo-Catholic	149,700	-4%	7%	93%
Broad Evangelical	189,400	-14%	8%	92%
Broad	295,000	-10%	10%	90%
Liberal	304,700	-16%	18%	82%

Churchmanship	Total UK numbers 2005	% Change in numbers 2000-2005	% Female ministers, UK 2005	% Male ministers, UK 2005
Low Church	214,700	-9%	15%	85%
Total	3,236,100			

Summary

There is a stark gender imbalance in the UK church, with proportions varying depending on how they are measured, but overall in the region of 40% male, 60% female. This equates to at least half a million more women than men attending church regularly in the UK, and up to about 2 ½ million more nominal female attenders. For regular church attenders, the gender imbalance is bigger among single people than married people. It is essential that the church recognises and addresses the hugely adverse consequences of the situation for men, women and children/young people, both in the church and wider society.

Action points

The national church
- Collaboration between leaders of denominations, networks and organisations is needed to create a standard approach to all relevant national data being gathered more regularly and longitudinally to monitor trends. This can then be used to inform action to redress the gender imbalance and other issues arising.

The local church
- It is recommended that individual churches regularly carry out anonymous demographic surveys of their congregation, asking the age, gender and marital status of their members (and allowing for the fact that some may prefer not to say). This is something ministers can do as soon as possible but ideally would link in with national data collection in due course (as above). Congregations will need to know that the purpose of the survey is to inform how the church can more effectively reach and support different people. A simple example survey is given on the Engage website.

- It will be also good for churches to audit the age and gender of those in their children and young people's groups, adult groups and ministries, and staff teams.
- Churches need to use information such as this to inform more effective evangelism and discipleship for different groups of people.

CHAPTER 5

Men and church: the 'Why?' questions

Annabel Clarke

I once went to an event for Christian leaders and was chatting to a small group of others. One man was very keen to start telling me why he thought there aren't as many men in church as women. He was pretty much cut short by the next person eagerly chipping in with their view, and before I knew it, they were all vigorously debating what should be done about the problem (in a godly way, of course!). Almost everyone has an opinion, it seems.

So *why* are men a minority in church, if the vast majority of church ministers are men (and have been in the past)? This is a crucial question. As far as we know, the factors causing the church gender imbalance haven't yet been investigated by much research. Like lots of complex situations, it's likely that there's not just one, but a number of interacting causes. In this chapter, although it won't be possible to cover every aspect of the discussions people may have around differences between men and women, we will look at some of the reasons that have been put forward, to help us seek solutions for creating a more gender balanced church.

God loves women more than men...?

"Either God loves women more than men, or we're doing something wrong," is how Carl Beech (President of Christian Vision for Men) has been known to summarise things.[1] Since God can't love women more than men, the church clearly needs to act on the alternative that "we're doing something wrong."

Men's and women's brains are just hard-wired differently...?

If you ever hear someone use this hypothesis to suggest why there are fewer men in church (or to suggest anything at all, actually), then it's time for alarm bells to ring. This one is actually listed as one of the *Great Myths of the Brain* in the book of that name by Christian Jarrett, a Cognitive Neuroscientist who is also editor of the British Psychological Society's Research Digest.[2] Here are some other popular, related but completely untrue 'neuromyths' (as they're known) that he addresses:

- Men's and women's brains are wired up differently and show different connectivity patterns: sometimes used to back the claim that women are better at multi-tasking and men are better at map-reading.
- Women's brain functioning is more balanced and global across both brain hemispheres, whereas men use a specific part of a single hemisphere to accomplish a task: this is sometimes used, for example, to explain that men tend to only think about one thing at a time and so forget to bring home the milk.[3]
- Men are more left-brained, women tend to be more right-brained: neuroscience shows that in reality we all use both our left or right brain hemispheres to different degrees depending on what mental activities we're currently doing. It's not valid to say that someone is 'left-brained' (analytic) or 'right-brained' (creative).

And an additional popular one:

- Men and women (or boys and girls) have different 'learning styles': this originates from work by people such as Honey and Mumford who proposed that people can be classified according to their 'style' of learning.[4] However, we've now known for a while that the concept of 'learning styles' is scientifically unsupported, although it's one of the most persistent neuromyths around.[5] Actually, everyone learns best when a variety of teaching approaches are used and these involve active engagement with the content in some way (not just passive listening).

Men and women are just very different...?

From a biological and physical perspective, yes, there are some obvious differences. Apart from that, members of the general public, perhaps influenced by books such as John Gray's book *Men Are from Mars, Women Are from Venus*,[6] often believe that differences between men and women are larger than are actually shown by research. This is a massive field of investigation, and one that involves significant debate (and sometimes controversy) between different scientists. Any attempt at a comprehensive review would be far beyond the scope of this chapter, but a few of the issues are outlined below.

'Oh yes they are...'

On the one hand, there are studies, including meta-analyses (where researchers combine the findings from multiple studies to draw a more reliable overall conclusion) which show sex differences for some behaviours. Here are a few of them.

- Risk taking: men showed more risk taking behaviours, but this varied depending on the type of risk, and the age of the men. Certain topics (e.g. intellectual risk taking and physical skills) produced larger gender differences than others (e.g. smoking). Gender differences were found to be growing smaller over time.[7] At the same time, other research demonstrated that the supposedly 'robust' claim that 'women are more risk averse than men' is far less empirically supported than has been claimed.[8]
- Interests: men preferred working with things and women preferred working with people, although the effect size varied depending on how the different studies were carried out.[9]
- Values: men attributed consistently more importance than women to power, stimulation, hedonism, achievement, and self-direction values. The reverse was true for benevolence and universalism values. Overall, however, differences in values were more to do with age and culture than with sex.[10]
- Sexuality: gender differences in sexual attitudes and behaviours were found, but these were small. Exceptions were masturbation incidence, pornography use, casual sex, and attitudes toward casual sex, for which male participants reported somewhat more sexual behaviour or permissive attitudes than female participants. Older age groups and cultures with greater gender equity had smaller gender differences for some reported sexual behaviours.[11]
- Aggression: Findings indicated increased male use of costly methods of aggression, rather than different levels of anger between men and women.[12]

'Oh no they're not...'

On the other hand, The Gender Similarities Hypothesis was developed by Hyde (2005, 2014) who found that males and females are similar on most, but not all, psychological variables.[13] This came after a large meta-analysis showed that 78% of the gender differences researched were statistically small or close to zero. In other words, there is much larger within-gender variation than between-gender variation. This has been shown to be the case for cognitive variables, communication (interruptions, talkativeness, self-disclosure, facial expression processing), social and personality variables (aggression, negotiation, helping behaviour, leadership effectiveness, self-esteem, depression symptoms) and moral reasoning. There were larger differences (higher scores for men) for physical aggression.

One problem is that the extent of the gender differences reported in research studies can depend very much on how the research is carried out. A key book about this is Cordelia Fine's *Delusions of Gender: The real science behind sex differences*. She notes the need to carefully investigate the specific details of the methodology used. One example given highlights the need to be cautious about drawing firm conclusions from brain scan results. Some researchers had suggested that brain scans showed statistically significant differences in men and women's brain activity when given 'empathising tasks' (suggesting men are more 'thinkers' and women are more 'feelers'). To show that the usual threshold for 'significant difference' is perhaps not high enough, other scientists "recently scanned an Atlantic salmon while showing it emotionally charged photographs. The salmon – which, by the way, 'was not alive at the time of scanning' – was 'asked to determine what emotion the individual in the photo must have been experiencing'. They found significant brain activity in one small region of the dead fish's brain while it performed the empathising task, compared with brain activity during 'rest.'" It was concluded that sometimes studies are inadequate "because they allow too many spurious results through the net."[14]

Other issues to bear in mind with research in this area can include the following.

- Small sample sizes.
- 'Self-report bias': people's self-reports of their characteristics don't always match objective measures.
- 'Stereotype threat': gender stereotypes are primed in our mind, and this interferes with our ability and interest in the task. For example, simply by recording their sex at the beginning of a quantitative (number) test can reduce women's scores.[15]
- 'File-drawer phenomenon': it may be that studies that do find sex-differences get published (and make the headlines), but those that don't just remain unpublished and unseen in a researcher's file drawer. Perhaps they're not as interesting?
- Impact of other variables: sometimes the extent of sex-differences found varies depending on the specific task, the way something is measured, the social context, or the location.

Nature or nurture...?

The extent to which any sex differences are due to any innate 'maleness' or 'femaleness', and how much due to social learning, context and experience, remains a matter for debate. In lots of ways, it is difficult, if not impossible, to establish a clear picture.

Can we expect men and women to change from being 'just the way they are'...?

By saying individual differences are 'hard-wired', people often mean 'born a certain way' which is 'unchangeable'. Some might think, "That's just the way I am due to my life experiences." From a biblical perspective, we are all created as unique individuals, with different gifts and characteristics. Paul describes in 1 Corinthians 12 that we're all needed for the full, healthy functioning of the body of Christ (the church). At the same time, as Max Lucado has said, "God loves you just the way you are, but he refuses to leave you that way. He wants you to be just like Jesus."[16] There are many passages throughout the Bible which encourage us to put intentional effort into changing our thoughts, feelings and behaviours, even though we're saved by grace alone. We're all called to grow in holiness, and the Lord helps us to change.

A significant field of contemporary science looks at 'brain plasticity', or the capacity of the nervous system to change its organisation and function over time. The good news from this is that learning and emotional/social development can take place, given the right circumstances. To use stereotypical examples, if a women finds map-reading difficult, she can learn to get better at it. If a man finds it hard to empathise, he can learn to get better at it.

There's also the influence of a person's mindset. Carol Dweck (Professor of Psychology at Stanford University) has shown how some people have more of a 'fixed mindset' and believe that their qualities and traits are 'set in stone' and not something that can be practised or developed. Others have more of a 'growth mindset' and believe that effort or training can change and develop one's qualities and traits.[17] Dweck's work has shown how important a growth mindset is in positively influencing personality, motivation and learning.[18]

How about children and young people...?

The international meta-analysis by Hattie (2009) summarises "There is more variance within groups of boys and within groups of girls than there are differences between boys and girls" (supporting Hyde's Gender Similarities Hypothesis). This came after he analysed nearly 3000 studies involving 5½ million participants. The things that help the effective achievement and development of children and young people are the same for both genders.[19]

Summary

The information summarised here illustrates that it's very difficult to draw simple and firm conclusions from research about the differences between men and women. One study might show a difference, another might not. Meta-analyses are useful (where researchers combine the findings from multiple studies to draw a more reliable overall conclusion).

Key points to remember are:

It will be helpful for people in church to avoid making stereotyped generalisations about men and women.

- It's not necessarily valid to try and apply research results to the church gender imbalance when this involves taking findings out of context.
- Some of us are better at some things than others, but personal growth and learning is possible for everyone.

Social issues affecting males more than females aren't always effectively addressed by the church...?

The latest copy of The Psychologist, the magazine of The British Psychological Society (BPS), came through my door this week. In it is a section headed "Pioneering new ways to reach men and boys."[20] This outlines that there are a number of well-researched and documented social and emotional problems that affect men and boys more than women and girls. In the UK today, young men make up less than 40% of those in higher education. Men make up 75% of suicides, and suicide is the biggest killer of men under 45, but men are less likely than women to seek help from psychologists. Men make up 85% of rough sleepers, 95% of the prison population, 75% of addicts, 40% of reported domestic abuse victims and 97% of those who die at work. The authors include a Consultant Clinical Psychologist and a member of Central London Samaritans. They are advocating setting up a Male Psychology Section within the BPS (there has been a Psychology of Women and Equalities Section since 1988). They call for psychologists to "pioneer new ways of reaching men and boys in need of our help...and create the research, teaching and interventions that can help boys and men, and by extension help also the women and girls who share their lives."

All of this has got to be of interest to the church, and I can't help noticing that that last sentence could relate to the work of Engage with the church.

Churches are ideally placed to further prevent and address the spiritual, emotional and social issues underlying the problems that men are facing. They can facilitate the connection and relational support that men need, but which is not always in place (whether for social, cultural or personal reasons). It could be that if churches did this more effectively, boys and men might be more likely to become, and stay involved in faith. The type of helpful men's ministry that Nathan describes in Chapter 6 would enable this.

Men don't feel that they belong...?

A key part of emotional and social wellbeing is 'belongingness' – the important human emotional need to be an accepted member of a group. It's about feeling that you're an important part of something greater than yourself, whether it's with your family, friends, work team, sports team, church or other group. Obviously this is equally important for men and women, whether single or married.

The YouGov (2014) survey for Christian Vision for Men and Single Christians found that if a man had children, they were more likely to attend church more often. Older men (40-54) with no dependent children said they were practising Christians but attended church less often. Many men were in churches over 10 years, but then appeared to leave because of finding little of real value other than their presence for their children.[21]

It's worth churches investigating how much the men in their congregation feel that they belong. Do they have a valued role both in the church and as part of a calling and purpose for their life? If not, how can we help them discover their part in God's big picture? Again, Nathan will explain more later.

Church is for more 'female' personality types...?

Let's look at this question separately, because there is actually some more relevant research available.

Personality differences in general

The field of psychology uses quite a number of personality models, and some research shows some differences in personality types between men and women. One of the most influential studies found that women consistently rated themselves as being warmer, friendlier, more anxious and more sensitive to their feelings than did the men. The men, however, consistently rated themselves as being more assertive and open to new ideas.[22] But what happens when you use an implicit measure of personality, so participants don't realise they're revealing what they think about their personality? Other research doing this found that sex differences were then still statistically significant, but three times smaller.[23] Some studies report very subtle differences, some report larger differences. The debate continues.[24]

Why are women more religious than men?

This has been investigated by a key study specifically focusing on personality.[25] Undergraduate students completed the Eysenck Personality Questionnaire, the Francis Scale of Attitude towards Christianity and measures of frequency of church attendance and frequency of personal prayer. Eysenck's model of personality has three main parts; Psychoticism (lower scores indicating self-control, higher scores indicating impulsivity and sensation-seeking), Extraversion/Introversion, and Neuroticism (lower scores indicating emotional stability, higher scores indicating emotional instability).

Overall, women scored more highly in terms of Extraversion, Neuroticism and having a positive attitude to Christianity. Men scored more highly in terms of Psychoticism. But both men and women who scored more highly for Psychoticism were less likely to go to church, pray and have a positive attitude to Christianity. In other words, differences in religiosity (worship attendance, personal prayer and attitude towards Christianity) were due to *personality differences* (the Psychoticism aspect of Eysenck's model about self-control/impulsivity and sensation-seeking), rather than because of being *male or female*. The authors suggest that future research would be useful to investigate this further, such as by using other personality measures with more people.

In practice, these findings indicate that in order to be more relevant to more men (and women of a certain personality type), it would be helpful for church to involve:

- Fewer repetitive experiences.
- More new experiences and choices.
- More thrill- and adventure-seeking.

Church leader personality

This theme has been researched quite extensively for years, particularly by Professor Leslie J. Francis and his colleagues. For example, one study used a version of the Eysenck Personality Questionnaire with Church of England clergy. Data showed that the usual sex differences found in the population as a whole were not reproduced among the clergy, as there were no significant differences between clergymen and clergywomen. However, when compared with the general population, the two key differences were that clergymen recorded significantly lower Psychoticism scores (closer to the female general population norms) and clergywomen recorded significantly lower Neuroticism scores (closer to the male population norms).[26] A similar pattern was previously found among Methodist ministers.[27]

Further research has shown that the personality profiles of church leaders are not proportionally reflective of society as a whole – there are more introverts, but that one of the strongest predictors of church growth is leadership by extraverts.[28]

It's worth remembering that results may vary depending on how the research was carried out, and what measures were used. Some work has involved the Myers-Briggs Type Indicator™ approach, and although this is popular in some fields, its statistical reliability and validity are questionable, and psychologists tend to use other personality models and measures.[29]

The very obvious question is: why are men in the minority in church congregations, when men are in the majority in church leadership?

Church leaders are probably going to most effectively relate to, and communicate with, people with personalities similar to themselves. Overall, the research therefore suggests that in order to develop a more gender balanced church, it will be helpful to develop a more personality-balanced church leadership.

This is clearly an ongoing issue for church leadership training institutions to consider in terms of recruitment and education. It's also important for any church leaders who are appointing staff or volunteers. How much do teams reflect different personality types? How much might this impact on the gender balance of the church? This doesn't mean everyone should take some sort of personality questionnaire. But we should intentionally involve a range of people with different gifts, skills and approaches.

Male ministers don't perceive the problem when it doesn't affect them...?

Most UK church ministers are male (84% in 2017).[30] Research by the Church of England found that in all age categories of its clergy, men are more likely to be married than women. The difference was extremely noticeable among those under the age of 32, with 73% of men being married, compared with 35% of women. More men than women under the age of 55 (and particularly under the age of 32) reported having children under the age of 16 at home.[31]

Some church ministers don't really understand the church gender imbalance because it hasn't affected them personally (e.g. they're male, and have been able to get married and have children). Because they haven't personally experienced the problems it causes, or the potential pain, they aren't so motivated to change things. If they've been a Christian for a while, they may also feel quite comfortable in church and be less aware of how it is experienced by non-Christians.

One session I did with some Christian leaders was particularly interesting. The group included men and women, all of whom were married and had children. They listened as I explained the extent of the church gender imbalance and some of the consequences, as I'd been asked to do. I then asked them to go round and tell everyone the name and age of one of their daughters, nieces, god-daughters, grand-daughters or female friends who is not married. "Beth, 17," "Katie, 4," "Sophie, 39," "Emily, 6." As each of them spoke in turn, I could almost see the 'light bulbs' going on over their heads as they realised that the church gender imbalance is a very real problem for them and their families. Suddenly the issue wasn't just theoretical. What if my daughter wants to marry a Christian guy when she's older but isn't able to? What if she can't have children as a result? What if I'm not able to be a grandparent? We then prayed together that all the females in our families would be able to get married one day to a Christian man if they want to, and of course we also prayed for all the males.

Over the last few years, we've had an increasing number of ministers partnering with Engage because they recognise that the church gender imbalance affects them personally. They want to reach and disciple their male friends and relatives more effectively. They want their female friends and relatives to have the choice of marrying a Christian man.

Male ministers are worried about excluding women...?

I've had quite a few conversations with male ministers or Christian leaders who are extremely reluctant to be seen to be specifically supporting or involved in 'men's ministry'. Even though they completely agree that something needs to be done about the church gender imbalance, their very real concern is that by 'doing men's ministry', they will somehow exclude, offend or alienate women. They worry about being associated with an unhelpfully old-fashioned, patriarchal church. It's understandable and commendable, however, let's think it through a bit more.

- Does supporting men's ministry mean you can't equally support women and women's ministry at the same time? No.

- Do single women want there to be more single men in church who are growing in their faith? Yes.
- Do Christian women married to non-Christian men want their husbands to find faith? Yes.
- Do Christian women married to Christian men want their husbands to grow in faith? Yes.

Overall, it's hard to think of which women will be offended about the church further encouraging men, as long as it's clear that the women are equally encouraged. Actually, many women have told me that they'd be absolutely delighted if their minister fully supported men's ministry as being a central part of the church.

Why men hate going to church...?

Some of you may have read the book *Why Men Hate Going to Church* by David Murrow.[32] The author is based in the US, but it's certainly an important read for anyone interested in developing a gender balanced church in other countries too. Some key points that he makes are:

- Your system is perfectly designed to give you the results you're getting.
- The church system is perfectly designed to reach a certain type of person. There are men and women who fit this type, but women are the majority. Therefore there are more women in church.
- High achieving, young, single and highly masculine men are missing from the church.
- There's a cycle: A surplus of women – softening of preaching/music/theology – softening of male clergy – explosion of female-oriented ministries – surplus of women etc.
- More risk/challenge/adventure is needed instead of just nurture/stability/predictability.
- Men believe that church is a women's thing.
- Feminine language is used in sermons and songs, and there is feminine décor in churches.

Murrow's suggested solutions for a more gender balanced church include:

- A 'manly' pastor, or a female pastor who intentionally promotes men's ministry.
- Excellence (preaching/music/facility/programs).
- Give space (no enforced hugs/hand-holding/prayer 'mushrooms').
- Make prayer real (no 'prayer-speak').

- Honour people's time (1 hour service rather than 3 hours).
- Intentional discipleship systems.

If some of his recommendations were implemented, perhaps churches would draw and keep greater numbers of both men and women?

What other reasons do people give?

Research work by David Pullinger on singleness in the UK church specifically asked respondents what they thought the reasons for the church gender imbalance are.[33] Suggestions included (with some example quotes):

- Romanticisation of the Church and its worship leading to passivity and more emotionalism. "Some song lyrics make it sound like Jesus is my boyfriend – why would a guy want to sing that!" (Male)
- The lack of masculine role models (carefully distinguishing the male gender from masculinity). Both men and women mentioned various aspects of men in their churches as being 'not manly'. "Fed up with girly stuff and 'wet lettuce' guys!" (Male)
- Lack of friendship patterns for men.
- Church creating a sense of passivity.

The solutions people put forward included:

- Present the gospel as difficult and challenging. "If we would occasionally show some fight, more men would be interested. The predominant mindset of my non-Christian friends is that it's a place for the weak and those who need to be told about love. They don't see God as a warrior." (Male)
- Get famous Christian men talking openly about their faith.
- Do Alpha or similar courses in pubs and golf clubs.
- Include more worship appropriate to men (songs, activities). "We stand around and sing songs to a man about how beautiful he is, then someone comes on stage and tells us to be nice to each other and get in touch with our feelings. When my friends come along, I just don't think they see many men in the church who they can look at and say 'I want to be more like him!' Perhaps they would if they understood who Jesus was." (Male)
- Do sports and activities.
- Value people behind the scenes, e.g. those doing church DIY, the church football team.
- Have events with speakers (although respondents said it was best to avoid "the usual curry nights and men's breakfasts").

Peter Brierley (Church Statistics Consultant) once did a poll in Scotland of why there were more women in church than men. The finding was that men thought the woman in their family went to church on *behalf* of their family, so if Mum went, there was no need for anyone else to go.[34] This is another indication that churches need to be aware of who the non-attending partners of the Christian women in church are, and to reach them more effectively.

The spiritual battle

The work of Engage includes showing how different ministry contexts interact and affect each other. This was illustrated in Figure 3 in Chapter 1. However, from a biblical perspective, we also know from Paul's letter to the Ephesians that we are all living in a spiritual context that is far bigger than we can see or imagine.

> *"For our struggle is not against flesh and blood, but against the rulers, against the authorities, against the powers of this dark world and against the spiritual forces of evil in the heavenly realms."*
> (Ephesians 6:14)

In July 2007, there was an article in *Christianity* magazine called "Getting Married in No Man's Land." In this, Diane Louise Jordan and Liz Speed clearly described the impact of the church gender imbalance on women and men. As Liz Speed summarised, "This is a kingdom issue, a generational issue, a national issue, and a critical issue." In the next month's edition was a feedback letter from a reader who made a foundational point: "Our understanding (is) that the enemy will seek to destroy Christian marriages, yet we do not seem able to make the tiny logical leap required to realise that it's an even better strategy for him to prevent these marriages from happening in the first place. No 'godly children' to worry about then either."

Marriage is a good thing, designed by God to be central to His kingdom on earth, to society, and to be experienced personally by most people. Marriage between Christians can be extremely powerful and have a spiritual impact across generations. The enemy doesn't like it. The church has to be alert to his strategies. This is why Engage and others are working to make more marriages between Christians possible, and encouraging every church to play its part.

Summary

Secular research about gender differences can only tell us a limited amount about why there might be fewer men than women in church. It can, however, remind us that it is unhelpful to make stereotypical generalisations about men and women. Research among Christians currently suggests that if church leadership and congregations involved a wider range of people and personalities, this could help improve the gender balance.

There are various other factors contributing to the situation, and these include:
- The need for men to feel they belong.
- Some male ministers not perceiving or understanding the problems due to their personal experience.
- The reluctance of some church leaders to support men's ministry.
- The call from both men and women for church to have more masculine role models and be less 'romanticised'.
- The fundamental issue – the bigger picture of our spiritual battle.

Further research would be useful, however no church can afford to wait and do nothing until the 'why' questions of the church gender imbalance have been fully researched and understood. We need to act now. Whilst 'evidence-based practice' is useful to inform what we do, there is also value in 'practice-based evidence'. In the next chapter, Nathan Blackaby shows us further practical solutions which can be implemented now.

Action points

Firstly, for everyone: pray.

The national church
- For ministerial training colleges and denominations to review the extent to which they are recruiting and training a range of students, in the light of the issues raised in this chapter.
- For theological colleges to specifically teach on the issue of the church gender imbalance and what to do about it. A few colleges we know have had input for all students, and one also runs a Certificate in Men's Ministry course.
- For denominational leaders to develop planned approaches for more effectively reaching and discipling men, perhaps in collaboration with each other.

- Collaboration between leaders of denominations, networks, organisations and researchers is needed to specifically investigate why there are fewer men in church. One approach to research particularly considers 'what works?'. It could be helpful to further identify the factors which seem to be involved where churches don't have a gender imbalance, or do have a thriving men's ministry. This can then be used to inform action to redress the national gender imbalance and other issues arising.
- It is recommended that researchers in the Christian context routinely analyse results by gender. It's interesting to note that it's standard practice for secular research to analyse relevant results by gender to see if there are any differences. A lot of research carried out in the Christian context (e.g. surveys) doesn't seem to do this, but it would be useful to help shed light on the reasons for the church gender imbalance.

The local church

- It is suggested that leaders in churches explicitly ask those in their congregations and groups (of different ages) what they think would help to reach and disciple more men and boys in their context. Obviously they can ask the same regarding women and girls too.
- Find out how much the men in your congregation feel that they belong. Do they have a valued role both in the church and as part of a calling and purpose for their life?

Further recommendations are also given in the following chapter.

Men's ministry: what would it look like if things were working well in the church?

Nathan Blackaby

Welcome to the chapter on men's ministry. From what you've read in this book so far, it's hopefully clear why the church needs to be doing things differently in order to reach and disciple men. Let me start by outlining the ministry that I represent, as this is specifically connected to this subject. Then we'll drill into some of the underlying issues around men's ministry and what it looks like when it is being done well.

My name is Nathan and I have been involved with Christian Vision for Men (CVM) for about five or so years, almost four of those as the CEO. At CVM we have a mandate and central driving vision to introduce men to Jesus. Year on year, we see hundreds of men respond to the gospel, and inevitably a percentage of them are single and go on to look for Christian relationships and marriage. However, as you have probably already seen from the presentation of stats and data in this book, we have a shortage of Christian single men in the UK and hundreds of thousands, if not a couple of million, of Christian single women looking for meaningful relationships. As Co-Chair of Engage and CEO of CVM, I'd suggest that we need to do a few things.

One of these is basically to win more men to Jesus, for their own sake primarily, but also for women and children. To do this we need to mobilise some effective ministry to men which builds itself around an evangelistic strategy, and I'll argue for this as we move on.

But let me also say that the need to make Christian marriage possible is a varied and complex challenge. Those involved in The Engage Network have been working on this for a few years now, and I am thrilled that this book is bringing together the thinking and action resulting from its work. As the UK church locally and across the nation becomes more aware of the multi-faceted strategies that can be utilised, we will see a Christian church that will thrive in relation to singleness, marriage and growing families of faith for the generations to come.

Having said that, let me now say something else. The arena of men's ministry can be a challenging area to map out in terms of robust data. CVM has been in existence for more than 25 years, and during that time we have been able to fund, support and produce some research.[1] But perhaps one of the richest sources of information is our experience of working with our grass-roots network across the UK and other countries internationally.

We have a team of committed staff members, volunteers and over 400 men's groups in the UK that have been journeying this path for decades, even forcing themselves to eat over 1000 cooked breakfasts in the meantime! These are our data-grabbers, and we as a ministry have learnt to trust them and lean into what they are seeing, week-in week-out. In addition to this, through Engage, we gathered together a group of ministry leaders who have an interest in men's ministry and what it can look like when it's done well. We shared lots of ideas and throughout the chapter I'll draw out some thoughts from this fantastic consultation process too.

So, enough of the background. If we are asking the question "What would men's ministry look like if it was working well for the individual, local church and national church?" then this assumes some sort of current state of existence, and one where things aren't always being done so well. So, the question I want to reflect on first is this: what does men's ministry look like if it isn't being done well?

The first and obvious answer here is that when it's not working well, men's ministry just isn't happening at all. So often at CVM we are contacted by men who are desperate for some sort of men's work in their church, but it just hasn't got off the ground. Nobody takes the initiative, there are no resources set aside for it, many people are not convinced that there even needs to be a male-specific 'something', and so the longing stays in the heart of one or maybe two men there and never gets birthed into anything more.

Then as we move up the scale of 'men's work that isn't being done well' we arrive at the stuff that has been bobbing on for years, but no one owns it, carries it in their heart or feels a burden for it. Often it might just be a monthly Bible study or pint at the pub. The guys turn up, but it floats along without sail and rudder and the passion just isn't there. Often at this point, the men's work is still heavy on one man's heart – you can spot him because he's the guy still inviting men along and paying for the tab when it comes to food or getting stuff printed. Usually at this stage, the heartbeat for it all still hasn't moved into the heart of the main church where the ministry might be plugged from the front, put in the notice sheet, or where some help and resources might be assigned.

The next level on from this is where the men's work has pierced the consciousness of the church on a spiritual level. Occasionally, prayer for the men is mentioned or a male testimony is heard on a Sunday. Also, on a practical level, for example, the church gets booked for a men's breakfast or day event. Let me stop here to clarify: what I'm NOT saying is that if these definitions describe your church, then it's not good enough and you might as well give up now! Not at all! But I am suggesting that in order to inspire men and encourage deep, life changing intimacy and accountability, you will also need something more.

Let's look now at effective men's ministry for the individual (both Christian and non-Christian), the local church and the national church.

Men's ministry: what would it look like if it was working well for the individual, both Christian and non-Christian?

For the Christian man

To kick this off I want to use the Engage consultation notes that we generated (given at the end of this chapter), then in addition to this I'll reflect, where appropriate, on the experience CVM has gathered.

So, let's make this crystal clear, the purpose of a men's ministry is to help men discover Jesus and grow in their faith in incredible ways, and it will encompass as wide a range of men as possible.

To broadly summarise the consultation thoughts in expanding this, the main emphasis was that a thriving men's ministry involves a small, tight-knit group, where the men know and deeply care for one another. It's a place where Christian men feel safe to be intimate and share within this trusting space. Deep relationships provide encouragement, challenge and accountability. A place where men look for the hero in one another and call it out, where they invite the men they trust to speak into their lives and maintain an undefended heart in this company of brothers. In addition to this, the consultation highlighted a theme of spiritual fatherhood. Men having a place where they can be fathered and learn how to father others with challenging honesty and truth. It was also recognised that this is a place or space of learning and teaching, following and leading which are all are continually part of the group's DNA.

The final key theme the group all felt was important, was that of a developed system of effective discipleship. When it's working well, this is spiritual and practical. Men will be repeatedly encouraged, built up, challenged and inspired. They grow to know their gifts and potential, to see God and discern his voice in their lives. What would that look like? In simple language: get men reading the Bible regularly and applying it to their lives with honesty and transparency. CVM have resourced churches to do this for years, and have seen it happen in pubs, men's homes, at church, on a mountain, and even in a curry house.

All these components of successful men's ministry that were raised by the consultation group strongly resonate with my own experience at CVM and what we see across the UK. I'd also like to add a few other ideas.

We've found that so often the message to men is to 'change'; be better men, dads and husbands. It's a message that is valid and needed, of course, but the message must encompass a clear process of 'how' men reach these targets. Effective discipleship includes setting out practical markers and goals in relation to things like holiness, honesty, trust, forgiveness, patience, kindness, gentleness etc. It also facilitates a clear process of how to achieve these steps, and how success will be measured and celebrated. Who will notice they've changed? Who will praise the effort and change? Without the process, the measurement, and the culture of celebration, men won't engage and instead may look elsewhere to achieve success and celebration for their efforts.

Relationships are central to growing a men's group and forging the right group dynamic; just throwing men in together doesn't always lead to the desired results. The group needs to be clear about its purpose. Certain values, activities and patterns need to be agreed which become the group's DNA, along with rules for how the group works (to support positive and helpful dynamics). These things need to be regularly discussed so that they're always at the front of the group's consciousness.

The DNA won't be established without the group owning it and holding each other in prayer and thought between the meetups. Meeting once a month might be helpful for men who are time pressured, but my personal experience is that as soon as men really see and discover the benefits of meeting in their group, they find the time for it. Twice a month can work better.

The final point I want to make here is that for me, the most essential ingredient to building an effective men's ministry is that evangelism is at the heart of the group and its men. We can get men meeting for years, studying the Bible and being real and honest, but without the end goal of evangelism, without the implementation of 'go' – what's the point? You might argue "Well the point is to be better men, fathers, husbands, elders or deacons etc.," and I am not arguing against that. But, if we don't inspire these men in the men's ministry to go, to care about the eternity of the men at work or at the squash club, or of their son's mates or their daughter's boyfriend then we have radically missed the point.

Discipleship misses the point without an outward spiral of 'building the individual to grow in his faith and then introduce Jesus to others'. Multiplication is at the heart of the gospel message. It is good news for all people, so our men's ministry is an extension of that missionary call. In my experience as a church leader and now as CEO of CVM, the one thing that has inspired men beyond everything else is seeing Jesus be welcomed by a mate who has been gradually introduced to him. As the group watch this man's life get saved and gradually (or radically) transformed by the Holy Spirit, this ignites a fire in the hearts of men unlike anything a curry or a breakfast each month will do.

CVM's long term strategy for introducing men to Jesus is essentially all about that. It takes a group of men, sharpens them up, encourages the relationships to be strong but makes sure there is an external radar switched on! We encourage men to build friendships, do stuff together they enjoy, but also maintain an evangelistic heartbeat as part of their core DNA. Who are the non-Christians they can pray for, encourage, give to, help or stand with? When the opportunities come, the group responds, they speak Jesus, they show his compassion, his grace and mercy and they invite these men to know more, to come and see. You might think this is wishful thinking, but I can tell you, we've seen it work countless times. We have seen men with ropes in the boot of their car ready to end their lives who surrender to Jesus because of a group that had evangelism in their heart. We have seen hundreds of men journey through the network and discover Jesus because their group's DNA is evangelistic, and spiritually they're on fire!

For a non-Christian man

Let's now build on the first section to look at what effective men's ministry might look like for a non-Christian man. I know for a fact that lots of men's ministry in churches across the UK is absolutely not ready for a non-Christian man to turn up – and if one did, there would be a lot of worried looks shared across the room – "What do we say? Do we need to change the Bible study somehow? Why has he come along?"

It sounds a bit funny really, but sadly it is true. If a group doesn't focus on this stuff, and if it establishes and builds a men's ministry without an evangelistic heartbeat, the chances are a non-Christian man will not feel like this thing is for him at all. However, having said that, there are of course some common themes and ideas that can be implemented that will help. In our Engage consultation we explored these and came up with a few suggestions.

The environment needs to be a place where a man will not feel instantly judged if his life and ideas don't match up to a certain standard. Men's ministry, when done well, should be a place where a non-Christian man feels welcomed and included. A place where his voice is heard, and he has the same opportunities as the others to build friendships, and he belongs. As the Christian men share their lives with the good, the bad and the ugly, this honesty will be an open invite for a non-Christian man to relate and connect at a base level. It's also important that the non-Christian man isn't seen as the new 'target', where every preach or spiritual message becomes tailored to his disbelief. Instead, his faith is allowed to unfold and be explored through activity and ongoing close relationships with friends.

At CVM we have seen this pattern develop slowly and gradually as the men's ministry builds and the guys 'do things' together. Initially, the activities don't need a 'gospel' slot; it's just about being mates and friends that are doing stuff together. Gradually, events can be planned around some food, with a talk/story/reflection from a guy who is a Christian, but can communicate clearly without lecturing. Invites can go out and all are welcome to come along, but the event does, at this point, talk more openly about faith and what it all looks like.

The '4 level strategy' is something CVM has deployed across the UK and internationally in helping churches build and maintain a long-term evangelistic vision to reach men. To be honest, it's so simple. First, it just starts with making friends, then secondly, speaking about Jesus over a meal or an activity. Then level 3 is to do a relevant and helpful Christian course, of which there are loads, then level 4 is to continue the journey for the years to come. We punctuate this journey with events that groups can come along to, where they'll have a relevant and fun morning, day or weekend, and the gospel is shared. Through this process, we see hundreds of men each year deciding to follow Jesus.

Men's ministry: what would it look like if it was working well for the local church?

I touched on this before, but it's a really significant transition when the men's ministry moves from being the passion of 'that guy at church' and into the heart of the wider church. Men's ministry isn't just the actual meeting on a Tuesday night when the men might gather. When it is prayed about and valued it becomes a spiritual movement, and it's something the local church owns and wants to invest in and see grow.

During our consultation we identified a few things that show what men's ministry looks like when it is being done well within the local church context. It is resourced, supported and funded at some level and not hidden away from the local church budget. Bacon isn't essential; the church is able to provide a broad range of events which helps welcome the whole plethora of men's character types and tastes. Also, the local church intentionally reaches out and welcomes the non-Christian male partners of the Christian women who do attend the church. The particular need to reach single men is understood and they are also included through a thriving men's ministry. The external activities that men are engaged in (e.g. sporting events that clash with the Sunday services) are recognised and valued.

The consultation involved a lot of 'out-the-box' thinking, and the chances are you are reading that and thinking "Yeah, just doing one of these things well would be a massive mountain for us to climb, let alone all of it!" But you're not on your own. CVM has written extensively on these issues (see our website). We work really closely with many local churches to equip, resource and stand with them as they introduce the church to men.

Our experience at CVM, having worked in this arena for over two decades, is that none of this will be achieved overnight, and it's almost impossible to forge a group that can 'be all things to every man'. However, we have seen that it's important to have a long-term strategy for both winning men to Jesus, and introducing the church to men. If men's ministry is working well in the local church, its role is to facilitate, empower and encourage the men's work to thrive. It's also a pathway to help men discover discipleship and long-term faith growth. If men's ministry is working well the church is fully supportive, committed to regular prayer, regularly announces the events and feeds back on the group's development.

A key success point is that the men's ministry has a level of integration across the services, sermons, worship, decoration, timings, newsletter, website, social media and mission. Let me explain by using a quick list of how men's ministry fuses itself (when being done well) into the core identity of the local church.

Services

Create a moment to call men to the front, hear about their story, their week ahead, the frontline or their frontier where they work, strive to be or fight for. Value their story and cheer them on. Encourage them from the front. If you have a police officer there, get him up the front and get the church to pray for his week ahead. If he has family, stand them with him. If it's a single guy at Uni, find out about him and his week; cheer him on publically. Call them up, don't let them hide. (You can do the same for women of course!) And hardly anyone likes services (or sermons) that are too long. Have you ever asked congregation members how they feel about the length of your services? Too short, too long, about right?

Sermons

Church leaders have a unique opportunity in sermons; it is a chance to be inspiring, dynamic and relevant and will impact heads and hearts. It will connect with your congregation's Monday morning when the Sunday service is miles behind. In a sermon at church I am thinking this: challenge me, poke me and wake me up with the relevance and edge of the Bible. Tackle the big stuff; if you don't know the answer then be honest about it. Invite me to count the cost, surrender to Christ, and help me to see what that will mean to my wallet, my time, my family, my heart and my passions. What does all this mean tomorrow when I am at work and with my non-Christian mates? What does this mean to me when I am battling that secret no one knows about? How do I apply this stuff to my heart?

When the men's ministry is working well, the local church will see the men, know them and be aware of who they are and what life is actually like for them. In turn, the sermon is crafted, built and inspired to reach into their lives with relevance and challenge. If I have learnt one thing about working with men on two continents for over a decade it's this: be direct! If something stinks, call it out, if something's broken or an idea doesn't hold water, call it out! If the Bible passage is a tough one and in reality it is hard to live, call it out! We must not sell or offer a version of Christianity to men that avoids the direct truth; we need both the comfortable and uncomfortable. The benefits and the cost must all be explored and made explicit, and sermons are a vital way to infuse this into the church culture. And the men will respond!

Worship

Now let me be clear on this, I don't use the term 'feminisation' when I describe certain elements or aspects of UK church culture. Some people do, but this has negative connotations for the term 'feminine', so I use the term 'romanticisation'.

For me personally, worship can be romanticised in the local church when it's gentle, nice, meek and mild, and communicates that a relationship with Jesus has a romantic dynamic. I have been a Christian over 30 years and have fallen in love with Jesus, so I get it. But, non-Christian men do not just walk into this stuff and 'get it'. We mustn't only present one picture of God's heart – the shepherd heart. There's the warrior heart too. What I mean by this is that I have been in church for three decades and learnt that we encourage the shepherd heart – love, peace, kindness, gentleness, patience – but what about the warrior part of us too? I feel it, wrestling within, wanting a contest. It's not something sinful that needs to be suppressed, it is part of who God's made me. I want a challenge to charge at, a hill to climb, for someone to see it and cheer me over the top. I want to push forward and achieve something. I want something that hurts, costs and impacts my life – and I don't just mean the collection plate as it comes around on a Sunday. This stuff connects with men, the shepherd stuff does too, but we can't ignore this warrior piece of the jigsaw. Why do some men spend hours playing sport or gaming? Because they're in an arena where their effort is seen – some competition, conviction and commitment is needed. The effort is also cheered on and encouraged. Do we nurture and encourage that in our churches for men? Do we lead them in the challenges of the gospel and the mission of seeing more men saved? When we encourage them to fully develop their shepherd-warrior heart, we will see them going full-tilt in their lives pursuing Jesus.

I am not suggesting scrapping songs that talk about love. Please understand that all of these ideas are motivated by evangelism, and usually just slight tweaks to the focus and direction are needed to be more appropriate for non-Christian (and Christian) men. When men's ministry is being done well in the local church there is a 'balance' to the worship, so that themes of courage, victory, battle, honour and might are also included.

Decoration

If your local church is equipped with all the lace, flowers and needle craft then we have realised that the men we work with will look and make a quick judgement 'this isn't for me!' Of course, I am not suggesting you hang chainsaws on the either side of the lectern, and yes, it is wrong to make snap judgements on superficial things. But please remember that we are trying to rescue these men from hell and that that snap judgement will reinforce the impression that church and its message isn't for them, and make them walk away. Decoration is therefore about relevance and awareness of the community of lost souls around the church. We need continual reflection on how well we're winning those around us to Jesus.

Newsletter, website, social media

This is just obvious stuff – churches with men's ministries that are vibrant and working well include information about men's work in their communications.

Mission

Finally, I want to suggest that the local church with a thriving men's ministry will have a clear definition of what 'mission' is and how the men can plug into it. The definition of mission won't only be about the 10-40 window[2] or the unreached tribes in the Amazon region. Mission will be about evangelism, reaching the guys down the pub, at work, on the terraces, in the social club, at the quiz night or on the street with vulnerable drunken parties at night, and more. If mission is to reach these places, then the men will need to hear about it, be inspired to engage in it, and not sold a version of 'missionary life' that only means Bible college, sandals and packing a bag for Africa.

As an over-arching practical thing, CVM also has found that it's helpful if the men's ministry group in a local church has an annual plan which is punctuated with some core events. We run a festival which is built around being easy to invite and welcome non-Christian men to (The Gathering). We have car days or even sport weeks in Lanzarote that enable men to get away and explore the gospel on their terms. This stuff isn't difficult to connect into, but it does need a plan for the year and a degree of intentionality and commitment.

So in summary, a local church doing men's ministry well with an evangelistic heart is a fun place to be. Men's lives get saved and transformed by Jesus. Men feel inspired and encouraged and able to share the deep wells of their hearts and minds. The church is blessed for them being there. Their influence and hearts, the passions and fight is included, seen and celebrated. The church grows, families turn up, lives in broken chaos find a place. How do I know? We have seen it; at CVM we see men in addiction, broken men and broken families healed and rebuilt. We see men who've been locked away with cynical hearts for over 20 years who are released and set free, men with pride-soaked minds broken by Jesus' love and grace. We are seeing it!

Men's ministry: what would it look like if it was working well for the national church?

Much of what we have already explored in this chapter would be exciting to see across the national church, right? Men giving their lives to Jesus in great numbers, men being discipled and encouraged, challenged and called out. Men living lives of integrity, holiness and truth! Men in business, in communities, men in all aspects of society seeking to be genuine followers of Jesus with conviction and passion, and living out their faith in the way they give their time, money and lives! Men who refuse the secret affairs building in their hearts because they brought them to the light of their men's group. Men who seek help with prostate issues when they were too embarrassed to do so before, men who talk about their suicidal thoughts rather than silently treading that path!

On a national level, the UK church could radically impact the work of men's ministry. Perhaps we need a coming together of denominational heads to develop a shared strategy which is based on theology and research? Perhaps as the national church moves towards more relational equity, sharing speaking platforms and working together, leaders can unite to promote our urgent need to reach men with the gospel in ways that work?

Wouldn't it be great if theological colleges equipped all students through specific training on how to effectively reach and disciple men? Plenty of resources to support this are available (see the end of this chapter). Once ministers are qualified, leaders' networks can run further regular training, as well as network events for men. At Christian festivals and holiday conferences, wouldn't we know things were working well if there was a seminar option on men's ministry during each week? All sorts of national leaders could contribute their skills and experience to further evaluating and researching what works for men and church. Everyone could benefit from this sort of collaboration – men, women, children and young people, as well as church leaders.

Is it too bold to dream that if men's ministry was being done well nationally in the UK, we would see less fatherlessness, fewer men in prison, fewer communities drowning in crime, and reduced violence against women? Would we see more social action and money poured into the fight for social justice? Would we see fewer men desperately ending their lives day-by-day? Would we see a decline in the UK rates of family separation and divorce? Is it too bold to suggest that a thriving men's ministry in the UK would lead to a wave of transformed lives, with people living by grace and holding on to Jesus with all they have? Isn't he the hope of the world? Isn't he the one to bring about transformation and new life? He did it for me and the men around me; we are just a few – imagine the whole nation transformed!

Action points

For individual men

- Talk with other men in your church, and your church leaders about developing men's ministry in your context.
- Make use of the resources out there to grow your faith and relationship with God.
- Go to events for men such as those run by CVM, New Wine, The Men's Convention, 4M.

For the local church

- Make men's ministry central to the church's life and mission. Remember, this will benefit everyone. Women will support you!
- Gather a small strategy group, and if you have a staff team, make sure a staff member is involved who's in a position to help develop culture.
- Make use of experienced organisations like CVM, who can chat

through the strategy, resources and practicalities of setting up a long-term evangelistic men's ministry in your setting.

For the national church

- Theological colleges: include what we've talked about in this chapter on your training courses.
- Church leaders' networks: run events on how to develop effective men's ministry, roundtables that help share good practice, and regular events for men.
- Denominational leaders: raise awareness of the issues and solutions in your denomination. Signpost people to solutions and resources in your communications and websites. Develop a specific strategy for making your denomination gender balanced.
- Festivals and holiday conferences: make seminars available each week on how to develop effective men's ministry.

Websites and resources

Christian Vision for Men

www.cvm.org.uk

Lots of resources, courses and events for men and churches, including on the 4 level evangelism strategy. Get in touch with CVM to discuss how we can support you and your church or organisation

4M

www.4muk.com

Mind, body and soul adventures for men, based on faith, brotherhood, adventure and justice.

The Men's Convention (London and regional)

www.christianconventions.org.uk/lmc/index.php

Christians in Sport

www.christiansinsport.org.uk

Reaching the world of sport for Christ.

Who Let the Dads Out?

www.wholetthedadsout.org.uk

Initiatives to give fathers, male carers and their children the opportunity to spend time together, have fun and engage with the church.

The Naked Truth Project
www.thenakedtruthproject.com
To open eyes and free lives from the damaging impact of porn.

Man-made
www.cvm.org.uk/manmade
A rites of passage course for teenage guys.

Boys 2 Men: Helping young men into adulthood
www.cvm.org.uk/news/news_detail.php?newsID=472
Helping young men make the transition into adulthood through a short course, a coming of age experience and through ongoing, one-to-one discipleship. Through collaboration with www.authenticdiscipleship.org.uk and using Man-made.

"Men's ministry: what would it look like if things were working well in the church?"

Engage consultation vision grid

An individual man	A local church	The national church
Evangelism *A non-Christian* • Has genuinely good friendships with a Christian/Christians, feels accepted and loved. • Is introduced to other Christians, so has opportunity to build several key relationships and be part of a group. • Feels listened to – Christian friend(s) meeting him where he's at and going at the pace he is going – on a spiritual journey over time. • Able to have real-life, honest conversations about real stuff – straight talking – say it like it is, with love (comes out of relationship) – nothing's taboo in conversations. • The Christian is 'real' about imperfections and struggles – so non-Christian sees similarities with themselves. • Non-Christian feels Christians are non-judgemental, un-shockable, helpful and have some answers to tough situations. • Knows the Christian will give ongoing friendship and support over time whether or not the guy comes to faith.	**Evangelism** • Money and time is invested in men's ministry. • Men's ministry is publically supported by women (and women's ministry by men, likewise). • Church leaders encourage men to develop deep non-Christian friendships around their interests out in the 'real world' – and male leaders model this. • Everyone is actively participating – a culture where men feel confident and competent about opening faith conversations. • Church culture celebrates steps on the journey to faith – the small steps early on are valued, prayed for, and highlighted through e.g. testimonies. • Personal testimony – honouring each other's steps in faith, wherever people are on the journey. • Church leaders model that it's not about 'success and failure'. • Men are involved in social justice projects – and involve their non-Christian friends. • Church holds events – though doesn't need to involve bacon or curry!	• CORPORATE PRAYER! • Agreed and accepted strategy for men's ministry that is based on theology and research. • Joined-up solutions between those working to develop men's ministry and between them and others. • A united approach to praying for men – grass-roots level work – the church is equipped to pray together for men. **Theological Colleges** • Central positioning of 'why and how' of men's evangelism and discipleship on the core curriculum – understood and promoted by Principals, staff and students. • Use of a cross-denominational module (e.g. the CVM Theological College week-long short course). • All students leave knowing how to effectively create a gender balanced and growing church (in numbers and spiritual depth). **Denominational Leaders** • Strong links to raise awareness of the issues and solutions, and provide ongoing training for church leaders.

An individual man	A local church	The national church
• Opportunities arise to comfortably talk about spiritual stuff without a sense that there's a hidden agenda. • Christians come alongside and ask whether they have any faith background – what the guy believes, but also about what they want their kids to believe (if relevant). • Can see that there are rational answers to questions that he has (including e.g. science/religion, other apologetics questions), Christian friends discuss or can signpost to answers. • Faith is seen to have practical implications/ applications – it feels uncomfortable – it involves challenge and risk. • Sees that Christianity is part of something bigger and beyond themselves/the individual – individual life transformation and also transformation of the world around them. • Hears stories of God working in Christian friends' lives. **Discipleship** *A Christian* • Part of a small group of men, with close, safe, intimate, trusting relationships that provide encouragement, challenge and accountability. • He has an in-depth understanding of all that discipleship means.	• Church culture around events is fun, light, easy-going, e.g. watch the rugby match at the pub, rather than in church/ elsewhere. • Men's ministry intentionally works towards the socio-demographics of the church reflecting society as a whole. • Church is intentionally reaching out to non-Christian husbands of Christian women. • Church has a specific focus on reaching unpartnered or single men. • Church is reaching men from different backgrounds (working class and middle class) with different interests (not all men are 'hunting/ shooting/fishing' outdoors types). **Discipleship** • All men are involved in lifelong intentional spiritual fathering – groups of 3 (for challenging honesty), groups of 7-8, and larger groups – membership of different group sizes for different purposes. • Leaders model and encourage the need to intentionally, regularly meet with a 'spiritual father'/mentor and also be a spiritual father/ mentor to others – relationships that intentionally encourage and challenge in all key areas of life and spiritual walk.	• Leadership networks promote effective men's ministry. • A church leaders survey could be done, including asking: – Do you feel you have healthy male engagement in your church? • Investigate differences between rural and city contexts – needs and solutions. **National Conferences** • Men's ministry is positioned centrally within mission/ evangelism and discipleship so that it is a 'main stage' issue literally and metaphorically. • Opportunity to address other individual issues more deeply in seminars. • All major national Christian conferences include input on how to develop effective men's ministry. • Stories/testimonies are shared about what it looks like when it is working well – from church leaders on the ground.

An individual man	A local church	The national church
• Is involved in spiritual fathering – is a spiritual father to others, has spiritual fathers himself – covering all areas of life honestly. • Is involved in both learning and also leading. • Feels safe and able to be honest with other Christians and in church. • Discipleship involves patterns that are relevant to him. • He is able to encounter God in his own ways – exploring different ways of a life of devotion within freedom. • Is pursuing Jesus increasingly whole-heartedly. • Knows discipleship involves cost and is willing to make appropriate sacrifices, e.g. time, money. • Is aware of his key strengths, gifts, callings/purpose and is using these – both within and outside of the church. • Knows he is called to bring justice where there is injustice. • Free from destructive behaviours and addictions, e.g. porn/alcohol/anger/other things. • Has been trained to, and can confidently pray for and reach out to other men effectively. • Feels able to facilitate non-Christians to take another step towards faith – doesn't feel it's all about one moment of decision.	• Intentional discipleship around relationships: healthy singleness, dating, marriage, friendship, loneliness, sex, porn, the way millennials do relationships virtually – encouraging 'real relationships' too. • Also addressing issues around fathering, food, money, power, dealing with guilt and shame, identity labels (e.g. 'Provider'), all passions moderated except passion for Jesus. • Church has good male role-models leading children's work and youth work – spiritual fathering (for boys and girls). • Church services/sermons are relevant to everyday life and work, e.g. prayers for work not just missionary work, sermon examples, testimonies of God at work – at work. • Groups are set up to work for the church's particular setting/context, e.g. rural/city life, e.g. at lunchtimes. • Going away together – allows honesty/vulnerability at another level sometimes. • Church is involved in networks empowering people in business or other fields to meet together and support each other. • Men are equipped to reach out to their friends (see 'Evangelism' above).	

An individual man	A local church	The national church
• Is involved in evangelism which is relational, based on genuine friendships, is intentional and visible, and jargon-free.	• Church recognises and values other activities – e.g. sports teams on Sundays – church service times are changed to take these into account – Sundays are most people's lie-in or sport day? • Involved in inter-church sports teams. • Involved in raising money for charity e.g. through sport.	

CHAPTER 7

Singleness: what would it look like if things were working well in the church?

Kate Wharton

Introduction

Singleness is one of the major realities facing the church in the UK today. A YouGov poll from 2014 stated that a third of adults in churches in the UK are single,[1] and an Evangelical Alliance survey from 2012 showed that 61% of adult Christians under 35 are single.[2] This large number of single adults has major implications for the church as we seek to engage with and support them.

Of course, singleness is not just widespread in the church. The 2011 census showed that 51% of the adult population of England and Wales were unmarried (up from 47% in 2001). That's 23 million people who were divorced, or widowed, or who had never married. 35% of the adult population in 2011 had never married (up from 30% in 2001). The Office for National Statistics analysis of these figures says this: "The rise in the single population could be the result of a number of factors, including the proportional decline in marriage since the 1970s and the increased social acceptability of remaining single or cohabiting (either never marrying or not re-marrying following divorce or widowhood)."[3]

UK society in 2018 looks dramatically different from how it looked 100, 50 or even 20 years ago. Today it is completely socially acceptable for a couple to live together before, or instead of, marriage. There is absolutely no social stigma around a baby being born to a couple who are unmarried. Divorce and remarriage are commonplace. 'Blended' families are the norm.

Singleness is common today both within society as a whole and within the church, and the likelihood is that it's only going to increase. Many people, of course, are happily single, but many others are not. A key challenge facing the church at the moment is how it can be genuinely welcoming of single people, as a place where they feel included, nurtured and valued.

I am absolutely certain that 'the church', both at a national level and at a local level, as well as the vast majority of the individual Christians who make up the church, want to be welcoming and accepting of single people. They want to be encouraging, understanding and affirming – not ignorant, hurtful and unkind. The problem is that churches are made up of humans and humans (whether married or single!) don't always get things right.

For instance, I was once at a Christian festival, and on my way to speak at a seminar on singleness. En route I was stopped by someone who engaged me in conversation, who asked me what my seminar was on. After I had told him, he sucked in his teeth and with a look of pity mixed with disdain said, "Ooh, singleness, it's SUCH a problem isn't it. I had a single friend once. Do you know, she was still single when she turned 30? It was awful for her." At the time I was a single, 33 year old woman, about to speak to a room full of single people. I mean – what?! On the plus side maybe he thought I was still in my twenties! Of course he didn't mean to be unkind. Of course he genuinely wanted to engage with the issue. But there were a fair few ways in which he could have done that better!

For around the past ten years I have spent a lot of time speaking about singleness at churches, Christian events and festivals, all around the UK and across the world. Whenever I am speaking to groups of single people I ask them how church feels for them. Without exception, the majority (and sometimes it is a huge majority) of people tell me that church, at least some of the time, feels like a really hard place to be as a single person. I have heard stories of people who have felt excluded, not part of the family, not valued as much as those who are married and have children. It can often feel like the vast majority of church activities are aimed at families, leaving single people feeling excluded. Single people often report not being asked to lead as much as their married peers, as if they are seen somehow to have not quite grown up yet. And often single people report feeling as if their married friends at church don't really understand just what their life is like.

Very clearly, this is not something those churches would want to happen. All churches would hope and aim to be places of welcome for all people, where everyone feels part of the family, loved, welcomed, valued and nurtured. For some reason, it seems that the church in the UK is, at least at some level, failing single people. But surely in an ideal world the opposite would be true? What could it look like for the church to be the very best place for single people – the place where they felt most welcomed, most included, most valued, most accepted? How do we enable our churches to step up to this challenge? What will that look like for churches and church leaders, and what would be its impact on individuals, the local church, the national church, and indeed society as a whole?

For individuals

I think that one of the biggest gifts which could be given to single people within our churches is simply the belief that it is possible to live well as a single person. Perhaps that sounds like a fairly modest goal! That it's possible for life to be whole, complete, and fulfilling even if you never marry, or if your marriage ends for some reason. However, unfortunately it seems to me that a lot of single people simply haven't been encouraged to think that it might be possible at all.

As single Christians, it is entirely possible for us to flourish spiritually and emotionally, to have a deep, intimate, growing relationship with the Lord, to have life-enhancing relationships with people around us – in short, to live what the Bible calls "life to the full."[4] It is possible for us to live in a way which is true to what the Bible asks of us if we are single, that is, to be celibate, and also to be whole.

It is vital that the church is equipped and able to support and encourage single people who have committed themselves to living life this way, as for many of them this is an area with which they really struggle. To live a celibate life is possible, to live a life that is whole and full while also being celibate is possible, but still there may well be a sense of loss for those who are living this way. As the numbers of single people continue to rise it simply will not do for the church to ignore this issue. It's vital that the church is able to embrace these issues, which may well be painful and difficult, in order that single people know that there is a safe space for these things to be discussed, where they can give voice to their everyday experiences of what it actually feels like to be celibate.

For single people living a celibate life there are a number of different issues which are relevant. One is simply the fact of living without sex. Very practically, this can be difficult to cope with as many people may experience strong sexual urges and desires. It can also lead to people feeling quite excluded, especially if they have never had sex – they may feel that they have missed out on a major life experience, or find themselves teased or ridiculed by non-Christian peers. Another is the fact of living not just without sex, but without close touch and intimacy. Often the lack of close personal touch, hugs etc., can be almost as difficult as living without sex itself. And finally of course there can for many people be the pain of knowing, especially as they get older, that they will not have children of their own.

Churches have a big part to play in enabling and supporting single people to live well. Churches need to be teaching what the Bible says about sex, marriage, relationships and singleness – clearly, truthfully and unapologetically.

For too long I believe that many churches have shied away from teaching this message, because it seemed to be too difficult. And it is difficult – but so are most things that are worthwhile! We simply must not shy away from this in our churches. If churches are not willing to speak out clearly and biblically on issues around sex, relationships, singleness and celibacy, then I believe they are doing single people (and indeed the whole church) a great disservice.

I think that what many of our churches do is that they teach their young people about sex and relationships, which of course is really important, but once the young people turn 18 all of the teaching stops. There is rarely any teaching on these issues within the adult programme of the church. Maybe it's because the church leaders are embarrassed. Maybe it's because they don't know what to say. Maybe it's because they have lost confidence in the message. Maybe it's because most of them are married so they don't know how to relate the message to single people, or feel somehow that they cannot ask others to live in a way which is difficult and which they are not living themselves. Whatever the reason, many churches are failing their single people by not helping them to navigate these important areas of life.

It is vital for single Christians that churches are clear and honest about what the Bible teaches about singleness and relationships. People hear so many different messages from the world around them – and biblical, Christian teaching is profoundly countercultural. We must help single people fully to understand how it is that God calls us to live.

The Bible calls us all to a life of holiness, purity, chastity. If we are single, that means we are called to live a celibate life. This is in profound contrast to the world around us, where we are all encouraged to fulfil whatever desires we may have, to please ourselves, to do what feels good (as long as no one else is hurt by it). The secular world's message about sex is a selfish one – it's all about me, what I want, what I need, what feels good to me. The Bible's message about sex is very different. Here it is something holy, something which is about covenant, and our bodies are temples of the Holy Spirit,[5] not simply ours to do with as we wish.

As Christians we long to grow and develop and flourish in our relationship with God. For all of us, there is a desire for a deep and contented relationship, and for us to be able to grow and develop spiritually, emotionally, socially and psychologically. This is obviously just as important and relevant for single people as it is for anyone else.

Churches can feel very alien to single people, perhaps most particularly those who are also younger. In the 25-39 age group in the UK, 13% of married adults attend church at least once a month, but only 5% of single people do.[6] This means that as single people seek to settle into a church and make friendships, they may struggle to find others in the same stage of life as they are. It is vital that single Christians feel able, within their churches and communities of faith, to seek help for any current or past issues within their relationships. If single people don't feel valued or welcomed in their churches then they might not feel able to ask for such help.

Single Christians also need to feel that they are treated the same as married Christians within their churches – this sounds obvious, but I know from many conversations with single people that it does not always happen. Single people need to know that they are valued just as highly as everyone else, and that their single status does not make people consider them to be not quite 'whole'. Clearly no individual Christian, or no church, would intend to make single people feel less than whole. But the way a church treats or values single people, and the language that is used to and about them, can mean that they end up feeling this way.

For instance, a phrase that an awful lot of people use to describe their spouse is their 'other half'. Obviously we all know what they mean – it's a common expression. But the problem is that this phrase can seem to suggest that each member within that relationship is only half of a person, and that only together do they make a whole. I would suggest that's bad enough for the married couple! But what about the single person who hears this expression used over and over again, yet has no 'other half'? Are they simply half a person, not a 'whole' unless they get married? It is easy to say "well, surely they understand what is meant." But when language like this is heard over and over again, it can make single people feel excluded and unwelcome.

Very often in churches and at Christian events, those preaching or leading give example after example and story after story about "my wife," "my children," "my family," etc. There is so often an assumption made that everyone listening will have had the same experiences, and will recognise the illustration. This can be incredibly alienating and isolating for all those listening whose life circumstances don't fit this neat pattern (and this may be for other reasons besides just singleness). Obviously there is a place for sharing life stories during preaching, but it would be good to have a wider breadth of stories being shared. This can happen both when preachers who are married with children think more creatively about the stories they share, and also when there are more single, childless preachers able to share their own stories.

In addition to this, there is something very important to be said for being able to get to know other people in the same life circumstances as you are. For all of us, to have someone to look up to, a role model, someone who is walking the path ahead of us and from whom we can learn, is a huge benefit, especially in our discipleship journey. For single people to see others ahead of them who are living life well, who are whole and fulfilled, is a huge encouragement, because it shows them that it is possible to live the single life well. Churches and Christian communities can really encourage this and foster these helpful role model relationships.

This can help to ensure that single people know that their lives have a purpose now – that it is not simply about 'waiting' but that they can use their gifts and serve the church right now, as single people. It can also help to ensure that single people have a balanced and healthy view of both singleness and marriage, understanding that both have their good parts and their difficult parts, that both take effort to live well, that neither one is inherently superior to the other. This will help single people better to understand their married friends, and also better to appreciate the positives in their own lives. Obviously, though, this helpful role modelling can only take place in a community and context where single people are welcomed, nurtured and valued, and encouraged to take their place among the worshipping, serving and leading life of the church.

It is frighteningly easy, as single people, for us to become bitter because we are unhappy with how our lives have turned out. We may consider that this is not the path that we would have chosen, and we may look at people around us and wonder why they have the thing that we want. It may be that we pray regularly and faithfully for a spouse or for children, and yet still we do not have those things, when others do. It is easy to become hard-hearted and to turn our backs on God – sadly I have seen this happen time and time again. In these moments we really need people around us who understand, who will not judge, but who will encourage and support us, pray for us, and help us to choose a life free from envy and bitterness – whatever our marital status. A loving church community which truly welcomes and accepts everyone can provide just this encouragement and support.

I would strongly encourage all single people (and all people, really!) to find some sort of small group or prayer partner with whom they can meet regularly. This should be a context where you can be completely honest about how life is going, and what is currently causing challenge or difficulty. Everyone will have a different view as to whether or not this should be someone who is also single or not – I don't think it really matters. But it does need to be a person, or group of people, who are empathetic and supportive.

I long for Christian single people truly to embrace Jesus' words in John 10:10; "I have come that they may have life, and have it to the full." What does living "life to the full" really look like when you're single? It involves spiritual, emotional and social flourishing, and support from close relationships. It involves help from others to deal with the many challenges that single people face in their daily lives, such as who to go on holiday with, how to cope when you're ill, financial struggles, finding a home, being self-employed, how to meet other single people. Advice on these and other things are given on the Single Friendly Church website.

How, then, can churches encourage single people to live life well here and now, recognising that they have a calling and a purpose, that their gifts are of value, that they have something to offer to the church and to the world?

For the local church

A few years ago I wrote a book called *Single Minded: Being single, whole, and living life to the full.* In it I wrote a chapter entitled "Living a God-obsessed Life in a Marriage-Obsessed Church."[7] That may sound a little harsh, but unfortunately I think that's how church often feels to single people. I understand how it's happened – over the years, the place of marriage in our society has been eroded, and its importance downgraded. It is no longer seen as special or lifelong. And so the church, rightly, wanted to stand up for marriage and family life, to champion it and promote it. Unfortunately, however, I think that some churches went too far, and made it seem as if marriage was the only proper way to live a godly life. This has led to the unintended consequence of anyone whose life did not fit the 'correct' model – because they were divorced, or widowed, or never married, or married without children – feeling as if they were somehow less valued than those with the 'ideal' family situation. I'm sure that this was never the intention, but I think it is the message that has sometimes been given out.

In healthy churches, the leaders (who are usually married) explicitly listen to single people and understand what life is like for them. Teaching from the front and in small groups involves as many illustrations about singleness as marriage. They give a balanced overview of the biblical teaching on sex and marriage. Right at the start of the Bible, in Genesis, we see God declaring, as he creates the world, that "it is not good for the man to be alone."[8] God has never before declared something in his creation to be "not good" and yet here he is clearly stating that 'aloneness' is not something that he wants for his creation. It is not singleness that is declared "not good", but aloneness. In response to this aloneness God creates Eve, and all of the people who then follow. Community has been established in God's creation right from the very beginning, and it is there as a remedy against the "not good" aloneness.

Marriage and family life was the norm throughout the whole of the Old

Testament period, and indeed in the society into which Jesus was born. It was very unusual to be single or not to have children – there was a stigma attached to it, and a concern about what would happen to single people in their old age. We see examples throughout the Bible of people (mostly women) crying out to God because they are unmarried or don't have children.

Jesus was single too!

Into the midst of this cultural context, Jesus' teaching and indeed his very life were countercultural. The fact that Jesus himself was single is hugely important. It is easy for us to miss, from our 21st century perspective, just how radical it would have been for a rabbi in his thirties to be single. But Jesus shows us by his words and by his life that it is possible to be whole and fulfilled and complete as a single person. And he created a particular type of community – the church – to provide a way in which all people could be cared for and supported.

Jesus also made it clear that marriage is an earthly state, not an eternal one. Jesus told the Sadducees that "at the resurrection people will neither marry nor be given in marriage."[9] We need to remember that (as important and valuable as marriage is in our society today) marriage is not to be placed on some sort of pedestal within the church, and seen as the holiest way of life, which should be achieved by all.

The apostle Paul is another role model for us as single people. He expressed his approval of the single life, and even said that he wished more people would remain single![10] He talked about the fact that single people were able to commit themselves even more fully to the work of the gospel.

Surely today we simply must take note of this. So often in many churches, it seems that marriage is valued and prized above singleness, and seen as 'the best' for Christian people – the goal to which we all should aspire. So often single people feel excluded in their churches, and report that they feel that people would prefer it if they were married. And yet here we are reminded that both Jesus and Paul were single! Perhaps there is something important for the church to consider in how it values and utilises the gifts of single people.

The American author Al Hsu wrote an excellent book a number of years ago entitled *The Single Issue.* In it he says this: "Without demeaning marriage, the New Testament gives a new dignity to singleness. Both are equally valid ways to serve God."[11]

The Single Friendly Church website puts it like this: "To many people, the church looks like a church of the married, for the married." Among the UK adult population today 47% are married, but married people make up over 60% of the church. And conversely 40% of the population are single people, but they make up just 32% of the church.[12] These numbers make a big difference to how welcome people feel within church, and to the extent to which they feel that 'people like them' are represented there.

I was once 'welcomed' to a church I was visiting by a cheerful older gentleman who asked "Are you lonesome?" I had absolutely no idea what he was on about so just replied "Err, pardon?" He tried again: "Are you here solo?" I was still so taken aback that I'm not even sure what I said next. I just grabbed a book and went to find a seat. Presumably he was just trying to make conversation, to welcome me, and presumably he didn't intend to rub my face in how lonely I was feeling that day, or how I'd had to stir up all of my courage to walk into a new church on my own – but I wouldn't recommend those as opening words when you welcome a single person to your church.

If a local church is going to be somewhere which truly provides a welcome to all, regardless of their relationship status and life circumstances, then it will have to mind its language, to be careful in its use of words like 'family', to treat everyone equally, and genuinely to say – and to mean – that all are welcome. 'Family' is a loaded word, and of course different people feel differently about it, but I would simply suggest that care is taken about when and how it is used. When 'family' means 'all of us in this church' then that's great – we're all family together. But when it is used in the context of 'a family-friendly service', and so clearly means 'this is for young married couples with children only', then that can feel difficult and excluding for anyone who doesn't fall into that category. It might be fine as a one-off, but if that sort of language use is common or regular, then it could be difficult for single people. The language that we use seems like such a small thing, but it is so worth our attention, since it can make such a big difference to how we make people feel.

Ideally, the local church will also be representative within its leadership structures at all levels, so that the only model of leadership given is not that of married couples with children. There will be single leaders too. This will mean that the church leadership is more representative of the church as a whole, and also of the wider society of which it is a part. Crucially it will also mean that single people within the church are able to see role models in leadership, and to be enabled to believe that it is possible for them as single people to be included within all roles in church life.

The culture of a church is of vital importance here. Leaders have a particular role to play in how a culture is formed, but it is the responsibility of every member to ensure that the culture is truly embedded and enacted. A church which is to be a safe and welcoming place for single people will be one where relationship issues are actively discussed, and where healthy relationships are encouraged and promoted. There is a balance to be found here. In some churches there is no mention whatsoever of dating and relationships. Single people are given no encouragement to think about dating or to consider (assuming they would like to be married) how they might go about finding someone to go out with. On the other hand, however, in some churches all single people are almost required to think and talk about possible relationships, and there is a strong matchmaking culture. I would suggest that somewhere between these two extremes is the healthiest place for a church to be!

In my experience, churches often also fall into one of two traps when it comes to single people and their availability for ministry. The first is when single people are treated as if they are not yet quite grown up. The model of leadership in action in the church is that married couples lead together – so single people are not invited to lead. This may well not be a deliberately thought-through position, but it is simply how things work out in practice. In fact, what is needed isn't a tokenistic, box-ticking representation of single people, but rather a genuine attempt for church to be a true cross-section of society, with both genders, a variety of disabilities, all ages, and all stages of life represented fully across the board, and involved in all aspects of church life.

The second trap is when single people are treated as if they have all the free time in the world, and nothing better to do than volunteer in church. It is assumed that they will be available to help with whatever is going on, and that, in the absence of 'family' responsibilities, they will be able to drop everything to help at a moment's notice. When things are working well, married people will realise that single people often have to do all the jobs at home by themselves, since there is no one with whom to divide the labour.

In addition to all that I have said so far about singleness in general, if a church is truly going to be a place of welcome for single people, it is going to have to work out how to support those who find themselves single again after being married, either because they get divorced or because their spouse dies. Often people who find themselves in these situations report finding it very difficult within church, because of the way they are treated by other people. There is often a lot of judgement of those who have got divorced. People may not have all of the facts, and so they make their own judgments based on what they think they know. They might decide that one party is in the wrong and one is innocent – that is rarely true in such a black and white way, but even where it is, we should offer support to both parties.

Where someone's spouse has died, hopefully in the short-term they will find that the church is kind and supportive. However, as time passes, those who have been widowed often find it hard within the church. Suddenly they don't quite fit in the same way as they once did. They are now single, but they are in a different category from other single people. They may well find that other people don't know how to treat them, and leave them out of social events or invitations, so a helpful and healthy church will intentionally address this. Those who find themselves single again may or may not wish to look for another relationship, but they require just as much support in living their single life as those who have always been single.

Churches, at their best, are communities of variety and diversity, where everyone has something to offer, and something to learn. In this context, single people can learn more about what Christian marriage, and Christian family life, really look like – not the rose-tinted versions, but the real-life versions. Also in this context, single people can be free to explore dating and to be supported and encouraged as they do so. At the same time though, they should be free from the pressure of feeling that they must explore the dating world if they don't want to, and from the expectation that the 'proper' end point for all single people is necessarily marriage.

Within our churches we have the opportunity to create genuinely meaningful relationships, which are honest and deep and challenging and accountable. There's so much for us all to learn from one another. I know that personally I hugely value the relationships I have with married people, of my age and older, and with their children. It's a huge privilege, within a church context, to be able to be part of the lives of different families.

A survey by the Office for National Statistics in 2013, the implications of which for the church were discussed by the Evangelical Alliance, showed that 29% of people who live alone reported feeling lonely some or most of the time.[13] Surely, as the church, we have an opportunity to do something about this. If we can create true community then we can ensure that no one has to spend significant days on their own if they don't want to, and no one has to go through tough times without someone alongside them.

For the national church

If attitudes within the church to single people are truly going to change, and if single people are to feel fully welcomed and included in church, then change is needed at the national level, not just at the local level. This is where culture and attitudes will really be changed for good, and where healthy patterns can be laid down.

The change needs to begin with training future church leaders, so that those who themselves are single are supported in order that their ministry is the best it can be, and also so that all leaders, single and married, learn about how to support and welcome single people within their churches.

Support for those who are single and are training for ministry is vital. While there are many joys involved in church leadership, there are also many challenges, and some of these can be magnified for single people. There can be a real sense of loneliness for church leaders, since they often work in quite isolated settings, are required to hold many pastoral confidences, and have to make complex decisions alone. Obviously this sense of loneliness can feel even greater for single people, as they don't have someone there to talk to at the end of a busy day, to support them when things are tough, and – crucially – to remind them to stop working from time to time!

In addition, it's really important that married leaders learn during their training about some of the pros and cons of the single life, in order that they might be better able to support the single people who will be members of their churches. Often the training for church leaders involves a lot of time thinking about ministering to married people and families, and a lot of time learning about preparing people for marriage and officiating at weddings. However it often does not involve very much time at all (if any) thinking about ministering to single people, and how to disciple and support them in their singleness. This is a huge omission. There are so many single people in our churches, and the number is only going to increase. We urgently need to equip church leaders to support them.

As has already been discussed, within society today there are a large number of single people, and some of these will be struggling with their singleness and feeling lonely. We have a huge opportunity as the church to offer them a welcome and to provide a place of belonging and community. I really believe that this is an evangelistic opportunity to which the church has not yet fully woken up.

There is also, I think, a specific evangelistic opportunity with regards to single men. This might sound a bit flippant, but it is actually a serious point. It is very obvious that within the church in general, and within almost all local churches specifically, there are significantly more women than men. There is then a very real need for more young men to come to faith in Jesus. This is not just so that they can be married off, but to address the significant gender imbalance which currently exists within the church, and to enhance Christian communities with a greater balance of qualities, gifts and strengths.

As future church leaders are trained they also need to be equipped to teach the Bible well, and to have confidence in teaching about relationships, sex and marriage, rather than shying away from these difficult subjects. Whenever I speak to groups of single people at Christian festivals and events, I ask them when was the last time they heard any teaching in their local church on marriage, sex, singleness or relationships. Generally fewer than 10% of people have heard any such teaching in the past year – and the numbers don't generally get better if you go back five or 10 years. We simply must teach about these issues in our local churches. It is unfair to expect single people to simply figure out for themselves what the Bible says about sex and relationships, and how to live faithfully within that. We must offer teaching and training and equipping and support as they seek to live faithful single lives, and if we are to do that well within our churches then future church leaders need to be trained in how to do it well.

Of course, this shouldn't just be something which is part of training for future church leaders, but then never spoken of again. There should also be ongoing training within the church's programme of continuing ministerial education. Single people are often an entirely forgotten constituency within our churches, and this simply has to change.

One thing I have been thinking about a lot lately is the representation of single people. If someone was planning their line-up of speakers for an event, or considering the overall makeup of a leadership team, they would (hopefully) very rightly and properly consider balance. If most of the group were male, they would aim to include some women. If most of the group were white, they would aim to include some people from different ethnicities and cultures. I am increasingly coming to the view that we should think similarly around singleness. If most of the group is married, let's aim to include some single people. If there are seminars and courses on marriage, there should be seminars on singleness too. This sort of attention to balance can only be helpful in terms of ensuring single people feel more represented, included and supported.

Conclusion

Singleness is a factor of modern day life – in the world and in the church. It isn't going anywhere. We as the church could get better at engaging with the issues which exist for single people. I long to see the church leading the way in supporting and encouraging single people to live the 'life to the full' for which they were created, and to become more like Jesus every day.

Action points

Some of the things which I've discussed above can be implemented fairly quickly and easily; others will require more time and effort but are no less worthwhile. Below are some suggestions for some simple starting points.

Individuals
- Find a small group or prayer partner to meet with regularly.

Local churches
- Think about your preaching programme and, if it doesn't currently feature, add in a sermon series about sex/relationships/singleness.
- Think about those who preach and teach, and ensure that examples and illustrations given are taken from the breadth of everyday life and not simply from marriage and family life.

National church
- Ensure that all training courses for church leaders include both specific support for single leaders; and also training in how best to minister to and support single church members.

Further information/resources

Books
- *Single Minded.* Kate Wharton (2013). Monarch.
- *The Single Issue.* Al Hsu (2009). IVP.
- *Party Of One.* Joy Beth Smith (2018). Thomas Nelson.
- *True Friendship.* Vaughan Roberts (2013). 10Publishing.

Websites
- www.singlefriendlychurch.com
  Comprehensive resource website for individuals and church leaders, with lots of practical advice based on research.
- www.engage-mcmp.org.uk
  Resources section on Singleness.

"Healthy Christian singleness: what would it look like if things were working well in the church?"

Engage consultation vision grid

An individual	A local church	The national church
Spiritual and emotional flourishing	**Language and representation**	**Initial theological training**
• Deep and contented relationship with God. • Continually developing spiritually, emotionally, socially, psychologically – confident to seek help if needed to deal with current/past issues including those to do with relationships/ parents' relationship. • Feels and is treated like a complete person as an individual. • Feels that singleness is do-able/plausible. • Free from pressure to get married – from family/ church. • Feel they have a purpose – not 'waiting until marriage'. • Sees own sexuality as a positive thing. • Aware of and grateful to God for the advantages of being single. • Aware of the reality of being married. • Clear on what the Bible teaches about singleness/marriage/ celibacy/sex. • Supported to consider how they feel about singleness and why. • Free from bitterness. • Healthy attitude to Christian dating.	• Language is completely balanced between 'singleness' and 'marriage/family'. • People are treated the same without regard to their marital status. • Church leaders are aware of the balance/ proportion of their congregation (single/ married). **Culture** • The views/needs of single people are proactively sought, listened to, and understood – whatever their circumstances. • Thriving, flourishing single people are very visible in the church community (a sign of a healthy community), and a witness to the difference between single Christian people and those who don't know the Lord. • Widowed/divorced/ others supported effectively – not viewed as a victim or patronised. • Leadership team has mix of single and married people.	• Training for ministry involves input on singleness, supporting single people, and evangelism to single people (a key demographic not effectively reached yet). • College staff enabling support for single people who are in training. • Leaders are trained to confidently teach what the bible teaches – including a positive vision of singleness. • Training includes basic socio-demographic information about society and the church around singleness/ marriage, psycho-social dynamics and other related issues. **Continuing training for leaders** • Ongoing regular training on the issues. • Continuing Ministerial Education – widespread input on issues covered by Engage. • Leadership networks have regular input. • People are trained to share in the Christian and secular media about what it's like being a single Christian.

An individual	A local church	The national church
• Understanding and embracing willingly that a key part of the Christian life is sacrifice – may include giving up the 'right to sex' (in contrast to sex-obsessed society). • Knowing and experiencing that Jesus understands – Jesus and Paul model how to be fully human and single. • A sense of humour around singleness as appropriate. • Being confident to seek help with the grief of childlessness. • Help to consider issues around fostering/ adoption as a single person with balanced, realistic and detailed information. • Feel free to ask questions about issues around singleness. • Able to raise the issues around singleness with church leaders.	• Actively promotes a culture that has balanced proportion of single people in congregation and leadership – actively avoids 'couples' culture. • Creates an emotionally safe environment to talk about issues honestly – whether single or married. • Church promotes healthy friendships between men and women whether single or married. • Co-leading between men and women whether single or married (not just married people leading with their spouse). • A named key leader in the church to support single people and representation of single people. • Single people quickly and fully included in the church if they're new, as well as married couples. • Staff acknowledge and address the challenges of encouraging a church culture that is welcoming for everyone.	**Denominations** • Proportional representation of singleness on leadership teams. • Churches within denominations are well connected, and with other churches in the community. • National debates and initiatives about singleness e.g. Church of England Synod. • Money/resources/staffing given to developing better evangelism and discipleship of single people. • Actively promote a theology of healthy Christian singleness. **National conferences** • Conference leadership teams have single members. • Speakers – balance between men/women, single/married.
Inclusion • Experience truly deep friendships. • Healthy 'accountability and encouragement' relationships. • In 'iron sharpening iron' relationships rather than superficial relationships or isolation. • Feels part of a community/family. • Feels fully integrated socially in church life. • Feeling genuinely understood by others regarding their age/ stage/circumstance.	• Healthy Christian single role models are evident – without a need to be 'outstanding'. • Church culture is free from assumptions about single people's time availability or skills. • The importance of spiritual heirs and not just biological heirs is highlighted. • Churches take proactive steps to be 'single-person friendly' as well as 'family-friendly'.	**Mission organisations** • Training/conferences include input about singleness on the mission field.

An individual	A local church	The national church
• Free from the impact of stereotyped ideas of men/women and what they may/may not find difficult. • Free to be honest about joys and struggles about singleness. • Has role models around of healthy Christian singleness, and is also a role model to others. • Is a spiritual parent to others (whether adults, children or young people). • Has people to spend time with – whether a 'normal day', holidays, special times of year, difficult periods of life. **Gifting** • Individual gifts are fully used. • Able to take part in all opportunities for church involvement, ministry and leadership – does not encounter a glass ceiling of gifts being used because they are single. • Single people aren't over-worked/exploited. • Has the courage to pioneer rather than just fit into what's currently going on.	• Church culture is free from assumptions about why single people are single (e.g. that healing is needed), but offers pastoral support and grace for those who do have particular spiritual, emotional, social, psychological needs. **Teaching/discipleship** • Church leaders read and use good quality UK books and resources about singleness. • Preachers are aware of the powerful impact (positively or negatively) of what they say. • Teaching involves as many examples about singleness as about marriage. • Teachers acknowledge if they are teaching on singleness/marriage and it is not their particular experience, and are sensitive. • Churches have a planned structure for teaching/discipleship that regularly and specifically covers singleness – and other issues – from the front as well as in other contexts. • Regular teaching around biblical perspectives on singleness/dating/sex before marriage. • Leaders apply biblical teaching to today's current social reality (not a rose-tinted bygone era). • Leaders provide a robust critique of a sex-obsessed world – including the challenges for everyone.	

An individual	A local church	The national church
	• Fact-based information is used to change thinking e.g. mental links/false attributions about single people. • Front-stage interviews of single people. • Everyone is happy that the church is teaching in a balanced way about singleness, dating/relationships, marriage – even if it's not directly applicable to them. • Short stories/interviews about singleness as well as 'sermons'. • Teaching is not just a one-off event, but there are ongoing illustrations/input about singleness. • The church addresses the issues that single people sometimes face, but which can also affect others in the church (e.g. loneliness).	

Dating and relationships: what would it look like if things were working well in the church?

Annabel Clarke

Introduction

"Christian dating and relationships": what are the first thoughts that spring to mind when you hear that phrase? For some people they will be positive thoughts, for others, perhaps not so positive ("cringe" is a common one!). For some who've been married a while, they might be along the lines of "I'm glad I don't have to do all that anymore." As mentioned in chapter 1, because of the church gender imbalance, and general lack of relevant teaching on the subject, there isn't much dating going on amongst Christian adults these days. Research has shown that 54% of single Christian adults said that they haven't dated for at least a year, or, it is many years since they last went on a date.[1]

But let's imagine – what if the church discussed and supported healthy dating and relationships as much as it discusses and supports marriage? What if everyone's automatic thoughts were not 'embarrassment' but 'empowerment', not 'hidden' but 'healthy', not 'paralysed' but 'proactive'?

Today's single Christians often seem to experience one of two equally unhelpful but opposite teaching and discipleship omissions.

- The assumption that everyone wants to or will get married one day. Teaching (if there's any) and discourse just focuses on marriage/ dating/relationships and ignores those who do not want to or will not get married one day. Many single Christians report that they feel unhelpfully pressurised to get married by those in their church. This leads to too much pressure on dating and relationships.
- The assumption that everyone wants to or will stay single for the rest of their lives. Teaching and discourse just focuses on singleness and ignores those who want to or will get married one day (there's no input for them on dating, relationships and marriage). This leads to too little 'pressure' or encouragement around dating and relationships.

Tim Keller has described how "single people cannot live their lives well as singles without a balanced, informed view of marriage. If they do not have that, they will either over-desire or under-desire marriage, and either of those ways of thinking will distort their lives."[2]

This chapter links with chapters 10 (about parenting) and 11 (about young people) in that all of them are about growing healthy dating and relationships, for the sake of those involved now, but also to help build stronger marriages in the future.

As I outlined in chapter 1, it is helpful for people to have a mental map to help them navigate both dating and relationships, and to view these as two distinct stages. The Engage consultation group for this theme considered what things might look like if they were working well for individuals, the local church and the national church, and then we also discussed the following in more detail:

- The spiritual, emotional and social foundations needed for healthy dating and relationships.
- What the dating stage would look like at the beginning, middle and end (with 'dating' defined as "getting to know someone with a view to seeing whether or not we want to be in a relationship").
- What the relationship stage would look like at the beginning, middle and end (with 'relationship' defined as "getting to know someone with a view to seeing whether or not we want to get engaged").

Individuals

Foundations

The foundations of healthy dating and relationships start with healthy singleness. A Christian single person's first life priority is to be rooted and growing in their relationship with God. Personal prayer and Bible reading, involvement in a local fellowship of other Christians, and wanting to grow in all aspects of faith will keep them connected to him. From this will develop healthy core life values which impact on choices and decisions. If someone is used to pursuing God's wisdom and discernment in all areas of life, it will be easier to apply this to dating and relationships. Encountering more of God shows them who they are in Christ, giving them a positive sense of identity and self-esteem, and they use the gifts and skills God has given them as they follow his purposes for their life. Having close healthy connections with others is the second essential aspect of singleness. This will help a single person's emotional and social needs to be met in appropriate ways, rather than them pursuing dating or romantic relationships to meet all these needs.

Everybody brings past experiences to dating and relationships, whether these have been positive or difficult. If things are working well in the church, single people will know where to go for support to gain freedom from the unhelpful 'baggage' of past relationships or from unhealthy habits. They'll be free from shame and free to choose to date from a place of wholeness rather than need. For some single people, it will be helpful to learn to be comfortable having friendships with people of the opposite sex. For others, the next step will be more about proactively seeking to move beyond friendship.

Simon (aged 38) told me a few months ago that the reason he is still single is because he works long hours. He was starting to see the tension – continuing to work at that pace was advancing his career, but not his desire to get married and have a family. For him, re-thinking how he spent his time was going to be helpful. Amanda (aged 32) once told me that while she had organised her schedule to make time for dating, she realised that for her, it was necessary to re-think how she spent her money. There weren't many single men at all near where she lived, but she met a nice guy through a Christian dating website who lived in a different part of the country. She then had to prioritise some more money for travelling to meet up with him.

A useful activity for single people to do is to list different areas of life, intentionally reflect on how those are going, and then decide whether it might be useful to make some adjustments to support their healthy living as well as dating. Some questions might be: is my life well-balanced? Am I involved in interesting and fun activities, including involvement at church? Is life 'moving forwards' instead of feeling a bit 'stuck'? Am I looking after myself physically, with enough sleep and exercise?

It's also worth thinking about possible barriers to dating and relationships, such as: how do I want my next date (or relationship) to be different from, or similar to the last one? How do I feel about the idea of committing to a relationship? How do I feel about committing to marriage in the future? How do I want my relationship (or marriage) to be different from, or similar to what my parents experienced?

This doesn't mean, of course, that a person has to 'get sorted' before they start dating, and it's important that this isn't the message they receive from the church. It's just that it's good for everyone, whether single or married, to regularly reflect on their life balance and relationships and make adjustments where appropriate.

One of the most helpful areas to have learnt about before dating is how to maintain healthy boundaries. In their book *Boundaries,* US psychologists Henry Cloud and John Townsend explain how boundaries are like a property line.[3] Boundaries distinguish what is our emotional or personal property, and what belongs to someone else. They define what we are and what we aren't, including our values and preferences, and let others know what we will and won't tolerate. They keep good things in and bad things out. Being comfortable with healthy emotional, relational, physical and time boundaries is a strong foundation for dating and relationships.

Being part of a good community and having close friendships who can give you feedback is also invaluable. Ideally, single people will know a range of people, and be able to learn from role models who are showing what healthy Christian dating, relationships and marriage can look like.

In his book *How to Get a Date Worth Keeping*, Henry Cloud has a chapter called "Get Your Team Together". He recommends having a small 'support team' of people (e.g. close friends, family, a mentor) for encouragement and accountability who can talk, pray, listen and feedback specifically around a single person's dating or relationship. The team doesn't need to necessarily have to all meet together (I know someone whose 'dating team' is a WhatsApp group), but this, along with meeting in person with some of them, can be very beneficial.

Some single people will need more encouragement from their team, some will need a bit more challenge, but this approach really supports the development of godly dating and relationships. Any unhelpful aspects of the psycho-social dynamics between men and women can be addressed (e.g. men sometimes wanting to date much younger women) and instead there will be a culture of mutual respect for Christian brothers and sisters. You might have heard of 'ghosting', which is a term used in dating when someone suddenly cuts off all communication without warning and 'disappears'.[4]When things are working well in church, this will never happen, and instead people will be respectfully responsive. I would suggest that a key principle is for people to always be 'clear, kind and honest' with each other.

Dating
As explained earlier, it is useful to define 'dating' as "getting to know someone with a view to seeing whether or not we want to be in a relationship." It's meeting up with someone between once and a few times. Let's now consider what this stage might look like at the beginning, middle and end.

Beginning
- People will intentionally think and pray about dating, by themselves and with other people. The phrase I'd suggest having in mind is 'intentional but not intense'. Intentional because dating should be

proactively purposeful, but not intense, because going on a date isn't about deciding if this person is your life partner. A coffee isn't a marriage proposal.

- Unless they live in a big city and go to a big church with lots of other single people around their age, many find it a challenge to meet potential dates. In *How to Get a Date Worth Keeping*, Henry Cloud emphasises the importance of 'getting your numbers up'. Single people often find that when they actually count up how many new people they meet per week, let alone those who are potential dates, the numbers are extremely low, if not non-existent. He gives lots of practical ideas to help with this problem, as does Aukelien van Abbema in her book *Dare to Date*.[5]

- Dating these days includes using online approaches to widen the net of people to meet. Some church ministers are unsure, anxious or sceptical about online dating, because it is so far removed from their own experience. However, it's now completely normal, and if a good website (such as Christian Connection) is used wisely, it can work very well for Christians and is to be recommended. You could try this experiment: ask a group of people to put their hand up if they know someone who has met and got married via a Christian dating website. You'll probably find that almost everyone does. It is helpful for everyone to be aware of how to make the most of online opportunities, such as through HopefulGirl's article on the Christian Connection blog "The Science of Online Dating – 10 Ways to Boost Your Success".[6] For more about online dating, you could also see the Dating and Relationships resources section on the Engage website.[7]

- Attitude is important. Looking for 'Mr/Ms Perfect' from the start is unlikely to lead to success, but when things are working well, Christians will be open-minded about dating a range of people to learn about themselves and others, rather than looking for a very specific 'type'. They'll be confident about their own attractiveness. Men and women will know that a feeling of attraction might not be there at the start of dating, but that's OK, it might grow. They'll confidently ask people on dates, and confidently accept date invitations unless there really are appropriate 'red flags' that their support team would agree with. As *How to Get a Date Worth Keeping* explains, 'go out with almost anyone once, and maybe again', but if someone does turn down a date request, then the person asking will be resilient. This is easier, if someone hasn't invested too much emotionally by spending a long time admiring someone from afar before asking them on a date.

Middle

- It's a good idea for people to think of a range of fun activities to do for dates. The resources at the end of this chapter give practical ideas. Especially if one date turns into more, doing different activities will mean getting to know someone better than just talking over coffee or a meal.
- Christians will be looking to make dating a positive experience for the other person. Kindness is crucial. Prayer about each date and the dating process continues to be essential.

End

- This again is where the 'clear, kind and honest' culture is so important. At the end of one date, one person will need to take initiative to communicate about whether they will meet up again. This might be in person at the end of the date, or just afterwards (e.g. within a day or two). If one person would rather not meet again, they will say so in a way that includes any general reasons which are 'owned' by the giver, and positive feedback for the other person. The same approach is helpful if they've met for several dates. One friend who has just finished dating a guy told me that he'd said to her "Well, I can't pretend I'm not disappointed that you'd rather end things. But can I say that I really appreciate how you explained that, in fact I think I might write down what you just said so I can say something similar to someone else in the future if needs be!" This is the sort of culture of kindness the church needs.
- On the other hand, one person may feel they'd like the dating to move to the next stage of a 'relationship', and then both need to have a clear, kind and honest conversation about this. In both instances, both people (if they're Christians) will be praying for wisdom and discernment, with input from members of their support team.

Relationships

A 'relationship' or 'going out' (the UK term) can be defined as "getting to know someone with a view to seeing whether or not we want to get engaged." This is an exclusive, romantic relationship. It is different from dating: the couple won't date other people and will come off any dating websites, and attraction becomes more important (whereas it's not essential in early dating). Here's an outline of how a relationship can work well.

Beginning

- If a couple want their relationship to be based on good communication, then it's worth them having a conversation early on about "What sorts of things would it be useful for us to talk about at the start of this relationship?" Some people might be used to having open conversations like this, but others might not. Do they have a shared understanding of how they would like things to be? When and how often will they see each other? What do they want their physical boundaries to be? How much time might they spend alone or with others? How do they want their faith to be part of their relationship? This doesn't mean immediately having a one-off very intense discussion at the very start, but when things are working well, these are issues that will be explicitly talked about near the beginning of a relationship, and will be re-visited as it continues.

Middle

- A healthy relationship will involve intentionally getting to know the other person's heart, character and values, and how they react in different situations. It will involve having fun! Over time, both people will initiate and openly respond to discussions about the future – their hopes and dreams about life and marriage. They'll both want to grow and learn about how to do relationships well.
- Christians will also want to intentionally support each other to love and serve God. This will include understanding why God's design is for sex within marriage, and honouring that. Their level of intimacy will reflect the level of mutual commitment.

End

- Bringing a relationship to a good ending requires prayer, courage and input from others to make wise decisions. When things are working well, the couple will be talking and praying together to mutually discern whether they should finish the relationship, or move on to become engaged. Any hesitations about engagement will be discussed and prayed through with friends, and preferably also an older, wiser married Christian couple. This can help avoid a relationship drifting on for too long for unhealthy reasons. Karen (36) told me a few weeks ago that she had finally decided that because her boyfriend of over a year was not willing or able to openly talk about the future of the relationship, she had reluctantly decided to end it. She was right to do so, because unfortunately he was not ready for commitment, and she was. Good 'closure' needs to involve discussion about what the new boundaries between the couple will look like.

- It seems that more churches are now becoming aware that it's probably a bit too late to only teach people about marriage when they're engaged. Couples in a relationship can really benefit from using resources about engagement, in order to help them make wise choices about whether this is right for them. Discussion and prayer together and with others will continue to be important. Sometimes, even just a short, direct conversation with a friend can be the prompt that's needed. Once, a good friend came round help sort out some problems with my computer. He was talking about Hannah, his girlfriend who he'd been going out with for three years. At one point, I carefully asked if he thought he knew whether she was the person he wanted to spend the rest of his life with, and he said that she was. We then carried on talking, mostly about new software. Two weeks later he rang me and said it was a "computer servicing courtesy call," mentioning that he was with Hannah. He asked how my computer was ("Fine, thank you") and I asked how Hannah was. "She's not my girlfriend anymore," he replied, "I've upgraded her, she's now my fiancée."

The local church

Foundations
The foundations for healthy dating and relationships for a local church involve two key elements: the gender imbalance and teaching.

Churches where things are working well understand that it's their responsibility to actively and intentionally work to make their congregation gender balanced, with about the same number of single men as women. To do this, regularly collecting relevant data will become part of the usual church systems, from doing an approximate count of the numbers of men and women at services, other meetings and small groups, to undertaking surveys, as outlined in chapter 4. This is an essential part of leading a church into healthy dating and relationships.

When things are working well, church leaders will be informed about how single people in their congregation are affected by national and local church gender imbalances and other current issues. It would be helpful if pastors met with the single women in their church as a group and listened carefully to their experiences of Christian dating and relationships, and then met with the men to do the same. This would be a good starting point to begin to address some of the needs. Group discussions could be structured through a simple format such as "What's not working well?", "What's working well?", and "How could we as a church help move things forward?" Another step could be to ask to meet up with a few men and women individually and ask them to share (confidentially) about their experiences of Christian dating and relationships. It would be best if the pastor has one other person present as 'co-listener' who is of the opposite sex for each of these listening contexts, so that their shared perspectives can help inform how issues are dealt with.

In terms of teaching, churches can support healthy spiritual and emotional foundations for lots of different people's wellbeing by sermons or talks from the front that address the life topics that people are dealing with. These include how to find freedom from past relationship hurts, from porn and from shame, why sex within marriage is God's design, and what marriage between Christians can look like. Testimonies can help do this really powerfully. During one evening service at my church, a married couple in their late fifties were interviewed about their marriage of 30 years. They were very honest about the joys and challenges they'd faced together, and it was really helpful for everyone. What was particularly striking, though, was to watch the reaction of both the youth group members and the students. They were hanging onto every word. You could tell that lots of them hadn't ever heard such a discussion, and that they found the combination of openness (they were allowed to ask questions) and humour absolutely inspirational. Some people will have seen healthy Christian marriage modelled at home by their parents, but many won't. Everybody needs to understand some of the potential of Christian marriage, whether they're single, dating or in a relationship.

There are some matters, of course, that it won't be appropriate to address just 'from the front'. Those who are divorced, widowed or older may have specific needs. There will be people (whether single or married) in every church who need to deal with deep emotional and relational wounds. One woman told me recently that for her, having an abortion when she was younger was now interwoven into the problems of longing for children, the pain of singleness and the lack of opportunities for marriage. She noted the need for churches to minister effectively to the many women who, for whatever reason, have terminated their pregnancies. It will be useful for small group or individual support to be available to address different issues and for people to know how it can be accessed, whether through the church or other organisations.

Overall, laying good foundations in a church for healthy dating and relationships can be more challenging if the church leader has limited or no experience of what dating is like for different people in today's Christian world. It may be many years since they were involved in dating, or even if it wasn't, male leaders will have had a very different experience of dating and relationships to female leaders, for example. For this reason, it's a good idea for any teaching and support around dating and relationships to be led by a balanced team of a man and woman, where one is younger and the other is older, and one is single, dating or in a relationship and the other is married. This can bring a credible blend of experiences that will be helpful for everyone.

Dating

One church I know is doing a great job at promoting healthy Christian dating. They decided to arrange a speed-dating event in a pub for single people from their congregation and other churches. They used the 'bring a mate' approach, which can work really well – where everyone brings a friend along of the opposite sex. This means you end up with equal numbers of men and women, and those attending have a 'wing-person' to go with, which makes the whole thing more relaxed. At the event, so many extra people turned up on the night hoping to get in that due to fire safety concerns there were literally bouncers on the door struggling to keep people out! I think the organisers were more than a bit surprised, but it was a very powerful illustration of how necessary it is for churches to facilitate healthy dating and how keen single people are to meet potential dates if an event is not 'cheesy'. This sort of gathering will probably work better in larger towns or cities where there are usually more single people, but imagine if churches across the country organised such speed-dating events a few times a year. It's intentional – people are looking for a date. But not intense – OK, the short speed-dating conversations might be in some ways, but you can go with a mate, meet lots of new people, and it doesn't take too long if the group size is kept manageable. This is just one example, but if churches network to promote events, this will help to widen people's social circles.

The obvious challenge, of course, with any 'bring a mate' events, is that there are often women unable to attend because they don't know any single men to go with – which returns us to the need for more men in church. However, it's usually when women can't see that anything is being done that they feel no one cares. If the impact of the lack of men in church on women's dating is readily acknowledged by church leaders, and if leaders are seen to be proactively trying to address the gender imbalance, then this at least is some encouragement to the single women.

When dating is working well in the local church, leaders will understand what a vision for healthy Christian dating can look like, and promote this from the front, as well as in other contexts. Information about relevant resources will be made readily available for everyone through all the usual communication channels – for those who are looking to date, as well as others, so that everyone is well-informed. If a third of the church is single, and most of them are looking to date, then lots of other people in the church who are acting as dating support team members will benefit from these resources too.

We need to move on from the 'cringey' connotations that are often present around Christian dating. Healthy dating can be normalised when churches have planned, ongoing, regular teaching and discipleship on all the issues involved. On the one hand, this will involve explicitly talking about the barriers, which include the gender imbalance, increasing numbers of single Christians, male-female psycho-social dynamics, 'don't date' messages and the spiritual battle around Christian marriage. On the other hand, it will also involve sharing the vision, such as outlined in this chapter, about what positive dating can look like in practice. This will really let single people know that their church leaders are encouraging and affirming healthy dating.

Some churches have a culture of match-making. This can either be helpful if it's done sensitively and appropriately, or be hurtful if it isn't. Some people have told me their stories.

> "In my church and family, getting married and having children is the top priority for women. My aunt told me that I must be demon-possessed because I'm still single. At church, people are always trying to set me up with unsuitable men." (Maria, aged 28)

> "We started dating when a mutual friend just asked both of us whether we were looking to date someone, and what sort of person we'd be looking for. She then tactfully and discreetly sounded us both out individually, and when we both said we'd be up for meeting, she put us in touch with each other." (Nick and Anna, in their late thirties)

Church leaders can explicitly teach and promote the sort of approach that helped Nick and Anna. It's just about connecting people. A coffee isn't a marriage proposal, so if nothing happens beyond a first date, that's OK. But who knows, it might lead to more.

This culture of encouragement will be greatly supported by local churches running specific seminars or courses on dating and relationships, just as many run marriage preparation, marriage and parenting courses. I know some churches that have run courses covering material such as we've been discussing, and drawing on resources such as those given at the end of this chapter. Churches can collaborate to do this, and successful formats I've seen include a one hour evening seminar, a course across three Sunday afternoons (single people are often free then), or one day workshop on a Saturday. When these are run regularly (e.g. two or three times a year) the church narrative around dating starts to change. People become more open to talking about dating and dating rates increase.

Relationships

Just as for dating, when things are working well with regards to healthy relationships, a church will understand what a vision for healthy relationships can look like, and this will be promoted from the front. Leaders will develop and affirm a healthy culture, with ongoing teaching that includes themes such as communication, commitment, resolving conflict and attachment patterns. Resources are available to help with this, although many of these conflate the terms 'dating' and 'relationships', which, as we've seen, can increase pressure on 'dating' unnecessarily. It is therefore suggested that the differences are made clear for the UK. *Boundaries in Dating: How healthy choices grow healthy relationships* is a very useful book by US authors Henry Cloud and John Townsend, for example, and mainly deals with what our definitions would describe as 'relationships'.[8]

Two of the questions that Cloud and Townsend address in this book are topics that are asked very often by Christians in romantic relationships: "Should I go out (be in a relationship) with a non-Christian?" and "What about sex outside of marriage?" For the first issue of going out with someone who is on a different spiritual level, the authors helpfully consider what the implications might be for couples who are Christian and Non-Christian, Committed and Uncommitted, and Mature and New believers. They advise that Christians should not be in serious relationships with non-Christians, and explain why. Secondly, in their chapter called "Set Appropriate Limits", they address the reasons why God's design is that sex is reserved for marriage. *The Marriage Preparation Course* by Nicky and Sila Lee[9] and *The Dating Dilemma*[10] by Rachel Gardner and André Adefope are other resources that cover this, within the context of their great teaching on many other aspects of relationships. Teaching about all these things must be explicit in the church to encourage a healthy culture. Of the respondents in the Singleness in the UK Church survey, 51% indicated that they agreed "Sex belongs only in marriage, and I'm fine accepting and living by this (even though it's costly/countercultural)." The rest weren't so sure.[11]

After a certain amount of time (e.g. usually between a few months and two years), a couple should decide whether to split up or get engaged. My friend Martin (aged 43) has been going out with Antje for about 5 years. They seem to get on well, but he seems in no hurry at all to make a decision about the future of the relationship, whereas she has felt from an early stage that she would like to marry him. Things are dragging on, and she would rather be with him than on her own. Who knows how long things will continue?

My friend Greg (aged 27) was in a relationship with Jane for nearly a year. Although they got on really well, somehow for both of them it didn't feel quite right. Was this to do with something that could be worked through, or because of more fundamental reasons that meant the relationship should end? Greg and Jane were both keen to put God at the centre of their decision-making. They each prayed about it alone, separately with friends, and together as a couple. They also went to talk and pray things through with an older, wiser couple at church. After this, they decided to end the relationship. Although they were both sad in some ways, they were also grateful that they could have as good an ending as possible – they had both been clear, kind and honest.

In a local church, it is very helpful for a couple in a relationship to have a married couple as mentors (it doesn't have to be formal), who can provide support, and if needs be, challenge. This would be particularly beneficial for Martin and Antje, for example. In addition, explicit discipleship conversations between Martin and another man in church would be invaluable (such as Nathan Blackaby discussed in chapter 6 on men's ministry), along with something similar for Antje with another woman.

The national church

If you're a church minister, think back for a moment to when you were training at college. How much input was there on your course about marriage? How much input was there on dating? It's likely that marriage was covered, and dating perhaps wasn't mentioned. Because the Christian dating and relationships culture has changed over time, now is an ideal time for all church leader initial training courses to include these topics on the curriculum. They are relevant for almost all adults, and are equally as important as marriage. When Engage ran a seminar at one theological college, several single students told us at the end that the dating input was actually really useful for them personally, let alone for members of their congregations. This is an important way to grow strong clergy marriages for the future.

For all leadership training, both initial and continuing, things will be working well when all leaders know how to actively work to address the church gender imbalance, and to make use of resources around Christian dating and relationships. They will know how to set up teaching and discipleship systems, and help develop a culture where talking about dating and relationships is normalised, just as talking about marriage or parenting is normal within churches. Church leader networks will have these issues on their agenda, literally, so that they can share best practice about how to move things forwards.

At the denominational level, when it's going well, leaders will promote healthy relationships (of all kinds) between men and women, whether single or married. As described in previous chapters, regular data collection and monitoring of the numbers of male and female members in their churches will be in place. Denominational leaders will also spearhead a national approach to increasing the number of men in their congregations, along with teaching and discipleship that promotes and facilitates healthy Christian dating and relationships. If the denomination's main website or communication channels signpost to resources on marriage, then they can also signpost to resources on dating and relationships. As sermons or talks are given, the outlines could be put online for others to use.

Annual national conferences are another ideal opportunity to help change the culture, narrative and practice around Christian dating and relationships. Imagine if everyone had equal opportunity to go to a session that was relevant for them and each conference week had a seminar on each of singleness, dating and relationships, marriage, and parenting. Along with these, it would be really helpful if each conference provided good quality, non-cringey, facilitated events for single people to meet others if they're looking to date.

In summary, the experience of Engage partners is that support for healthier Christian dating and relationships has started to grow over the last few years. This has been encouraging to see at national, local and individual levels. Much more change is needed however, so let's take a pioneering step forward into an exciting future where things are working really well!

Action points

Individuals

- Prioritise your relationship with God, make sure you're plugged into a good Christian community, and get yourself a dating support team or relationship mentor couple.
- Read a good book on Christian dating and relationships (see below).
- Join a good Christian dating website.
- Be 'clear, kind and honest' throughout dating and relationships.

Local churches

- Use approaches given elsewhere in this book to proactively address the church gender imbalance.
- Arrange to meet with single women in your church as a group, and single men as a separate group, to listen carefully to their experiences about current Christian dating and relationships (as described earlier in the chapter).
- Talk and teach about healthy Christian dating and relationships, so that this becomes a normal part of your church culture.

The national church

- Include input on how to support healthy Christian dating and relationships on initial and continuing church leader training courses.
- Have a national strategic approach to addressing the church gender imbalance and promoting teaching on dating and relationships, created by denominational leaders.
- Include a seminar on healthy Christian dating and relationships at each annual national conference week.

Resources

Books

- *How to Get a Date Worth Keeping.* Henry Cloud (2005). Zondervan.
- *Dare to Date.* Aukelien van Abbema (2017). SPCK.
- *The Dating Dilemma.* Rachel Gardner & André Adefope (2013). IVP.
- *Boundaries in Dating.* Henry Cloud & John Townsend (2000). Zondervan.
- *Single, Dating, Engaged, Married.* Ben Stuart (2017). Passion Publishing, Thomas Nelson.
- *The Meaning of Marriage.* Tim Keller (2011). Hodder.

Websites

- www.engage-mcmp.org.uk
  The Engage Network website with resource sections on singleness, dating, relationships and engagement.
- www.ntrelationships.com
  André Adefope's Naked Truth Relationships website with dating and relationship advice.

- www.christianconnection.com
  Online Christian dating website with additional weekly blog giving dating and relationships advice.
- www.singlefriendlychurch.com
  Information and practical advice on dating and relationships for church leaders and individuals, based on comprehensive research.
- www.restoredlives.org
  The Restored Lives course supports and empowers people to move forward from divorce and separation, or the breakdown of any serious relationship, to live a full life, free from past issues.
- www.restoreandrebuild.org
  A post-abortion healing course bringing restoration to women affected by abortion.

"Dating and relationships: what would it look like if things were working well in the church?"

Engage consultation vision grid

Foundations

An individual	A local church	The national church

Spiritual/emotional/social wellbeing
 	
• Rooted and growing in relationship with God.
• Clear sense of identity.
• Positive understanding of healthy boundaries.
• Good self-esteem.
• Positive body image.
• Sense of purpose/destiny/calling in life.
• Understanding that you and everyone is on a journey of personal growth.
• Being comfortable having healthy intimate relationships with people of the opposite sex.
• Freedom from baggage from previous relationships.
• Free from shame/unhealthy habits.
• Choosing rather than needing a relationship.
• Knowing and owning your values.
• Being open about emotional needs and desire for relationship.
• Bringing God into all relationships.
• Pursuing wisdom, grace and discernment in all areas of life, including relationships.
	• Church leaders understand that it is their responsibility to actively and intentionally work to make their congregation gender balanced so that healthy dating and relationships are possible.
	• All churches regularly collect and monitor data on numbers of male and female attendees of different ages to inform action.
	• Church leaders understand that it is their responsibility to promote a healthy culture of dating and relationships in their congregation so this is 'normalised'.
	• Church leaders regularly speak about the relevant issues from the front, including:
	  – A positive view of marriage between Christians.
	  – A positive view of sex only within marriage.
	  – How to overcome issues resulting from previous relationships.
	  – Freedom from shame.
	  – Freedom from porn.
	• Single and married people are all included and part of the community – not segregated.
		Church leader initial training
		
		• Includes input on how to promote and create a gender balanced church.
		• Includes information on how to support healthy Christian dating and relationships.
		
		Church leader continuing training
		
		• Church leader networks run regular training so all church leaders take responsibility for making their churches gender balanced and know how to do this.
		• Church leader networks run regular training so all Church leaders know how to support and signpost to relevant resources to promote a culture of healthy Christian dating/relationships.
		
		National conferences
		
		• All annual national conferences provide equal opportunities for teaching through having seminars each week on healthy Christian
		  – Singleness.
		  – Dating and relationships.
		  – Marriage.
		  – Parenting.

An individual	A local church	The national church
Support/accountability • Good community and healthy friendships around you who give honest feedback. • Role models of healthy dating/relationships/ marriage. • A small 'support team' of people (e.g. close friends/family/mentor) for encouragement, discipleship andaccountability who talk/pray/listen/feedback specifically around dating (though might not meet as a group). **Healthy male-female psycho-social dynamics** • Commitment to being clear, kind and honest, with ongoing 'DTR' conversations when appropriate (Define The Relationship). • Treating each other as brothers and sisters in Christ. • Gender equality rather than stereotypes. • Partnership, respect for each other and for marriage. • Men guarding the hearts of women, and vice versa. • Respectfully responsive (no 'ghosting'!).	• Church leaders and others model healthy relationships between men and women. • Men and women involved in reaching and discipling men. • Church leadership teams are intentionally diverse and include single men and women, and married men and women. • Church leaders explicitly encourage and facilitate systems of discipleship/ support/accountability. • Mutual conversations – leaders listen in depth to current experiences of those in their congregations and take supportive action. • Joint leadership responsibility for changing things – between church leaders and those who know from experience what the current Christian dating/relationships scene is like. • Church leaders identify the people in their congregation who could be key in leading/ inputting in the area of dating/relationships, and facilitate this. • Healthy attitudes and teaching about it being OK to want to get married, empathy, practical help (not "it's a sin to want to get married because that means you're not content with your singleness").	• All annual national conferences provide good quality, non-cringey, facilitated events for single people to meet others if they're looking to date. **Denominational leaders** • All denominations regularly collect and monitor data on the numbers of male and female members of different ages in all their churches. • All denominations run regular training so all church leaders take responsibility for making their churches gender balanced and know how to do this. • Church leader networks run regular training so all Church leaders know how to support and signpost to relevant resources to promote a culture of healthy Christian dating/ relationships. • Take responsibility for making their churches gender balanced – and explicitly lead the way in this. • Understand the current national Christian context around dating and relationships. • Explicitly promote and facilitate healthy Christian dating and relationships. • Promote high positive values around self and relationships (not defining people by their marital status).

An individual	A local church	The national church
	• Encouraging single people that it's OK to look outside their own church for dating/relationships. • Divorce recovery support is available e.g. the Holy Trinity Brompton 'Restored Lives' course.	**National resourcing/networks** • Model sermons/outlines are available online around healthy Christian dating/relationships. • Church leaders have somewhere to go for advice – online forum/Facebook page/network/coaching? • Divorce recovery support widely available e.g. Holy Trinity Brompton 'Restored Lives' course.

Dating: "getting to know someone with a view to seeing whether or not we want to be in a relationship" i.e. meeting up with someone (once to a few times)

An individual	A local church
Beginning • Intentionally thinks and prays (alone and with others) about dating in a godly way. • Knows how/where to intentionally find good people to date. • Intentionally active about meeting lots of new people and 'potential eligibles'. • Confidently asks people on dates. • Confidently accepts date invitations and says 'yes' unless there are appropriate 'red flags' (and knows what are/are not appropriate red flags). • Is resilient if people say 'no thanks' and keeps asking others. • 'Intentional but not intense' approach: honest, up front. • Open-minded, not looking for a 'type'. • Sees dating as an opportunity to learn about yourself and others. • Comfortable with own attractiveness. • Realises that attraction might not be there to start with but might grow. • Choosing fun activities to do together. • Comfortable with asking someone if they'd like to meet up again, either at the end of the date or afterwards.	• Church leaders understand what a vision for healthy Christian dating looks like and teach and promote this from the front. • Church leaders and congregations know what resources are available to support healthy Christian dating, and use and promote these for all who are looking to date – including good Christian online dating. • Church leaders explicitly and actively address the barriers to dating: societal influences, church gender imbalance, increased numbers of single Christians, unhealthy male-female psycho-social dynamics, 'don't date' messages, need for teaching on healthy dating, spiritual battle around Christian marriage. • Church leaders explicitly encourage and facilitate systems of discipleship/support/accountability which address dating. • Planned, ongoing, regular teaching and discipleship about healthy Christian dating including developing prayerful wisdom and discernment.

An individual	A local church
• Wisdom and confidence to use good quality online dating approaches, e.g. see Hopeful Girl list "The science of online dating": https://blog.christianconnection.com/the-science-of-online-dating • Comfortable with either accepting a second date invitation or saying 'no thanks' in a clear, kind, honest way. **Middle** • Intentionally continues to think and pray (alone and with others) about dating in a godly way. • Being willing to go on another date unless there are appropriate red flags. • Fun dates involving activities, rather than just talking over coffee/meals. • Intentionally getting to know the other person beyond a superficial level. • Making dating a positive experience for the other person. **End** • Clear, kind, appropriately honest. • Ending by building up, with positive feedback for them as a person along with any general reasons given which are 'owned' by the giver e.g. "at the same time, I don't feel we have as much in common as I'd be wanting/I feel that I'd rather not pursue things further", rather than needing to give specific justifications unless this is particularly appropriate. • Communication of ending method is appropriate to how long you've been dating and how you met. If met in 'real life' – face-to-face best. If met online, it may vary, e.g. by text/email OK if just 1 date, phone call if 2/3, face-to-face if several dates. • Resilient and comfortable with rejection and being rejected. • A good ending, with discussion to agree boundaries around friendship after dating if are in the same social circles/church. • Using wisdom and discernment (with input from support team) to be pro-active in either ending dating or moving onto a "going out" relationship.	• Church leaders give permission and affirm healthy dating, from the front and to individuals. • Promote a culture of encouragement. • Promote a culture of people asking others on dates, and people saying yes. • Training for group leaders on dating/relationships. • Promote a culture of sensitive match-making between mutual friends – with education on how to do that. • Promote social events that are connected with dating or dating teaching – networking between different churches to increase their effectiveness and widen people's social circles. • Church leaders and congregations understand and proactively meet the needs of those in their congregations (e.g. some older/divorced/widowed people may have specific needs).

Relationship/'going out' (UK): "getting to know someone with a view to seeing whether or not we want to get engaged" i.e. an exclusive, romantic relationship

An individual	A local church
Beginning • Clear, kind and appropriately honest. • Defining boundaries e.g. social, time, physical. How are we going to help each other with holiness/purity in our relationship, or set and maintain appropriate boundaries? e.g. Henry Cloud and John Townsend's book *Boundaries in Dating.* • Graciousness. **Middle** • Talking about the future – hopes, dreams about marriage and other things. • Understands that the level of intimacy matches the level of mutual commitment. • Having fun! • Intentionally getting to know the other person's heart, character, values. • Understands why God's way is for sex only within marriage, and both intentionally supporting each other to honour that in the relationship – spiritually, emotionally, physically, practically. **End** • Clear, kind and honest, courageous. • Input from support team to help make wise decisions, whether you're taking the initiative to end the relationship, or propose, or knowing how to respond when the other person does either of these. • Not waiting too long to make a decision (support team may need to challenge about this).	• Church leaders understand what a vision for healthy Christian relationships looks like and teach and promote this from the front. • Church leaders give permission and affirm healthy relationships, from the front and to individuals. • Planned, ongoing, regular teaching and discipleship about healthy Christian relationships, including developing prayerful wisdom and discernment. • Provide support and accountability – mentoring available with older couples. • Church leaders and congregations know what resources are available to support healthy Christian relationships, and use/promote these. • Teaching and resources are provided on attachment, commitment, how to resolve conflict. • Practical positive teaching about healthy relationships is 'normalised' – including a positive view of sex only within marriage which enables an understanding of why this is God's way.

An individual	A local church
• If considering engagement: - Use pre-engagement and engagement questions/books. - Attend an engagement course together (even if not yet engaged) to help make wise and informed decisions. • If ending the relationship: - Carefully and prayerfully done. - Face-to-face. - Involve your community. - Not ghosting/ignoring. - Clear-cut, agree boundaries, clear signals.	

CHAPTER 9

Marriage: what would it look like if things were working well in the church?

David and Liz Percival

"Marriage is more than your love for each other. It has a higher dignity and power for it is God's holy ordinance through which he wills to perpetuate the human race till the end of time. In your love you see only your two selves in the world, but in your marriage you are a link in the chain of the generations, which God causes to come and to pass away to his glory, and calls into his kingdom. In your love you see only the heaven of your happiness, but in marriage you are placed at a post of responsibility towards the world and mankind. Your love is your own private possession, but marriage is more than something personal – it is a status, an office."
— Dietrich Bonhoeffer, in a letter from prison to his niece on the eve of her wedding.[1]

Introduction

Our story
My (David) journey to faith began, aged 11, on a series of Christian Union camps from my school. Whilst I had been raised in a nominally Christian home (church at Christmas and Easter), I had little real understanding of what Christian faith meant. On my first camp I was struck by a young couple who together led the worship in a draughty barn we used for communal times; there was something about their warmth and gentleness with each other that stirred and attracted my heart. On the first camp they were boyfriend/girlfriend and my interest in the Christian faith was stirred; on the second they were engaged – and I gave my life to the Lord. On the third they were married, and I left that camp determined to live my life in a way that attracted others to Jesus.

Sadly, in the years that followed my faith proved to be like the seed that fell on the path – I was in an environment with no support, and where my faith rapidly became the cause of much bullying, and within 18 months I had walked away from the Lord, making my way through the challenges of adolescence and university in very much the world's way, meeting Liz at university and marrying three years later.

I (Liz) was raised in a strong Christian household but my faith had been dormant for many years. Fast forward to the point where we had been married six years with one son, and once again a couple was to have a profound impact on both our lives. In them I saw an authentic faith which I had been hungering for. Their love and care for us as a young family, and their example of care for each other seemed to strike David in a deep way. Gradually they told us that much of what shaped their life had come from what they had discovered on a Marriage Encounter weekend.

Although I (David) heartily rejected the idea that I had any need of such a weekend, I was drawn by this couple's love, and ultimately agreed to go, mostly because Liz wanted to. On that weekend two things happened: first I shared with Liz my early journey of faith – something I had never done in over ten years of being a couple! And then I had a clear encounter with the Lord. He was standing at a fork in the road ahead, hand in hand with Liz. He simply looked into my eyes and said, "We can walk together as three you know, we've walked together before." I knew at that moment I either "walked as three" with Liz and our Lord, or I walked away from both and headed down the road alone – the answer was a no-brainer, and as I write this we are about to share our 39th anniversary – all three of us!

God's purpose for marriage

We share this story, not just by way of personal introduction, but because it illustrates for us a very important truth about couple relationships, and marriage in particular – they are a place where God's character and love should be very visible (and attractive).

Marriage is used by God as an important sign throughout the Bible: clearly the creation account sets the scene in establishing the joining of man and woman as part of his created order, even before the fall. In the stories that follow there are innumerable examples of God revealing his nature through marriage – everything from the glorious celebration of love in the Song of Songs, to the command to the prophet Hosea to take to himself an adulterous wife (Gomer) as a sign to the nation. At the very end in Revelation 19:9 we are told that we are invited to the "wedding supper of the lamb" – a time when all who have been saved through faith in Jesus will be joined with him for eternity – all will know and be fully known – a state of complete intimacy both with God and with each other.

If God, through the Bible, uses marriage as a sign of his nature, then we should not be surprised to find that marriage has a purpose in his order. In the Genesis accounts of creation God sets out his purpose for humankind – it starts with man giving names to all the animals, and the calling is to steward his whole creation. It is in this context that God declares that "it is not good for man to be alone" (Genesis 2:18) – he's never going to accomplish all that stewardship on his own – he needs a "helper" or "companion". Together (as man and wife) they can procreate and so begin their task of stewardship.

This model of two people working together to steward creation and to create the next generation, and in so doing to reflect something of God's nature, is fundamental to understanding marriage in the Christian context.

Christ's instruction to his disciples was to "seek first the Kingdom of God" (Matthew 6:33), and to live by its principles in their time and context – and he foretold that it would be countercultural and would be rejected by many. His words are as relevant today as they were in the first century – Christian life is profoundly countercultural. Living in such circumstances was foreshadowed by the people of Israel, most clearly when they were taken into exile to live in Babylon. In Jeremiah 29 we find God's clear instructions for such times: 'settle down, marry and have families, and pray for the good of the land'. The wisdom is clear: the well-structured family, framed around marriage, offers a micro-culture in which God's way of life can flourish even if the external culture is very different. That message remains deeply relevant today.

The culture today in the UK and the West is profoundly self-centred – it revolves around seeking my own wellbeing through material goods, experiences, even relationships, that will enhance and make fulfilling MY life – we are told we should 'be the best version of me!' Our lives are to be viewed as a journey of self-actualisation, defining everything ourselves from our personal identity, gender and sexuality, and on our terms.

Marriage is regarded primarily as a status, something to be attained typically after having achieved certain milestones in terms of career, life experiences etc., often even the birth of children, with the wedding a sort of 'cherry on the cake' to celebrate having 'arrived'. It attracts certain 'rights' and benefits framed in law.

However, if marriage has a purpose in God's plan over and above just being a convenient social contract to cement the love of two people, if he intends it to be a living sign to the world, then we can be assured of two things: it will be profoundly countercultural; and it will be a calling, or vocation, to which he calls us.

And from this flow two important thoughts: the first is that the calling to marriage is complementary to other callings, be that as a teacher, or apostle, or prophet, or even to be ordained. It sits alongside, not in competition, to other callings. The second, especially for those who long for marriage but have yet to reach that goal, is that the church needs to be firstly aware of the pain of holding a calling that is apparently unachievable, and then teaching actively about what it means to live for God in such a compromised place — often with pain, anguish, self-doubts and God-doubts.

Finally, by way of introduction, we need to emphasise that everyone is of equal value before God, whatever their calling, and whether married or single. All Christians are called to be 'other' focused, we are called to lay down self, and focus our lives (time, skills, experience, work) on enabling others. At the core, we are called to be prophetic — that is setting out clearly God's holy nature, and pastoral — that is showing God's compassion and justice, bringing care and nurture to all, especially the marginalised and weak in our midst.

In this context, marriage is perhaps the easiest of callings. God gives us one person who above all we are called to love into the very fullest version of themselves that they can be — this is what Paul talks about when he talks about laying down my life for my wife (Ephesians 5:21-33) — being prepared to expend everything I am for my spouse.

Our task is to discern what God is calling us to, and then to live out that calling in the fullness of his grace and spirit. For many, for the purpose of creation of the next generation if for no other reason, marriage will be a calling on their life — but that doesn't in any way detract from those who are called to singleness, or other ways of life.

Doing marriage well as a couple

So, we think we'd like to get married! What happens now?

Listening to the stories of couples over the years, there seem to have been as many different ways of arriving at the decision to get married as there have been couples, from a surprise romantic proposal at the top of a mountain in Wales, to one lady who said, "Well, when he asked I didn't actually say 'yes'. We just started planning the wedding."

However attractive a surprise romantic proposal is, there is no doubt that careful discussion about the future while in a relationship provides a good basis for the decision to marry. In announcing their engagement, a couple signal that there has been a change in their relationship to each other and to others around them.

They have already taken the first steps to be set apart for each other, but it's very easy to get sucked straight into the excitement of planning the wedding and to lose sight of the huge lifelong commitment they are about to make. The period of an engagement offers a unique opportunity for a couple to explore why they are getting married, what it means and what sort of marriage they wish to build. By intentionally using this season in this way they can build foundations for the future. There are lots of resources and courses to help them and many find the support and mentoring of a more experienced married couple invaluable.

In our dating and 'going out' days we may think we have discussed and talked through everything there is to consider, but there are subjects we can subtly avoid or haven't thought about. How will our different family backgrounds, cultures or even faith (or lack of it) affect our attitudes, expectations, communication, decision-making and how we bring any children up, now and in future? Are there past experiences, relationships or even addictions which need to be faced up to, and healing sought for these? What personal awareness and growth do we need? Are we willing to be completely honest and open with each other?

What boundaries – physical, emotional and spiritual – do we need to establish? What does unfaithfulness look like for each of us? Is it a flirty text, a kiss and cuddle with a colleague at the office party, sharing personal details of our marriage with friends without our spouse's permission, or does it have to involve the sexual act? How do we prepare for the sexual union in marriage, while honouring God's design and will for this? Do we have a clear vision of what Christian marriage is and what its purpose is?

For those who come from very different faith and cultural backgrounds there are further challenges that need to be faced and prepared for. It is important to explore each other's beliefs, values and expectations. Can the Christian partner accept that things may not change or do they perhaps hope that they will? Is the non-Christian open to attending church? Can they drill down to real scenarios around children, family expectations, practical things like tithing and giving? Some of the inventory-based preparation programmes with a mentor or formal course may be helpful here.

We cannot avoid all the challenges that lie ahead, but by God's grace we can use the time of engagement to prepare well for married life. In dating and 'going out' much of our focus has been on 'attracting' our partner – now is the time we need to face up to the realities of who we, and our partner, really is. More than anything we need time to shift our focus away from 'being me' towards what it will mean to 'be us!' – to actually live with a priority order that places 'enabling you to be you' at the top, with 'the good of our relationship' second, and 'self' third. 'You – Us – Me' – we need to develop a 'YUMmie' mindset!

The Bible and the marriage service have a rich vein of wisdom to help us to live a godly married life. For Christians, marriage has God at the centre. In God's eyes it is a lifelong commitment of unconditional love and mutual support, dependent on God's grace and healing. Spiritual growth and deepening emotional intimacy complement physical intimacy.

Marriage is a calling in which we are to serve God, and far more than the legal contract that many in society see it as. It is a bold and hope-filled way of life involving a commitment and determination to love and support one another through the ups and downs of life and to serve God together. It has the potential to illuminate the gospel and the love of God as each marriage partner sets themselves apart for each other, committed to mutual support and stewardship of the gifts and resources God has given. In this way it is outward-looking not inward-looking. It is not an answer to loneliness or to meet my needs, but a state where we can serve others together alongside single people who are also serving God. It will involve hospitality, the nurture of children (usually, and where possible), support of the elderly and all forms of Christian service and evangelism.

Christian marriages are subject to all the same pressures that other couples experience. So once the honeymoon is over, how do we live out God's desire for our marriage as a couple? What does that look like and involve in reality? The heart of the answer lies in communication – deep meaningful communication that goes way beyond the facts and opinions we each hold, and instead seeks deep understanding of the heart – that builds empathy and unity.

Take, for example, the young married couple who have a young baby to look after – suddenly they have responsibility for a small human being and sleep is disturbed; one is back at work and the other has to negotiate their return after maternity leave. This is when good and thoughtful communication can become particularly important – notes left on the fridge door will not cut it. The efforts they have made at less stressful times to be open with each other, to share expectations and feelings and to listen wholeheartedly to each other, to be gentle and loving will pay dividends in the times of stress. We live out our vows for better for worse, by building openness and intimacy in the good times. That security in each other's love helps us to make the decision to love and go on loving when life is stressful and we don't feel very loving towards each other.

There needs to be a willingness to go on growing through the ups and downs of life. Many couples don't admit to pressures and difficulties until they have gone too far. There are lots of courses and resources to encourage couples in their relationship. Our Marriage Encounter weekend gave us tools and a fresh vision for our lives together and set the pattern for us to attend some form of enrichment on a regular basis – a constant attention to our communication and reassessment of our priorities has helped us through many challenges. It's just good to step aside from the pressures of life sometimes and enjoy the beauty of what we have. Regular date nights that focus on our relationship, rather than issues we are facing, can help us to feel united and ready to face the issues later.

Cultivating a healthy sex life is another important aspect of a strong marriage, but this is not just about the sex act itself. We relate all day as man and woman, through gentleness, respect, tenderness and playfulness – the squeeze of a hand, the gentle tone of voice and smile as we come home in the evening, the tender kiss on the back of the neck while cooking, the snuggle together on the sofa – all express our sexual love for each other. Our love-making is the culmination of all the loving communication that has been going on. As we give attention to the needs, concerns and presence of our loved one, we build the intimacy that strengthens our unity.

Prayer and how we involve God in our relationship is another key aspect of building a godly marriage. Many couples find prayer together very challenging, but coming together before God with our concerns and needs allows him to speak and be an active part of our marriages. David experiences faith in pictures, Liz more in words. Liz has had to learn to respect David's sometimes fragile images of what he is hearing from God rather than demand that he explain in a way she can understand. It has taken time to accept our differences but we have been greatly enriched by it. The When2Pray network have an excellent booklet to help couples grow in this area. For couples where one is not a Christian, the support of Christian friends to pray with will be important, but the couple will still benefit from being able to look at aspects of their marriage and challenges they face in a spiritual values-based language they have developed together.

Living counterculturally is not easy and we need the support of likeminded people who are committed to following God's ideal for marriage. There may be support networks in our church or we can gather round us friends who we think will strengthen rather than undermine our marriage. This is not to say we just restrict our friendship to like-minded people, because part of our calling in marriage is to share hospitality and our love with others, but it may mean we limit our exposure to people who might be toxic to our marriage.

For married couples where one is not a Christian, it is good to have a support network where both of you are welcome and to know where to turn when life gets difficult. A strong faith, spiritual humility and the ongoing guidance of the Holy Spirit are all essential to living out a godly marriage in these circumstances.

In a good support network there will be others who will encourage us and hold us to account, gently challenging us to engage with an issue before things go badly wrong. In fact regular re-evaluation is a valuable tool to keep our marriage healthy. It's easy to get into bad habits and not spot the damage until it's done. In his book *Let's Stick Together*, Harry Benson describes the corrosive STOP signs that can wreak havoc in a relationship; Scoring points, Thinking the worst, Opting out, Putting down.[2] A subtle change of priority, an independent attitude, a lack of caring and tenderness can all creep in. A marriage remains healthy when each spouse takes time to reflect on their attitudes, actions and the impact they are having, and to choose to change, seek forgiveness and healing and a fresh start, through the boundless grace that God pours out as his wedding gift to us. The humility to recognise a more persistent issue, e.g. anger management or addictive behaviour, and seek counselling are important too.

In a world which values hedonism, individual fulfilment and success, and discards the old or broken for the new and shiny, marriage holds out a reality of self-sacrifice, forgiveness, healing, holiness, commitment and hope – and it is fun too! It has the potential to illuminate the gospel and God's loving longing for relationship with mankind. Each couple's unique story and journey can be used to inspire the next generation through family life, couple mentoring, service in the church or community, and even through schools programmes like Explore (married couples sharing their stories with young people).

Doing marriage well as the local church

There are of course many different local churches, and each will have its own character and sense of its purpose in its locality and community. However, it's probably fair to generalise that they will see two threads to their purpose: firstly to nurture their people in their relationship with God; and secondly to enable their people to reach out and show God's love, and the good news of Jesus, to the world.

A Christian married couple is in many ways a 'little church' – two believers working as a community of love, learning constantly about and from God, and reaching out both to their own family, and to the wider community. In the Nicene Creed we pray that the church should be one (embody unity), holy (be 'set apart'), catholic (accessible and welcoming to any and all), and apostolic (sent out with a purpose).

A healthy local church will have both a mature sense of its own identity and role in the wider body of Christ, and a clear sense of its purpose to enable and equip its members for mission in a world that generally doesn't want to listen, and may indeed be actively hostile! To do this it will need to develop its own ways of helping each member discern their own calling and sense of God's purpose for their life, provide a place of nurture and safety to enable them to live out the calling, and a place where all can celebrate, or commiserate on, the milestones of life. This is true for everyone – single, married, mother, father, child, friend or anything else.

So what specifically should the local church be doing to support those who are married to live their marriage as a calling from God?

Engagement (or betrothal)

The decision to 'get engaged' can be, as we have seen, a simple conversation between two people, or may be an elaborate romantic act in a special setting, which today's society celebrates with video clips on social media, the exchange of rings and gifts, and a huge focus on 'planning the wedding'.

To the local church community, whilst clearly an event to be rejoiced over, an engagement should represent a clear call to action! Two of our community, or just one if the partner worships elsewhere, have jointly discerned God's calling on their lives – how can we as their Christian family support and enable the couple in this decision?

Probably the most important support is to help the couple to resist, or at least balance, the pressure from today's society to put all the focus on the wedding. Whilst the big day is of course important, it is only 'a day' – a marriage is a lifetime! Couples need the space and focus to prepare well for all the changes that will come with the commitment to marriage.

The most obvious (stock) response is to offer some form of marriage preparation programme. This may take the form of one-on-one (or couple-to-couple) support and mentoring, or where there are several couples then some form of course. Most of the available courses have all the proven core components of teaching the main skills needed in marriage (shared expectations, communication, conflict resolution, and general life skills around jointly handling finances, family relationships etc.). Most will include some aspects of living a healthy sexual life, and some include aspects of shared spirituality and prayer.

Today's individuals and couples face particular pressures in the area of sex! The free availability of pornography, and the pervasive world view that sex is governed by rules of consent and the pursuit of pleasure, have deep and far-reaching consequences, and many individuals coming to marriage will already have full experience of both. The challenge to the church is to help the couple move from this world view to one where sex is a wholesome part of their mutual self-revelation, and a means of deepening and enriching the full intimacy of relationship God calls married couples to.

For some this may also raise other questions around healing and wholeness from previous relationships. Every individual comes to marriage with their own unique story and baggage, some more 'heavy' than others. The church has a clear role in helping each person come to terms with aspects of their character or life that have failed to live up to God's ideal, to accept his forgiveness through the cross, and to live lives which reflect our new nature in Christ, enabled by the Holy Spirit. This isn't just at a spiritual level – there are often real practical challenges such as existing children, blending two families, dealing with ex-partners and a third set of grandparents, handling parents who have divorced or separated etc. Each of these situations is a pastoral opportunity to help the couple discern God's will and nature in handling our brokenness.

The core role for the local church is often to help the couple really think through "What is our marriage for?" This should take the conversation beyond "for our mutual companionship and support" into a conversation on 'calling' both as individuals and as a couple – a sense of purpose for their own marriage. The book *Married for God* (Christopher Ash) can provide a good starting point, perhaps with ongoing mentoring and support from a more experienced couple.

Weddings

Clearly the actual words and form of the wedding service itself are a matter both of national law, and of the particular requirements of the different denominations. However, weddings themselves offer great opportunities in three regards.

Firstly, they are an opportunity for the community of members of the church to come together to demonstrate their love and support for the couple. In our own case, in a small Durham village church, the ladies of the parish had made two beautiful cream kneelers for us to use in the service. There are a host of welcome and hospitality opportunities, provision of music and worship etc., all of which can be a way of involving the wider church community.

Secondly, the couple can be encouraged to actively involve Christian friends and family members in every aspect of the wedding. This can be a particularly important witness to non-believing family members, and a way of signalling 'our faith sits at the heart of our marriage'.

And thirdly, weddings are a tremendous outreach opportunity – here we have the opportunity to welcome large groups of non-believers into our church with an opportunity to share the good news of Jesus with them. If the couple has done the preparation with the church, and has developed a clear sense of their purpose, this can also be a chance to 'commission' them in this calling before all their family and supporters, who also have a responsibility to encourage and support the couple in their mission.

For those already married

The wedding is simply the celebration on Day 1 of the marriage – what happens afterwards is life!

A Christian couple, as we have already seen, is being called to live a countercultural life in a world that places little value on marriage and all it entails. So the role of the local church is to enable, encourage, support and where necessary be a place of sanctuary and healing for each couple. Of course the church has to be all these things for those not-married as well, so the challenge is to identify the particular needs and opportunities with couples and to ensure these are met alongside the care of all individuals.

Perhaps the single greatest challenge to church leaders is to recognise that, if they are married, their own marriage, whether they like it or not, is going to be viewed by their congregation as a model. Today more than ever, young people seek, and intuitively recognise, authenticity, and if the words and the perceived relationship between leader and their spouse do not match up, then no amount of preaching and teaching will ever get through. The pressures of church leadership, coupled with the 'goldfish bowl' visibility of their marriage, means that they are under more pressure than ever before. That means they need nurturing and input on a regular basis for their marriage. Leadership couples need 'couple time', opportunities to celebrate their love for each other, and a shoulder to cry on when things are hard, every bit as much as the rest of us! Organisations like Marriage Encounter welcome clergy and leader couples, Time for Marriage runs weekends specifically for Christian leaders, and all these offer a great opportunity to get away from church life to really focus on 'us'!

With their own marriage being regularly fed, leaders are in a position to create a culture in which couples are regularly fed and encouraged to live their calling to marriage to the full. Such a culture will encourage couples to regularly undertake some form of marriage enrichment, whether that be studying some book or video appropriate to their stage on the journey of life, or going on one of the various marriage enrichment programmes available nationwide.

Some couples may want the support of others in the church; resources like *Together* (FamilyLife) provide a discipleship framework for couples to encourage couples in mutual support on the journey. Specific times too are known to be points of extra stress: parenting and early years; teenagers; children leaving (or not!) the family home; our children struggling with their own relationships and marriages; the challenges of ageing parents and bereavement – the list is almost limitless! In each of these cases perhaps the greatest support the church can be is to help the couple draw strength from each other – to recognise they face each challenge not as an individual, but as a team in which their key calling is to love each other through the challenges.

Because the couples will, over time, develop their own sense of being a team with complementary skills and experience, they also become an important resource for the church. Marriage is never intended to be an inward-looking institution, but rather one which faces outwards in the secure knowledge that someone has 'got your back'. So, a culture in a church which encourages couples to serve as 'couples' will encourage them to bring their capabilities to the fore.

There are, of course, a special set of problems which can arise for couples, and which create special pastoral challenges. These typically flow from unhealthy spiritual roots around abuse of power and a failure to recognise and live out the call to mutual submission. Such problems will include domestic violence and abuse, abuse of children, coercive control, infidelity, and a range of addictions from alcohol and drugs to pornography and prostitution. Much of the response is mandated by law, and by guidance available from the national churches. Perhaps the greatest challenge in most of these cases is establishing relationships and structures which reflect both the prophetic role of bringing light to the darkest of places, and the pastoral role of caring for both victims and perpetrators. Such problems arise in all types of couple relationship, and are actually much less common in marriages than in less-structured families; the challenge in a married family is how to honour both the safety of each individual and the mutual promises that underpin marriage – pray for the Wisdom of Solomon!

For most couples, these problems will not arise, and the needs for ongoing support are essentially those of good discipleship in their calling to be married – plenty of warmth and encouragement to both partners, social activities they can share in, and hospitality in small groups (not splitting them up so one can 'babysit' for the other!).

Young families may need support in how to encourage an active faith in the home, and in understanding how faith develops from the earliest days of life – simple activities like learning to pray together at the start of meals can be effective in helping children 'normalise' faith as part of life.

There are, of course, special pressures when one partner in a marriage is of a different (or no) faith. In such relationships faith may represent a source of friction and division rather than a unifying force, and the Christian partner may need special support to be able to live out God's call in marriage without necessarily receiving reciprocal support from their spouse. Such a couple needs to know that Jesus walks with them in the dark places as well as the light, and the church needs to do likewise.

And finally, we need to remember that marriage is a calling for life, and as such is ever-changing as circumstances and the processes of ageing change us. Those at the twilight end of life have much to teach all in the church about how to be fruitful in ever-changing circumstances. It was probably only as my mum slowly lost her faculties through dementia that I learned what it means to love with patience, and to value all that she had done for me over the past 60 years. It was a privilege for Liz and I to sit and quietly pray with her in her final hours, sending her on her way to glory in peace, and together quietly closing another chapter in the book of our family.

Doing marriage well as the national church

The national church has been associated with various issues about marriage, and as important as they are, the effect has been to render many churches singularly silent about a positive vision for marriage between Christians. Our focus is therefore on looking at things the church at national level could be doing to better support a culture which values and supports Christian marriage.

The first, and perhaps most important, role the national church should have is that of being a champion for the profoundly countercultural calling that sits at the heart of marriage – which is that in marriage each of us is called to a life that is focussed on the good of our spouse – a message of unconditional love, modelled on the gospel, and lived out in the security of the foundational promises of marriage that it is lifelong and faithful.

From these very specific foundations flow the personal and social benefits of marriage which organisations such as Marriage Foundation are regularly researching and highlighting. In particular, the commitment embodied in the marriage promises is demonstrably the best and safest environment in which children may be conceived and nurtured. The church, over and above every other organisation, should be able to articulate the reasons why such benefits flow from lives which embody the Christian faith and should do so without fear in a manner that is both prophetic and pastorally sensitive.

The church is called to bring the gospel, "good news," to all – it isn't called to be popular, or to espouse the culture of the times, though clearly it must speak into the society in which it exists. The opportunities to speak in the public square today are many and varied, and the national church needs to find its voice, speaking in terms that frame the message about marriage in positive and forward-looking terms. We tend to speak of things like 'traditional marriage' as if some model from Victorian times is likely to attract or motivate. Young people today need to hear about marriage as 'natural', part of creating a sustainable, healthy, organic society in contrast to a dystopian, industrialised future in which children are mere commodities to be created in some laboratory process, schooled and raised principally by the state, taught humanist values, and then released as 'economic production units' to support the national economy.

The church, through its websites and social media presence, should be clearly articulating the call to all to live out their faith 24/7 in the world, and to be seeking and then living to the full God's calling on their lives. For marriage, it could do much to signpost to resources and organisations which offer understanding, skills, training and support.

The church has great opportunities to engage actively with national events, not only the obvious major ones like royal weddings, but also annual events like Marriage Week UK.

One of the major functions of the national church is the training and development of the leadership of the church. Most churches have some form of 'Continuing Ministerial Development' or similar – but how many recognise the huge pressures on the marriages of their leaders and encourage, or indeed sponsor, ongoing enrichment in their calling as a married couple? Those coming into leadership roles through the theological colleges need proper formation both in understanding marriage as a calling (vocation) and a sign (sacrament) so that they can lead others, and support in developing their own personal models of what this will mean in their own relationships and families.

There are a number of national 'para-church' organisations whose understanding of marriage could be usefully harnessed by the wider church – conferences aimed at informing and equipping church leaders, both ordained and lay, could form part of the agenda for the national church to spread best practice more widely.

Much work is going on worldwide pushing the boundaries of understanding of the processes of conception, of sexuality and relationships, indeed to what it is to be truly human. Whilst these debates and advances may seem far from the daily experience of many people today, they will have a profound cultural impact on coming generations. The church needs to be at the forefront of the ethical and philosophical debate around these issues, speaking God's wisdom to shape and guide, and to bring God's sovereignty into clear view.

Each of these issues has deep implications for the everyday experience of the majority of believers as they form lasting intimate relationships, conceive and nurture children, and care for the weak, elderly and infirm in society. And at the heart of these very natural human processes sits marriage, a framework formed by God in creation, used by him throughout his revelation of himself in the Bible, and to which ultimately we will be called with joy at his wedding feast.

The church must speak out on marriage!

Action points for church leaders

Local church

- Preach regularly on the different callings God has for each of us, including marriage and relationships, and related topics – fidelity, forgiveness, seeking help, life priorities, and faith in the family – at least once a quarter.
- Identify 'marriage champions' and encourage them to actively enrich their own relationships.
- Ensure you have all the information to signpost people to marriage support and marriage enrichment services.
- Establish or strengthen your marriage preparation programme or signpost to local or national providers. Make attendance mandatory for those getting married in your church.
- Put regular articles in your newsletter about marriage-related issues (and others about singleness/dating of course too!).
- Create time for your own marriage and discuss with your spouse whether to attend a marriage enrichment weekend or day away from the parish/locality for your own benefit.
- Celebrate Marriage Week UK (February 7th-14th) in the church.

Local church – longer term strategies

- Build a team focussed on strengthening marriages from your marriage champions.
- Establish a marriage policy for your church. Articulate clear theology on marriage. Reflect on how church life supports or hinders healthy family life in your church. How do you encourage growth and support

in times of need? What are the local issues relevant to your church? How can you encourage married couples to serve others?

- Offer your marriage preparation course to other local churches or build joint programmes and advertise beyond the church.

National church

- Develop clear biblical teaching on Christian marriage, and articulate it effectively.
- Make sure there is comprehensive signposting available for marriage preparation, enrichment and support through the church's national website (along with signposting around singleness, dating and relationships).
- Appoint a Marriage Champion or Officer to articulate theology around marriage, and develop resources and information on services available.
- Develop easy-to-pick-up resources for local churches; sermon topics, summary of theology of marriage, draft policy formats, re-affirmation of vows services, prayers for marriages.
- Work with existing organisations focussed on marriage – no need to re-invent the wheel.

National church – longer term strategies

- Ensure theological training colleges and programmes equip future ministers to support and enrich marriage at all stages.
- Encourage all married minsters to take time out to strengthen and enrich their marriages.
- Engage with the national press and media on issues relating to marriage.
- Review the hurdles to marriage – charges for marrying in church, choice of venue – and the barriers to living out healthy marriage in church life.
- Engage with issues around cohabitation, mediation and divorce – offering messages of grace, healing and hope.
- Provide thought-leadership on the profound challenges of what it is to be truly human, and our need for relationships that reflect the qualities of our creator.

Resources

Resources for couples

Marriage Preparation courses
- Engaged Encounter weekend: www.engagedencounter.org.uk.
- A Day Together. Familylife: www.adaytogether.org.
- One for Life. 2=1: www.2equal1.com.

Marriage Enrichment courses
- Marriage Encounter weekend: www.marriageencounter.org.uk,
- www.beofme.org.uk and www.wwme.org.uk.
- Time for Marriage weekend: www.timeformarriage.org.uk.
- A Day Together, Familylife: www.adaytogether.org.
- Married for Life, and Intimacy Courses, both with 2=1: www.2equal1. com.

Books
- *Married for God.* Christopher Ash (2007). IVP.
- *Sex, God and Marriage.* Johann Christoph Arnold (2015). Plough Publishing House.
- *Loving Against the Odds.* Rob Parsons (2005). Hodder & Stoughton.
- *The Marriage Book.* Nicky and Sila Lee (2014). Alpha International.
- *How Women Help Men Find God.* David Murrow (2008). Thomas Nelson.
- *Surviving a Spiritual Mismatch in Marriage.* Lee and Leslie Strobel (2010). Zondervan.
- *When2Pray.* Barrie and Eileen Jones (2004). RoperPenberthy Publishing Ltd.

Online
- Prepare Enrich inventories: www.prepare-enrich.co.uk.
- Toucan, an app to help build relationship skills: www.toucantogether.com.
- The Marriage Challenge Podcasts: www.careforthefamily.org.uk.
- When2Pray network to help couples pray together, overseen by Time for Marriage: www.when2pray.net.
- Christian Muslim marriage: www.christianmuslimforum.org/index. php/about-us/areas-of-work/family.
- Interfaith Marriage Network: www.interfaithmarriage.org.uk.

Resources for churches

- The Marriage Preparation Course. With an extra session for blended families. Holy Trinity Brompton: www.themarriagecourses.org.
- Marriage by Design. Care for the Family: www.careforthefamily.org.uk.
- Preparing Together. Marriage Care: www.marriagecare.org.uk.
- From This Step Forward. CD based marriage preparation course for those forming a step family: www.careforthefamily.org.uk.
- The Marriage Course. Holy Trinity Brompton: www.themarriagecourses.org.
- The Marriage Sessions. Care for the Family: www.careforthefamily.org.uk.
- Together Course. Family Life: www.togetherinmarriage.org.
- Explore (enabling young people to explore the realities of lasting relationships): www.explorerelationships.org.uk.
- Bereaved parent support. Care for the Family: www.careforthefamily.org.uk.
- Whole Hearted. Support for spouses, Naked Truth Project: www.thenakedtruthproject.com/wholehearted/landing.

Resources for the national church

- Faith in the Family conference, based on research by Care for the Family.
- Marriage Foundation: www.marriagefoundation.org.uk.
- Marriage: Sex in the service of God. Christopher Ash (2007). IVP.

"Christian marriage: what would it look like if things were working well in the church?"

Engage consultation vision grid

Foundations: A gender balanced church that teaches about healthy Christian singleness, dating and relationships for young people and adults

A couple where both spouses are Christians

A couple	A local church	The national church
Engagement • Intentional period of preparation for marriage, not just the wedding. • Understanding the value of engagement – richness in waiting. • Discussing, and managing shared, realistic expectations around marriage. • Making intentional decisions to be different from the 'world'. • Understanding and living out God's design for sex within marriage. **Marriage preparation** • Considering it normal to do a marriage preparation course. • Freedom to make a clear decision (about whether to get married or not). • Talking about and addressing issues needing emotional wholeness and healing (from previous experiences, or ongoing addictions, e.g. porn). • Understanding and valuing each other's differences. • Healthy self-identity.	**Pre-engagement** • Helping couples to explore marriage, e.g. through using marriage preparation resources/ going on a course. **Engagement** • Celebrating engagements. • Running regular engagement courses. • Teaching on understanding and living out God's design for sex within marriage. • Mentoring, support and teaching in place for engaged couples. **Marriage preparation** • Running regular marriage preparation courses. • Expectation that couples will attend marriage preparation courses. • Mentoring, support and teaching in place for couples.	**Collaboration** • Articulating the vision for Christian marriage. • Support portal/'map' of all resources available. • Marriage ministry members working together to promote the uniqueness of Christian marriage. • Marriage Week. • Churches and organisations being seen to be working together. • Openness within the Church – through building relationships between the leaders. **Denominational leaders** • National leaders role-modelling healthy marriage. • Denominational leaders encouraged to attend marriage retreats if they are married. • Denominational leaders promoting marriage support as normal in all churches, including for church leaders. • The Church removing rather than creating barriers to God's plan for marriage.

A couple	A local church	The national church
• Being 'real' and honest. • Establishing boundaries – physical, emotional, spiritual. • Having a clear vision of Christian marriage. • Understanding what a covenant contract means. • Establishing life aims. **Marriage** • God at the centre. • Lifelong commitment. • Praying together daily. • Reading the Bible together regularly. • Unconditional love. • Forgiveness. • Hospitality – open-hearted in practical ways. • Missional. • Openness and transparency. • Vulnerability. • Sacrificial, unselfish giving. • Fun! • Understanding of equality. • Mutual submission and absence of control. • Continuing and deepening intimacy; emotional, spiritual, physical. • Comfortable with sexuality. • Commitment to personal and emotional growth. • Commitment to growing together. • Commitment to ongoing investment in the marriage. • Accountability to each other, and to identified, trusted others. • Countercultural. • Increasingly reflecting the fruit of the Spirit. • Reflection of the gospel and the church.	• Support to talk about and address issues needing emotional wholeness and healing (from previous experiences, or ongoing addictions, e.g. porn). • Teaching and support for children of blended families. **Weddings** • Engaged couples are welcomed in church. • Missional opportunity (marriage support). • Church community involvement. **Marriage** • Leaders modelling healthy Christian marriage. • Leaders regularly attend clergy marriage retreats. • Training for leaders on how to support marriages. • Expectation that couples will be followed up by mentors after the wedding. • Ongoing support from marriage mentors – e.g. meeting six months later. • Regular marriage courses. • Mentoring, support and teaching systems in place. • Promoting and providing a variety of resources (including online). • Marriage (and singleness) talked about freely and sensitively by ministers. • Providing social activities – for couples and single people.	• National Church leaders accepting appropriate responsibility for what's gone wrong. **Initial and ongoing ministerial training** • Theological/training colleges train future church leaders on how to support marriage. • Ongoing training provided for church leaders to know how to support marriage. **National conferences** • Always have an accessible marriage seminar. **Communication promoted by national leaders** • Approaching the topic of marriage – knowing when to speak out and what to say. • Have a positive pro-marriage message that doesn't marginalise others. • Respected spokespeople for marriage. • Academic and secular world encouraged not to be threatened by marriage – supportive and enthusiastic instead. • Positive messages about 'natural' marriage (instead of 'traditional'). • Taking opportunities (e.g. royal wedding) to talk about marriage. • Promoting positive messages in media. • Influencing culture.

A couple	A local church	The national church

• Being family to other people.
• Mentoring the next generation.
• Sharing stories and demonstrating the benefits of godly marriage.
• Going somewhere for help with the marriage when either or both feel this would be useful.
	• Providing additional practical support and care at times of particular stress, e.g.
	  - Meals for new parents.
	  - Lifts for elderly/infirm spouses etc.
	  - Babysitting.
	• Church/'rest of life' balance promoted for leaders and congregation.
	• Enabling couples to serve together.
	• Celebrating anniversaries.
	• Aware and explicitly talking about challenges and opportunities of marriage.
	• Supportive environment for all couples – whatever the circumstances.
	• Named contact person within the church – for those seeking help.
	• Clear signposting for further expert support.
	• Understanding and support for infertility.
	• Support for being countercultural.
	• Acknowledgement and practical support for those dealing with issues around porn (and other addictions).
	• Understanding of domestic violence and abuse – and how to deal with it appropriately.
	• Acceptance and support for step families/blended families.
	• Support and resources for children of step families.
	• Support for those separating, divorced or widowed.	

'Mixed' marriages where one spouse is a Christian and the other isn't

A couple	A local church	The national church
Engagement • Negotiation of how the spiritual difference will be handled. • Planning ahead around what the potential implications of the difference might mean. **Marriage preparation** • Exploring and understanding each other's beliefs and values. • Counting the cost of not being able to share faith (for the Christian). • Being aware of both potential difficulties (reality check) and potential opportunities (celebration of coming to faith). • Awareness that things may or may not change. • Planning around scenarios e.g. how our beliefs and values affect our approach to children, finances, time etc. • Understanding and managing values around generosity e.g. tithing and giving. • Explore potential churches for both to attend if the non-Christian is open to going to church (e.g. one that is more suitable for them which may be different from the type of church the Christian is used to attending). • Open communication.	• Church knows which couples fall in this category. • Openness and both welcomed. • Welcomed for who they are. • Welcome the whole family – reach them where they are at. • Plenty of social activities to build relationships. • Involvement in projects that relate to their interests. • Hospitality in small groups. • Recognising 'church' is in weekday activities, not just attendance on Sundays. • Treated as a married couple rather than one person feeling 'spiritually single'. • Recognising the tension the Christian may face – e.g. regarding time with family/church commitments. • Prayer support for the Christian. • Signposting to supporting resources. • Marriage support. • Support for Christian parent to pass on faith sensitively to children. • Involve children in Church activities. • Mentoring (either or both). • Awareness of other potential spiritual similarities and differences of religion.	**All national leaders** • Normalising this as a common issue and churches addressing it relevantly. • Recognising the evangelistic opportunity. **Initial and ministerial training** • Clergy training addresses this issue (theological/ training colleges). • Ongoing training for church leaders. **Networks that need to be set up** • National support networks/inter-church networks for Christians who are married to non-Christians. • National support networks for those in inter-faith and/or inter-cultural marriages **Resources that are needed** • More resources available, e.g. websites, podcasts, books etc. – practical advice.

A couple	A local church	The national church
• Acknowledging that there is potential for change in the future. • Both being aware of biblical teaching on marriage. **Marriage** • Christian would know where to go for support. • Having a support network that's welcoming of both. • Christian sharing, modelling and being a channel of God's love. • Ability to cope with other's opinions. • Christian being strong and secure in their own faith. • Spiritual humility (not superiority). • Ongoing guidance from Holy Spirit.	• Resources and understanding for those with spouses of other faiths. • Valuing the marriage regardless of where the non-Christian is faith-wise. • Equipping all church members – not just leaders to do the above!	

CHAPTER 10

Parenting and discipleship around young people's dating and relationships: what would it look like if things were working well in the church?

Paula Pridham

The Problem

15 years ago Care for the Family introduced a parenting programme called *How to Drug Proof Your Kids – steering children away from the harmful use of drugs*. I cannot tell you the number of times we were asked to produce *How to Sex Proof Your Kids*. Mums and dads, of faith or none, wanted help navigating the minefield of dating and relationships that the onset of puberty brought. They wanted to be given a set of steps to follow that would ensure their children never engaged with risky, sexual behaviour – or preferably any sexual behaviour at all! Unfortunately it's not quite that easy.

In addition, parents of faith wanted their children to share their values relating to dating, sexual activity and marriage. Yet at the same time they often felt painfully inadequate, and lacked confidence in knowing how to do this. Fast forward 15 years and the primary concern over whether a son or daughter in a Christian home remains a virgin until marriage almost pales into insignificance when faced with modern-day dilemmas. Sexting, gender identity, sexuality, online pornography and a plethora of TV programmes such as Ex on the Beach, Love Island and other reality shows have added a layer of complexity never previously dreamt of.

Postmodern culture may have said 'if it feels good do it', but Millennials and Generation Z (11-18 year olds) are now encouraged to do it, let others see you do it, do it front of everyone else and do it to pass the time of day. And if you don't do it, and do it this way, then obviously there's something wrong with you.

Online pornography has been a game-changer when it comes to where young people first find out about relationships and sex. Various studies put the average age of first viewing between 8 and 11 years old. Often they weren't even looking for it, but by typing an innocent phrase into a search engine they encountered stuff that at the least would previously have been hidden behind the closed doors of a backstreet sex shop.

In the 2017 annual Girls' Attitude Survey from Girlguiding, 25% of girls aged 18-21 thought sexting was a normal part of a relationship, and 16% felt pressurised to send nude pictures.[1] But it's not just girls that are being affected. An NSPCC report in 2016 *I Wasn't Sure It Was Normal To Watch It* cited 53% of boys believing what they saw online was a realistic portrayal of sex.[2] One boy in the study said "One of my friends has started treating women like he sees on the videos – not major – just a slap here or there."

It might be tempting to think that young Christians are safe. That they are immune from the machinations of the world they live in, or not even curious. That is probably a very naïve and potentially harmful way of thinking. Without effective discipleship, strong support networks, an understanding of what healthy relationships look like (including sexual intimacy) and the skills to build those relationships, they may be as vulnerable as any other young person.

It's not just about sex though. In a world where family breakdown is widespread it is imperative that parents, and the church, do the very best they can to help young people have the fulfilling, committed relationships that God intended. And that is still the aspiration of most young people, even those who wouldn't consider themselves religious.

With the backdrop of changes in the provision of Relationship and Sex Education in schools in England, the Centre for Social Justice and Family Stability Network surveyed over 1000 young people aged 14-17 to understand their views.[3] They found that 72% wanted relationship education to understand how to build lasting relationships, 78% said they wanted to get married, 56% thought forming lasting relationships is harder than for previous generations and 77% believed long-term relationships are important. When asked where they would get the relationship information and advice they needed, more than half said they would go online. But the good news (although perhaps daunting), is that 66% said they would talk to their parents, only just beaten to first place by friends at 72%. The importance of the role of parents as influencers and advisors is echoed in many other studies. Yet so often mums and dads believe, especially when it comes to teens, that they have lost all credibility, they don't know enough or that others have more influence over their young people's thinking. A report from Youth for Christ, *Gen Z: Rethinking Culture* should provide encouragement. In their research they found the Number One positive influencer for 11-18 year olds was family.[4]

By working together, parents and the church (both local and national), can address one of the last taboos – talking about sex and relationships. This is more than just telling young people to remain abstinent until married. And what do they do if they don't marry? It's about open and honest dialogue, addressing uncomfortable issues and intentionally creating a culture where we all learn about relationships from each other.

> *"I know the Bible says you can't have sex before marriage. But why can't you, if you're in love with the person? It doesn't feel wrong."* (Kyle, 14)

> *"My boyfriend and I don't want to mess around anymore. But how do we keep this commitment? I never realised how powerful passion can be."* (Shari, 15)

> *"I feel cut off from God. I want to do what's right, but I can't seem to. Recently I had sex with a guy, thinking that it would bring us closer. I know now that was a mistake, and I feel totally ashamed."* (Aimee, 16)

What would it look like if things were working well for parents?

> *"Start children off on the way they should go, and even when they are old they will not turn from it."* (Proverbs 22:6)

> *"Give me a child until he is seven and I will show you the man."* (Aristotle)

At Care for the Family we often say "Don't expect your child to listen to you when they are 15 if you didn't spend time listening to them when they were 5." Discipleship issues around dating and relationships may not manifest until a child is in their teens, but the foundations of how they are dealt with are laid much earlier. The writer of Proverbs, and Aristotle, knew without the benefit of modern scientific and psychological discovery, that those early years in a child's life are some of the most formative. It's vital for those of us with children to realise that.

We can go right back to birth and those first few precious months. This child will be learning all about safety and security, and does this through attachment. 'Attachment' is the phrase coined in the 1960s by psychologist John Bowlby to describe the emotional, and physical, connectedness between a child and its primary caregiver, usually one of the parents. Strong attachment enables a child to feel safe and stable, and as they grow allows them the confidence to explore and be adventurous – knowing they have at least one person who has their back, so to speak. It's developed through physical presence, touch, attention and being aware, and taking care, of the needs of the child.

Without this attachment a child may become fearful and less willing to engage in new experiences. With secure attachment children are more able to grow into confident, caring and capable young people. They are less likely to engage in unhealthy behaviours and be better able to cope with the emotional and physical changes that they go through. Secure attachment is no guarantee but it does provide a firm foundation. The attachment we have experienced as children, whether secure or otherwise, will also follow us into our adult relationships. It may mean the difference between looking for love in all the wrong places or holding out for something that is of value and mutual satisfaction.

Every child and young person needs to know that there is at least one person who has them in mind – at least one person in the world who is there for them and that they can turn to. I remember attending a seminar on teenage mental health. The speaker, from Young Minds,[5] recounted the story of a young girl, let's call her Clare, he had been supporting. She was a teenager, excluded from school, very disruptive and angry and he was finding it difficult working with her. On his way home from work one day he called into the local supermarket to pick up some bits and pieces. He was due to see Clare the next day and found himself already beginning to feel stressed about it and unsure of what good he was doing. As he turned the corner of the aisle he bumped into the back of someone. As she turned, he saw it was Clare and automatically said, "I was just thinking about you." Usually Clare's responses to him were aggressive and sarcastic, but in this instance she burst into tears. He asked what was wrong, and she replied, "No one has ever said that to me before." Now the truth is, what he was thinking wasn't particularly good, but for Clare, for anyone to have her in mind was a powerful experience. He said that after this encounter it totally changed the dynamics of their relationship, becoming much more positive and productive.

During the primary, formative years a child also watches everything... absolutely everything. Not only do they watch, they imitate. You stick your tongue out – they do too. You blow a raspberry, and they'll try really hard to do that too. You mutter under your breath when you're frustrated, they'll do the same. You kick the cat when you're angry...you get the picture. But at this early age they're unable to discern which are the good things to copy and which are the not so good.

Children are watching the way we handle our own relationships, particularly with our closest family and friends, and also the way we handle our relationship with God. We are modelling to them what relationships look like and we can either show them 'done well', or not. But this is not about being perfect, it is more about being intentional. Because we are frail and human we are not always going to be on our best behaviour.

Even as Christians with the transforming power of the Holy Spirit available to us, there are going to be times when we just get it wrong. That in itself though is an opportunity to model repentance and forgiveness, for when our children let us down – as they most certainly will – they will have seen that there is a way back and the opportunity to start again. It is perfectly OK for a parent to apologise to a child if they get something wrong. If they see Mum and Dad having words with each other but then watch as they 'don't let the sun go down on their anger' but restore their connection to each other, that child is learning how to do relationships well.

Another key foundation stone is setting and keeping boundaries. This isn't about control, but about security. There is nothing more certain to make a child feel insecure than to know they can do what they like without any consequences. However, how those boundaries are set and implemented will be the difference between a child feeling loved or not – even though they might not be able to articulate that themselves. Their immediate reaction to any boundary is that you are just trying to stop them having fun.

More often than not when we become parents we don't really think about it, we just get on and do. But that doesn't necessarily mean that what we are doing is right. It's useful to consider whether some ways of parenting are better than others.

At Care for the Family we talk about 3 different styles of parenting and use these illustrations.[6]

Authoritarian

Parents who are authoritarian know how to put their foot down. Typical comments to the children are "Just do it!" or "Never mind 'why?' It's because I said so." If the family were the Army, these parents would be the sergeant majors. They expect their orders to be obeyed instantly and don't encourage discussion.

Permissive

These parents are, in some ways, the opposite of the authoritarian type. They do not like either setting or enforcing boundaries, and they back away from confrontation. They are often warm and accepting of their children, but rarely demand high standards in behaviour. If the child of an authoritarian parent left their chocolate wrappers and trainers on the floor in front of the television they might expect to be yelled at. The child of permissive parents, however, would expect that their parents would probably clear it all up after them.

Authoritative

These parents believe that boundaries are important, but are careful not to back themselves into a corner over things that don't matter. They are unlikely to hit the roof over minor issues, but on the other hand they will be very firm over things like curfews or homework. They take time to explain why the rules they set are important and are prepared to listen to an opposing view. Their children know they are accepted and loved, but equally know that Mum and Dad are not an easy touch. The children are encouraged to be independent.

Rob Parsons, founder of Care for the Family, sometimes tells of the time he once saw a blind man walking along a long hospital corridor. Rob says "He was tapping his white stick against the wall at the side of him. After a while he stopped tapping – he knew where the wall was. But after he'd gone almost the whole length of the corridor, I saw him reach out with his stick again and tap it against the wall a few times. He needed to test that it was still there – test where the boundaries were. Our children, too, will test the boundaries – push against them every now and then to test they are still there. They will actually feel more secure knowing they are in place."

Most agree that the authoritative style of parenting is the one to aim for. It lets children know that boundaries are there because Mum or Dad care, not just because they are bigger and in charge. Underpinning this style of parenting is love, and as our children grow older we will be able to explain why this or that boundary was important to us. Perhaps it was for safety reasons, such as asking the child to be home on a certain time, or because of our values, such as we don't believe sex outside of marriage is God's ideal.

If we can get these early years right – and none of us are going to be perfect – we are likely to raise young people who are resilient, can weather the knock-backs life will throw at them and are able to form good relationships. It'll make it much easier to have important conversations with them when they are older and we should find they do actually want to talk with us.

And prayer. From even before they are born, our children need our prayers.

> "In modern society, raising emotionally healthy children is an increasingly difficult task...If children feel genuinely loved by their parents, they will be more responsive to parental guidance in all areas of their lives." (Chapman and Campbell, 2016. *The Five Love Languages of Children*.)[7]

As we move into the dating phase there is more that can be brought into young person's life to help them, especially if we are asking them to be countercultural. It's here that discipleship complements the 'training' of those early years.

Even though we have seen that parents are the greatest influence on a child's life and that most teens would want to talk to their parents about relationships, sometimes they may need to outwardly process their thoughts and feelings to another significant adult first. Ideally, this should be someone who is trusted by Mum or Dad, someone that they have actively put into their young person's life. It could be another family member, such as an aunt/uncle or grandparent, but it might be a mentor or a church youth worker.

As well as significant adults, young people need the opportunity to have Christian friends of a similar age. Preferably in the same school. It can be much easier to stand up for what you believe in if you have at least one other person you know who believes the same as you. Young Christians will need to understand why not just they, but their parents believe what they do. If we want to be able to discuss those beliefs and our values with them, Youth For Christ's *Gen Z* report gives three reasons why young people will explore ideas: 1) because something makes sense, 2) it could be worthwhile and 3) it's presented in an interesting way.

Young people no longer believe just because someone said so. Which brings us back to modelling by parents. If we want our young people to believe prayer is important, they need to see us praying. If we want them to believe the Bible is true, then they need to see us engaging with it. (And I use that word advisedly – we don't have to be seen reading a physical book, this could be online, audio, podcasts as well as in print.)

Young people will need to know what we believe about dating, relationships and marriage. They will want to hear our views on sexuality and diversity and share theirs. Our commitment to them, their wellbeing, and understanding their world view will let them see how we don't just give up when things get difficult or if we don't agree on everything. We teach an understanding that commitment to faith and people means being in it for the long haul, and that that brings its own rewards.

As well as parents sharing their own views and values, they do need to address the whole online world, which can so easily ensnare even the most confident and well-adjusted young person. Engaging in conversation about screen time, the kind of content being viewed and apps being used is vital. Our young people need to know that a lot of what they see are unhealthy relationships and not ones to aspire to. Additionally, mums and dads should find out what is being taught in Relationships and Sex Education (RSE) in their school and be able to talk about it with their own child. If the foundations of positive relationships and communication between parent and child have formed, these should be natural conversations rather than 'we need to talk about' ones.

Some parents will have come from challenging family backgrounds. They may never have themselves experienced the positive parenting that is needed to raise secure, independent, confident adults. Perhaps they too have a background of unsatisfactory relationships. Does this disqualify them from becoming effective parents themselves? By no means, but they may need some extra support along the way. And it's never too late to start. Although those early years are foundational, teens go through another spurt of brain development, and inputting positive messages at a later stage will never be wasted. Getting together with others in a similar situation will encourage and build confidence.

Mums and dads who come to faith later in life will also need additional support. They are going to have to balance their own discipleship journey with discipling their children. It may be a temptation to leave this to the local church who are the 'professionals', but as many others have said, 'it takes a whole church to raise a child'. Parents and church working together will be the most effective way of helping young people do dating and relationships well.

Here is what it might look like for parents if things are working well:

- Christy is a single mum with twin girls, nearly 17. One of the girls has told her their sibling has been meeting up with a 20 year old on the way home from school. Christy doesn't like the sound of this, but rather than just wade in, she phones her Parenting Prayers buddy first for some support.
- Jon and Amy have just dropped their 13 year old son off at the church youth club. They decide to stop on and call in to the informal Parenting Café that gets together once a month. It's a good place to catch up with other mums and dads. They often watch a vodcast on parenting teens and then have a chat about it afterwards.
- Clare has heard the church are putting on a seminar about the digital world and young people's engagement with pornography. She encourages her husband that this is something they should go to.Their children are only in Years 6 and 7 but she wants to be on the front foot.

What would it look like if things were working well in the local church?

When it's at its best, the local church is a great place. It can be vibrant, hopeful, loving and serving. A place of encouragement and support, helping individuals along their own spiritual journey as well as drawing in those outside the church to "taste and see that the Lord is good" (Psalm 34:8). But we know that some churches aren't doing so well and others are overwhelmed by the barrage of requests they receive to become involved in another campaign/outreach/event.

Whether successful or going through a difficult phase, what most churches don't need is to be asked to enter into another project or programme. But when it comes to helping parents engage with young people's dating and discipleship, it's not another programme that's needed. This is more about developing a culture, led from the front, of spiritual, emotional and social wellbeing for all. A whole church culture which encourages people to develop meaningful relationships, not just with God, but with each other.

It can be hard as a leader to be vulnerable and share from the front the challenges you face. Yet there is amazing power in doing just that. When a mum or dad in the congregation hears in a Sunday sermon how you got it wrong in your parenting that week, there'll probably be an audible sigh of relief. That sort of vulnerability says 'me too', 'this is normal', 'it's not just you',

'you're not a bad person'. It allows conversations to be had that may otherwise never see the light of day.

Families come in all shapes and sizes and a congregation should reflect the community it lives in. This means it may include a large number of single parent families, blended families – some quite complex, foster and adoptive families. No church leader can meet all their needs themselves. They need to include the whole church family, bring in other organisations and also know where to signpost people if they need additional support. This in itself models to parents that it's OK to seek outside help when you need it. It normalises the use of relationship support – and it's even better if, say, the church runs a marriage enrichment course and the church leader joins in too. It doesn't have to be formal though. Just getting mums and dads together for coffee and cake and asking how their week went creates the space for conversation.

Alongside supporting parents, churches need to provide welcoming and innovative youth ministries. Young people need to engage with authentic, godly relationships with young adults they can identify with and who can disciple them. Yet in Youth for Christ's *Gen Z* report, only 2% of young people said youth club was their favourite place to spend time and only 69% ever attended one. Now that could be because of the competition. In the same report, when asked about hobbies/activities they do on a daily basis, 94% spent time on social media, 75% watched YouTube, and 73% said 'gaming'.This is a challenge for the church but also a great opportunity.

Here is what it might look like if working well in the local church:

- Sean and Kemi have been asked by their church leader to run marriage enrichment sessions. She's concerned about the number of pastoral conversations she's been having with couples who are struggling.
- Valentine's Day is on a Sunday and the youth group lead the service. They unpack the various Greek words for love found in the New Testament and interview a couple who have been married for a long time about what love means for them.
- The church puts on a course for those parenting early teens and organises youth activities at the same time so no one has to worry about finding someone to be at home with their children.
- One of the mums in the congregation has set up prayer triplets amongst the parents to pray specifically for their children.

What would it look like if things were working well in the national church?

> *"So Christ himself gave the apostles, the prophets, the*
> *evangelists, the pastors and teachers, to equip his people for*
> *works of service, so that the body of Christ may be built up*
> *until we all reach unity in the faith and in the knowledge of*
> *the Son of God and become mature, attaining to the whole*
> *measure of the fullness of Christ."*
> (Ephesians 4:11–13)

There are two key areas that impact on the national church engaging well on this agenda. The first is the initial training of church leaders. Whether or not a student has chosen a 'family ministry stream', all potential leaders need to have an understanding of the issues facing families today and the complexity of their lives. In particular, parents are looking for clear guidance on, or at least the opportunity to discuss, issues around emotional and relational health, self-identity, sexuality and gender identity. Parents try to talk to their church leaders, who also feel these subjects are beyond their capacity. There are no easy answers, but church leader training must address how to support families who have questions about what is appropriate sexual activity before marriage through to more challenging circumstances, and how to positively engage with Relationship and Sex Education (RSE) in schools.

Thinking of RSE has just brought to mind a recent story from a colleague of mine. Her daughter, six years and seven months, had just had a first lesson on anatomy. They had learnt the names for the 'private parts' of the body of both boys and girls. My colleague asked what she learned about girls and daughter couldn't remember that at all. So what had she learnt about boys? Her daughter responded. "Are you sure?" my colleague said. "Yes," says daughter. "Are you sure they didn't call it something else like…?" "No, no, no," says daughter. "I do think that perhaps you mean…?" "No Mummy, you're wrong – it's definitely called a peanut!" It could happen to any of us. But on a serious note, information from the national church on RSE policy and guidance on the rights of parents, and potential ways of responding to what is being taught would be invaluable for mums, dads and church leaders.

Initial ministerial training should also include how you set the culture within church where relationships, and the quality of them are not taboo subjects. This would include the importance of looking after your own relationship with partners and children.

And we need more ongoing training for church leaders. The longer you are in church leadership, the more you see the same pastoral challenges come around. Having the opportunity to meet with others and share experiences of how to deal with these can make a leader more effective. It may also protect them from thinking that this is something they need to always handle themselves, rather than getting input from other sources.

Church leaders also need the opportunity to care for their own relationships. Leadership can be stressful and couples need to have built up their own resilience to pressures the role puts on their marriage and family life.

Here is what it might look like if working well at a national level:

- A ministerial training college wants to help its students understand the cultural pressures facing young people about dating and relationships and what is being taught in schools. As part of the curriculum, they bring in an outside organisation such as acet UK to run a session to raise awareness.
- Leadership network training days which include how to support parents to engage with their children around dating and discipleship.
- Regular marriage enrichment weekends for church leaders that are offered throughout the denomination.

Action Points

For parents

- Parents need to:
    - Start on this journey before their young people get to the dating stage, providing a warm, structured and secure home environment.
    - Be intentional about modelling 'good' relationships and discipling their own children.
    - Be able to identify other significant adults who can be part of their child's life.
    - Know what is being taught in RSE in their child's school and be able to talk about it with them.
    - Have their own support network of other mums and dads going through the same stage.
- Young people need the support of Christian peers to help them be countercultural.
- Parents need support from the whole church community, especially those who are parenting alone.
- Prayer underpins everything.

For the local church

- Identify what relationship support (both parenting and marriage) currently exists in the church and ways to fill in the gaps – perhaps by partnering with another church or training people in the congregation.
- Have a go-to list of other organisations that support parents.
- Include messaging about healthy relationships in sermons.
- Identify those with mature faith and sound relationships who can mentor younger couples and young people.

For the national church

- Identify what training to support parents around young people's singleness, dating, relationships and sex/sexuality is currently part of the theological college curriculum, and how to fill in the gaps.
- Liaise with other organisations which can provide specialist input.
- Develop a culture of preventative support for church leaders and their families.

Resources

Parent workshops/resources around emotional wellbeing, relationships and sex

- acet UK: www.acet-uk.com
- Romance Academy: www.romanceacademy.org

As well as referring to the resources suggested by Laura at the end of chapter 11, I would signpost to general parenting support.

- www.thenpi.org.uk
  The National Parenting Initiative was set up by senior church leaders as a one-stop shop for parents to find out where church-led parenting courses are running across the country.
- www.careforthefamily.org.uk
  Covering all aspects of parent and marriage support via books, DVDs, courses and online information. Specialist support for those who share a Christian faith is available through the "Faith in the Family" section of the website.
- www.themarriagecourses.org/run/the-parenting-courses
  Courses developed by Nicky & Sila Lee, Holy Trinity Brompton.
- www.new-wine.org/resources/family-time
  A collection of family resources from New Wine.

"Parenting and discipleship around young people's dating and relationships: what would it look like if things were working well in the church?"

Engage consultation vision grid

Parents	A local church	The national church
Spiritual/emotional/social wellbeing • Intentionally develop their own spiritual, emotional and social wellbeing. • Model a growing personal relationship with God and encourage that in children and young people – parenting for faith, so that children/young people know faith is authentic. • Pray for their children/ young people. • Model prayer, understanding and applying the Bible to life, engagement in church. • Model how relationships are done well. • Are discipled themselves – including those new to faith who haven't seen good Christian parenting modelled. • Have an understanding of attachment and how to develop healthy attachments. • Provide warm and structured parenting. • Provide love and freedom within realistic boundaries. • Parents able to articulate their values and reasons for them.	**Spiritual/emotional/social wellbeing** • A culture, lead from the front, of intentionally encouraging spiritual, emotional and social growth for everyone. • Intentionally encourages a culture where everyone is learning about relationships from each other. • Promotes and encourages conversation amongst parents – parenting in community. • Supports parents to be able to articulate their values and reasons for them. • Intentionally proactive in addressing issues that parents need support for, signposting to resources. • Vibrant, godly modelling of effective parenting. • Church practically enables parents to get involved, particularly single parents. • Addresses holistic needs of children/young people – effective teaching about all areas of development. • Modelling by godly youth leaders of spiritual, emotional and social growth, and positive relationships to support parenting.	**Initial training of church leaders** • Students understand the issues people are actually facing. • Practical training (e.g. from acet UK). • Practical pastoral aspects (e.g. Care for the Family Bereavement Care) not just theological only. • Understanding how you set the culture of your church (e.g. Care for the Family doing 3 days training on parenting for students, also developing similar for marriage support). • Understanding how to support blended families and parents in different circumstances, including single parents. • Input around sexuality follows through to parenting. • It's put on the agenda – 72% of churches are not engaging with young people – go and find them! **Ongoing training for church leaders** • Good quality courses/ support is available to develop the culture outlined in 'parents' and 'local church' columns.

Parents	A local church	The national church
• Supportive about issues children/young people are facing, rather than judgemental. • Focus on questioning rather than telling. • Open communication. • Take and retain responsibility for discipling their own children and young people. • Are in Christian community. • Understand the challenges their children/young people are going through. • Feel and are capable and confident to disciple their children/young people (see *Gen Z: Rethinking Culture* Youth For Christ research report). • Are confident and faithful about having a long-term view of children/young people's spiritual development. • Encourage involvement in church groups and youth groups. • Involvement of youth workers/youth work to support discipleship by parents. **Discipleship around dating/ relationships** • Prayer! • Age-appropriate support/discipleship for pre-teens as well as teenagers. • Bring their children/ young people up to be God-connected, with a heart wanting to please him.	• Focus on developing healthy youth ministries in churches – welcoming and innovative, relevant, in different church contexts. • Church recognises that God can use children and young people as much as adults. • Opportunities for growth in gifts and leadership for children and young people in different contexts in the church. • Intergenerational discipleship encouraged within church – young people want a grandparent figure in their life. • Those who are older in faith are willing to be flexible in 'how we do church' – and this is modelled by church leaders. **Discipleship around dating/ relationships** • Leaders are interested in young people and these issues! • A culture of honesty led from the front about needing to learn and develop in addressing these issues. • Helping parents have a healthy relationship between themselves (marriage enrichment). • Normalising use of support, courses and resources for marriage and parenting. • Teaching and signposting parents to relevant resources. • Age-appropriate support/discipleship for pre-teens as well as teenagers.	**Heads of denominations** • Recognise that these issues need to be addressed by all leaders. • Church to be clear on what its message is in terms of how to develop healthy spiritual, emotional, social and relational wellbeing. • Leading on how to articulate values and reasons for these. • Set up systems to ensure these things happen. **National Conferences** • Run a parenting stream/ seminars.

Parents	A local church	The national church
• Have thought through their understanding of biblical teaching on relationships and sexuality and how it's applied to today's experiences. • Support young people to be countercultural, recognising relativism, how to understand the importance of authenticity of scripture. • Can explain biblical teaching on marriage – the 'why' as well as the 'what'. • Address question of relationships/marriage with non-Christians. • Encouraging good Christian peer friendships with both sexes. • Model relationships/communication/clear expectations and boundaries. • Teach an understanding of commitment, to faith and people, rather than 'random dating'. • Aware of what the context is for this generation – starting from their world. • Understand the impact of the digital world and the influence of porn/drink/drugs. • Have clear expectations and talk about issues openly and constructively. • Hold young people accountable – ask clear and direct questions. • Know what to say in certain situations. • Know about resources on relationships and sex education for young people, and share these with their young people.	• Support parents to have confidence to effectively parent in this area. • Church is a place of support for parents – it's OK to have difficult conversations, even if a young person is going 'off-track'. • Culture of grace and love, vulnerability, don't have to be perfect to be accepted. • Churches liaise with and use organisations that provide support and training e.g. Romance Academy/acet UK/Youth for Christ. • Churches work/group together to support and resource each other and parents. • Churches are in relationship with local schools to support young people and adults who support them.	

Youth work and discipleship around young people's dating and relationships: what would it look like if things were working well in the church?

Laura Hancock

For most of my childhood the internet didn't exist. If you say that in a room of 11-18 year olds today, you can watch as their world begins to deconstruct and their brains fall out of their ears (hopefully not literally). Whether in my role as Church Resources Director with British Youth for Christ or through my church where my husband is Next Gen pastor, I spend a lot of time with young people. As many of us will be aware, youth culture today feels different. It can feel quite intimidating to think about supporting and discipling young people when, at times, current youth culture can feel so alien, let alone trying to talk to them about dating and sex. But whilst culture has certainly shifted, the basic narrative and needs of a young person trying to find their purpose and place has not. A generation is crying out for people to stand alongside them as they navigate what, to us, may look on the surface like unfamiliar terrain.

Helping young people to know Jesus and be known by him is our first task, in order that they flourish spiritually, emotionally and socially as individuals and in all relationships. These are the foundations for any healthy dating and relationships later, for teenagers and adults. Discussing everything that is involved in building these foundations is beyond the scope of this chapter, however, as we start, I want to acknowledge that they're essential.

Before we press on to speak specifically about young people, dating and discipleship, I would like to take a moment to sketch you a brief picture of today's cultural landscape for a teenager. That's because understanding their context will enable us to aid their journey better. Young people today do not know of life before the smartphone or what it is to be unconnected and uncontactable. They have never known a world without terrorism, where war looks like an unforeseen danger at any moment. They have grown up in economic uncertainty, where jobs are to be fought for or self-created rather than offered. They do not know a world without social networking and the fine balance between constant critique or affirmation, coupled with the chance to post their opinion and receive immediate responses to their requests.

They live in a world in which they are saturated with adverts and so they've actually learned to discern what's authentic. But this is a world shaped by media they don't believe, governed by world leaders that they don't trust and adults who voted for them. We are dealing then, with young people who are ethically minded, authentic, creative, constantly connected, entrepreneurial, partially attentive and well-informed. Into this mix is included the complex minefield of building and sustaining relationships. A desire and need for relationship is part of our shared human narrative, although not every young person in western culture would hold this view. The connectedness of young people today has also added complexities that other generations have not had to face.

At Youth for Christ, we carried out a survey of young people across Britain called *Gen Z: Rethinking Culture* in which we questioned over 1000 young people across Britain on issues of culture, influence, priorities and faith.[1] As Paula mentioned in the previous chapter, in that survey we found that 94% of the young people asked were on social media every day. 75% of young people accessed YouTube every day and 73% of young people were gaming on a daily basis. Many of the young people were 11-14 years old and may not have been old enough to be allowed a social media account or access to YouTube by their parents. So, we see that even the way relationships are formed and maintained is fundamentally different. Often this is not in person but through the social use of media.

From my own observations, young people are experts in the art of initial connection but seriously lacking in knowledge of how to form and maintain healthy relationships. Unfortunately, one is often mistaken for the other. These connections are often a cheap counterfeit of the real relationships that they long for but have not learned the skills to build. The addictive chemical in their brain (dopamine) that is released when a notification sound comes through on their phone only amplifies this feeling of excited infatuation.[2] Into the fray then comes the quest for love and acceptance that is in the fabric of every human, yet it's made more precarious because it's conducted on social media. Connection is therefore mistaken for relationship and even for love.

It's a world where images and words can be edited and filtered, where nude pictures are as easy to request as they are to send and it's free from the awkwardness of face-to-face intimacy. The digital age makes sending indecent images quick and simple to do but leaves long-lasting regrets. I am deeply grieved by the number of teenage girls that have sat in front of me having mistaken connection for intimacy. They are often known better by their profile than their personality, with images that were meant for one person being easily circulated in local schools. Then the online comments and messages begin.

The constant access to technology in the digital age has also impacted the availability of porn for young people. I am reliably told that porn is not like it used to be, with content that includes violence and bestiality now easy to find. Some believe that this, again, has affected the quality of teenage relationships. A 2014 study across high resource countries, including the UK, found that half of all young people, irrespective of gender, reported emotional abuse within a relationship. Most often this was being shouted at or called names. A third of adolescent girls and a quarter of boys reported sexual violence through pressure or physical force.[3] We could go on to talk about young people being trafficked and groomed around our local towns or our nations, or the brokenness that a young person carries when they have suffered sexual abuse.

I do not share these things to scare us, and thankfully, this is not the experience of the majority of teenagers. But pornography, sexual abuse and pressure are features of the world in which they are being formed. So how do we as adults and role models speak into this world? How do we disciple young people so that they are flourishing spiritually and emotionally, and tell them what dating and relationships might look like if they were working well? These are the questions that we will begin to explore in this chapter.

An individual young person

Throughout the Bible we see the importance of story. A central tradition in ancient Jewish culture was the art of storytelling and narrative. We read in Psalm 78:5-7, "He decreed statutes for Jacob and established the law in Israel, which he commanded our ancestors to teach their children, so the next generation would know them, even the children yet to be born, and they in turn would tell their children. Then they would put their trust in God and would not forget his deeds but would keep his commands." In fact, if you have a moment I would recommend that you give the whole Psalm a read. Why? Because it highlights the importance of story and narrative when discipling the next generation. When communities began to share the bigger story of God together, the whole community began to understand their collective narrative. From this, individuals could then start to see their place in the story and their purpose. This is the narrative that they were created for, were created to thrive in, and which explains how relationship, romantic or otherwise, works best.

When we look at discipling young people in the area of dating, I believe we have a crisis of narrative. Through song, screen and social media, young people are being told an ever-changing narrative of what singleness and dating should look like. By comparison, the narrative that the church offers young people just doesn't seem credible to many of them. Glynn Harrison has done some great thinking around this in his book *A Better Story*. Young people are broken from their culture and are looking for people to come alongside them with a better and alternative story. This wider narrative of humanity's brokenness, its need and desire for relationship and intimacy helps me to make sense of my story and my identity, my place and my purpose. This is where we must begin.

In many ways, we have failed young people in our silence. You don't have to be a seasoned youth worker to build enough of a relationship with a young person to ask about their relationship status. We will speak more of this in a moment, but by not asking a young person what currently 'is' in their world of dating, we're less likely to paint them a picture of what 'could be'. We could be sharing a narrative about their value, purpose, identity and the value of others. When young people begin to understand their place in a wider narrative, they see that they have high worth in the eyes of a God who loves them. They see that he cares who they date or if they struggle with loneliness. They come to realise that God the Father loved them so much that he sent his only Son to give his life for them! The sacredness of relationship is demonstrated by this supreme act of love on God's part. We must help them to see that their core purpose is to love God, love others and help draw others towards him. Then the foundation by which they see themselves and others begins to change.

We talk to our youth group a lot about their own identity, because out of it comes understanding of the value of others and how you should treat them. We know we shouldn't use others to fulfil our own need for self-worth. Instead, we need to help young people understand that they are a complete individual because of their part in the greater narrative, whether they are in a romantic relationship or not. They are not one half of something looking to become a whole. As young people begin to understand their identity and place within a bigger story, they will learn to stop looking for silver bullets or equations to work out if they should date someone who isn't a Christian. Instead, their imagination has been captured by a wider, alternative narrative for being a teenager, whether dating or not.

However, the stage must be set to tell this narrative and that happens best through relationship. The importance of open and honest relationships with adults cannot be underestimated. Whilst this might include their youth worker, young people must not exclusively relate to their youth worker in this way. Each young person should be in relationship with a variety of adults who have a range of relational experiences, and with whom they are comfortable having meaningful conversation about these themes. They must be the kinds of relationships which are honest, real and, as far as appropriate, vulnerable. How can we expect young people to share the intimate details of where they are at or their struggles of identity and sexuality, if we are not in turn willing to open our lives to them in an authentic and appropriate way?

Young people need wise and mature adults who will model healthy relationships and lifestyles and know when to share, when to challenge, when to listen and what not to share. This can't only fall to a church's youth team (you might not have one anyway!). We all can talk to them about matters of the heart and vulnerable areas, such as addictions or negative patterns of self-worth. Often a mature follower of Jesus sharing their story and life makes a huge difference. As these relationships begin to form, we can model realistic relationships to young people instead of the types they've been led to believe in by culture's narrative. We must help them gain realistic expectations of singleness, sex, break-ups and friendships.

However, this is not the only battle fought through the forging of cross-generational relationships. As we see an increase in the use of media to communicate, the art of face-to-face interaction and basic people skills become increasingly lost. A short time ago, I sat with a girl who had decided to sleep with her boyfriend for the first time. When I asked her if they had talked about it beforehand, she looked at me like I was crazy. She shared that it had been really awkward afterwards, so they went and played a computer game and that made it all OK again. Young people are losing the art of having difficult conversations face-to-face. The screen is the easier option but face-to-face interactions offer them the opportunity for learning.

In our youth work settings, countless hours have been spent resolving relational fallout that's rooted in the loss of the ability to form loyal, trustworthy, secure friendships. Yet, as we step in front of a young person, we can begin to model something different. Having open and honest relationships with young people, where they learn how to say 'no' and how to manage relationships online, can change the course of a young person's future. Some young people I work with have a dangerous mix of poor self-worth and poor conflict-navigation skills. So, if a guy asks for something, then their answer is always 'yes', no matter what the cost is to them. Our presence as adults in the lives of young people is vital as we teach them what healthy face-to-face relationships look like. But what about when we can't be there? What about the times when a young person has to make decisions on their own?

As a youth worker (and parents may also relate to this), some of the most difficult and frustrating times are when you can't follow a young person to school or to that house party and make their decisions for them. When you send them off and you can't even remind them of some of the deep wisdom you have imparted in your time together. I have wanted to offer to go to parties with young people, but it definitely comes across as a little odd! Due to it being socially unacceptable, not to mention physically impossible to follow each young person around, we decided to change tack in our youth ministry and try to get ahead of the curve. It's vital to give young people the tools to make wise decisions as part of our discipleship around friendships and dating. We talk through strategies in our teaching and one-on-one relationships, when they're safely away from any potential difficult situations or reactive moments. So often, we don't plan to make bad dating and relationship choices, we just don't plan not to. By talking about things in advance of actual situations arising we can give young people a better chance of making the right choices when they find themselves negotiating relationships on their own.

We talk to our youth group about putting wise boundaries in place, what those might look like practically, what happens if you cross them and about accountability. We also talk about how to have healthy relationships with both sexes and what is wise and unwise in that context. We must teach them one-on-one about hearing the voice of God, how to identify triggers that kick off unhealthy behaviours or thought patterns if they are struggling with singleness, how to manage relationships and how to pray with their partners. We need to tell them how to handle online dating, conflict and breaking up well. We must speak to them and teach them about these things before they find themselves in the moment. As we teach them to be wise, they can apply that wisdom to whatever situations they encounter, but this must be a part of their language way before it is part of their experience.

In summary then, for a young person to have positive experiences of dating and relationships, they should first be clear and confident in God's desired narrative for the whole of humanity in this area and their place within that. They should first know that they are loved and of value, no matter what their mistakes or experience may be. They should also understand that God loves and values others as much as he does them. A young person should be surrounded by adults of varying experience who are willing to form honest and meaningful relationships with them. That way, adults can give the young person time, and model what realistic, healthy relationships look like close-up. All whilst reminding them of the larger narrative they're a part of. Friendship groups should also be encouraged to be accountable to each other, to encourage and challenge each other and to form examples of healthy community and relationships. Finally, each young person should be equipped with the tools they need to make wise decisions and discern the voice of God outside of a reactive moment. Young people are then better able to understand their own story in such a way that they might model something of the nature of God in their relationships and communicate God to their friends.

The local church

If we, as the wider church, want to see dating and relationships working well for the young people in our care, then there are some really easy wins – things that aren't difficult to do, as we'll see in a moment. Let me ask you two questions. When you get in from a long day, what is the first thing you do when you walk into your home? Stop and think about it. You might take off your shoes, greet a pet, go and make a cup of tea. I just drop everything in the middle of the floor, much to my husband's frustration, but whatever it is that you do, I expect that you do it instinctively.

Now for my second question. What is the first thing you do when you walk into the home of someone that you don't know that well? Again, stop and think about it. For me, it's easy. When I get to someone's house, I will ring the bell or knock on the door. Once the door is open and I have said "Hi," I check to see if they are wearing shoes. I realise that to some people this might sound odd, but as I step into their home I want to understand their way of doing things, their culture. If they don't have shoes on I will take off my shoes because this may be a 'no shoes on the carpet' household. You then might go through to the living room and after a while I look to note if this is the kind of home where it's acceptable to put your feet up on the furniture. When having food, I would never be the first person to start eating because this might be a household where each meal begins with saying grace. If I want to form relationship then I watch and listen for that home or person's culture and I react accordingly. This should be our starting place.

If we, as a church, want to disciple and raise up a generation of young people that follow Jesus and learn how to have healthy relationships, we must first understand the culture they are living in and the narrative being spoken over their generation. Here are the quick wins. Begin by finding one or two young people in your church or community to have a conversation with and get to know them. Next, maybe you could ask them which artists they are listening to at the moment, then head to YouTube and check them out. Hear the lyrics that are being filtered into them each day. Once you have done this, go back and ask them what they are watching at the moment, log into Netflix and watch a series. Now, I can't promise you that this will be painless but I assure you that it is not a waste of time.

In our *Gen Z: Rethinking Culture* research, we asked the young people: "What are the top 3 things that make you feel bad about yourself?" Social media was in the top three for 67% of young people, while 41% said their friends, and 40% said YouTubers. These three things are also the ones they said they spend time on most regularly. When asked what the top three things are that they are most worried about, 54% of young people said school and exams, 33% said their appearance and 30% said "what other people think of me." Again, for the second two answers, social media will directly affect each of those issues.

We need to be watchful of the world young people inhabit in order to know how to speak. However, the most direct way of understanding a culture is by engaging with it. Intentionally seek out time when you can visit, volunteer with the youth group or provide support to young people. A healthy church needs people of all ages and relationship status engaging with the young people. In their book *Sticky Faith: Youth Worker Edition,* authors Powell, Griffin & Crawford share that in order to raise a healthy child, they need at least five significant adult relationships in their lives.[4] The youth team can't do that for each young person alone and so we must come together as a church family.

As a wider church, we need to be supporting families with young people as they have conversations around dating and relationships. Within the same *Gen Z* research, we asked the 11-18 year olds: "Who do you enjoy spending time with most?" Of course, friends from school came out top at 63% and family were a little further down the list at 9%, but only third in popularity. The real surprise was that a young person's boyfriend or girlfriend came at the bottom of the list at 1%, with the teenagers saying that they would rather be on their own! But, whilst family may not be seen as the primary source of fun, it does hold influence. Throughout the research, the theme of family kept coming up, as the primary influence on thought, the importance of making our families proud and of family being a positive influence. This points towards the importance of speaking to young people about relationships in the family home and demonstrating healthy relationships in that space. It may be that as a church, we even want to bring in external organisations to run training days to help us navigate having those conversations. This will speak volumes to our young people as they see healthy relationships modelled, and for those of us who aren't married or don't have children, we can model other varying stages of relationships. Being a healthy church family and teaching young people how to have honest and open discussions about relationships is key. But as the wider church, we must be helping families initiate this and find creative and natural ways in which to have those conversations. Maybe everyone in the church would benefit from creating a small, supportive group of people where we invite each other to ask questions about our friendships, singleness, dating, marriages etc. We all need encouragement and accountability.

As a church, we also need to be better at speaking into these areas corporately and sharing our narrative of purpose, wholeness, selflessness and covenantal love. Being able to give really practical advice and teaching alongside it is vital. Young people are being spoken to about singleness, sex, dating and relationships, make no mistake. But if we don't speak up, then they are only hearing one side of the story – the world's. In my church and through the church resources that I help to create at Youth for Christ, we ensure that sex and relationships is a regular feature on our teaching curriculum. One of our link churches, for example (signposted at the end of the chapter), has been addressing this issue with resources on a YouTube channel. Unless we are speaking regularly into this, both in a youth setting and a wider church setting, young people will not consider the church to have anything to say on this topic. Nor will they consider it somewhere that they feel they can discuss what matters to them – they will look for wisdom and role models elsewhere.

We cannot be fooled into thinking that this is only a 'young person's issue'. It is a whole church issue. Year after year, you will see young people become adults and these issues surrounding relationships, dating and sex will fill your entire church, unless we tackle them together and tackle them early. This open culture must be set top-down by church leaders and youth or children's leaders, who are willing to speak into whole-life discipleship. They need to be willing to put topics on the agenda that some may find a little awkward to talk about but are shared with a balance of honesty and sensitivity. It would also be helpful for us to know what we as a church believe about some big issues that young people are encountering regularly, either face-to-face or online. These include topics such as same-sex relationships and perspectives around the transgender community. Whilst this may not be what we speak about from the front on a Sunday morning, our silence doesn't help young people. If we don't speak biblical truth into that space then they will fill it with information from elsewhere.

As we, in the local church, begin to understand the world in which our young people live, and we have open and honest dialogue in the context of intimate, supportive and varied community, our hearts will begin to be softened. Communities of truth, grace and patience must be built where individuals feel safe enough to be vulnerable, where no question is out of bounds. These communities must be places where failure is acceptable and a range of people are there to get alongside you, pick you up and help you to move forwards. As a wider church family, we must extend empathy, patience and grace to young people (and adults) who are from different backgrounds to us. Young people may not know Jesus or have any idea what healthy and positive relationships look like. If we really want to impact the lives of young people in our communities, our churches might need to become messy places, full of young people who need a lot of healthy investment. Then the wider church family (not just the church leader or youth leadership) must gather round and demonstrate covenant relationship at its best.

In summary, for dating and discipleship to work well amongst young people in a local church setting, we need to intentionally make an effort to understand the world in which our teenagers live. The messages they are hearing and seeing on a daily basis are also things we must understand. We need to be equipping families through training and support, to be having conversations and modelling healthy relationships and identity at home. As part of a wider church family, we must be gathering around these young people and providing safe environments where they can hear about their identity and be encouraged not to conform to other narratives that they will hear. We also need to intentionally speak into areas of sex and relationships on a regular basis and make sure these are seen to be on the agenda for people of any age. We must be mindful of those who haven't had healthy relationships modelled to them or have suffered abuse at the hands of others. There must be space for this mindfulness in our church communities, and we've got to be prepared to be patient, extend love and model healthy relationships to those that have experienced them least.

The nation

What would it look like for a generation of young people across our nation to be doing dating and relationships well? That's an exciting question, but let's start with the detail and work outwards. I would be interested in knowing how many of our nation's church leaders feel suitably trained or equipped to speak to their churches on this topic? Are they prepared to give biblical teaching and practical advice not just to adults, or even unchurched adults, but to teenagers as well? Are they prepared and trained to work alongside young people and to understand current youth culture and where it is heading? We need to be equipping our leaders to do exactly that and to lead in these areas.

In practice, that might involve inviting experts on youth and sex and relationships into theological colleges to speak as a core part of the curriculum.

It may be offering ongoing training through church denominations, church networks and leadership conferences. For those of us who work with young people a little more regularly, plugging into something larger than ourselves can be really helpful. Journeying with young people on this can be exhausting, so wider conferences can be a great source of rest, encouragement and equipping. These conferences are brilliantly placed to regularly address issues of dating, relationships and sex and can be great opportunities to learn from others. It might also be helpful for conferences to be equipping church leaders on how to teach on this to a wider congregation. Teaching and support is key for families who are looking to disciple their children effectively in the home.

Nationally, family homes might be hubs for discipleship in this area. Parents should know how to have conversations about dating, relationships and sex, and understand their own influence over their children. Where young people are from homes that are relationally dysfunctional, they might find role models in the families of their friends. This might be their only opportunity to see a positive narrative lived out. Churches need to work hard to support families in their discipleship. If they do, unchurched families in the local community might find themselves at home in a church community, unable to resist the magnetic pull of a healthy, grace-filled narrative around the family home. There might be communities of adults modelling healthy singleness, dating and relationships and involved in communities with families, couples, other single people, older people and younger people alike.

From these communities, a younger generation might see God's narrative of relationship for humanity come to life. They could give a generation of young people confidence in their identity and the narrative that God is calling them to live out, however countercultural. This certainty in identity and intimacy with Jesus would lead to young people being grounded, having wise boundaries in place and the confidence to stick to them. But this narrative would not stop there.

Nationwide, there might be a generation who are able to connect to a healthy community that they could call family, no matter where they are at with God. We would see a movement of young people who can confidently articulate a better story, who aren't crippled by fear and insecurity. Their identity would not be fused to their relationship status but they would confidently live out their sexuality in a God-honouring way. This generation wouldn't be relationally crippled by their phones and tablets. They would know God's narrative for their lives and be able to tell and share it, both in person and digitally, so that a better picture might be drawn for their peers. They might be a generation whose desire for the authentic stretches beyond brand and advertising to authenticity and quality of relationship. They could be a generation who care about and protect each other because they are secure in themselves. Crucially, they could act as relational models for the generation below them, passing on the narrative of God from generation to generation. This is a wonderful vision for the future, but the future begins with the immediate and that starts with us.

Action points

- If you don't normally, go and spend some time with a young person. Check out your church's safeguarding policy but start to build a relationship with someone you don't know that well. See how they're getting on, maybe even find out what they're watching at the moment and check it out yourself.
- If you have a family, intentionally spend some time reflecting on what you are teaching your children about relationships. Maybe even include your children in these conversations.
- Have a think about the last time you were taught or lead teaching on singleness, dating, relationships and sex. Plan an opportunity to do this as a church and/or youth group and work out how regularly you would like this to be a part of your church's rhythm. If you are looking for youth resources, email us at resources@yfc.co.uk and we will happily send you a relationships teaching series to do with young people for free!
- Spend some time thinking through what you would describe as the relational narrative that you believe that God has called humanity to. Work out how to articulate that and think about how you might creatively share that with others.
- Finally, check out the resources in the list below. There's lots of stuff out there to help you out, so go and have a look around!

Resources

Teaching/course material
- Youth for Christ resources on sex and relationships: www.resourcesyfc. co.uk.
- Andy Stanley, *Guardrails* teaching series: www.northpoint.org/ guardrails-2017.
- LifeCentral Church, YouTube *Get real* teaching series.

- *Man-made*. A course for teenage boys. Christian Vision for Men: www.cvm.org.uk/manmade.

Training and resources
- Romance Academy: www.romanceacademy.org.
- acet UK: www.acet-uk.com.

Books/research
- *Gen Z: Rethinking Culture*. Youth For Christ (2017). www.yfc.co.uk/rethinkingculture.
- *A Guide to Growing Up: Honest conversations about puberty, sex and God*. Sarah Smith (2017). Lion Hudson.
- *Cherished: Boys, bodies and becoming a girl of gold*. Rachel Gardner (2009). IVP.
- *A Better Story: God, sex and human flourishing*. Glynn Harrison (2017). IVP.
- *The Dating Dilemma*. Rachel Gardner and André Adefope (2013). IVP.
- *Pure: Sex and relationships God's way*. Linda Marshall (2010). IVP.

Other websites
- www.moreprecious.co.uk
  Resources for young women, including on relationships.
- www.thenakedtruthproject.com
  Resources, programmes and support to help tackle the issue of pornography.
- www.xxxchurch.com/products
  XXXchurch accountability software to tackle use of porn. The website also lists courses and books for adult men and women.

"Youth work and discipleship around young people's dating and relationships: what would it look like if things were working well?"

Engage consultation vision grid

Foundations: A gender balanced church that teaches about healthy Christian singleness, dating and relationships for young people and adults – including all other aspects of discipleship and wellbeing

A young person	A local church	The national church
Spiritual, emotional and social foundations • A safe network of people in church to talk to, so experiencing emotional safety and grace-filled relationships, meaning that they are confident about talking to relevant people honestly. • Intimate relationships in the body of Christ with people of various ages, and through participation. • Positive sense of self, and self-identity whether single or in a relationship. • Strong sense of belonging and healthy friendships of both sexes. • Feeling a complete and valuable person whether single or in a relationship. • Healthy understanding of self-control and how it can be freeing, and why it's a good thing. • Intentionally discipled by healthy single adults, including seeing singleness as a positive option.	**Spiritual, emotional and social foundations** • A key church leader who facilitates a discipleship culture that speaks to every area of people's lives, including around dating/relationships. • Intentionally facilitating a safe network of people in church to talk to – need at least five key relationships with people of different ages/stages (*Sticky Faith* research, US). • Intentionally facilitating a culture of honesty, vulnerability, emotional safety. • Church leaders are freed up to do the above by a mobilised congregation. • Youth are being taught to disciple younger youth. • Empower young people to have a voice in church, so they are involved and sharing input, leadership, thoughts, testimonies. • Frequent opportunities for all congregation members to interact with, engage with, and get to know young people, e.g. visiting the youth group.	• The national church has, and is articulating a clear and inspiring vision for relationships/sex. • Sacrificial giving to organisations that are working to support church leaders/young people. • Every church in the country is linked with and is supported by a relevant expert. **Church leaders initial training** • Theological colleges teach future church leaders to be confident to teach on these issues. • They invite RSE experts to speak to ordinands as a core part of the curriculum. **Church leader ongoing training/resourcing** • Training for clergy from acet UK, Romance Academy and others. • Church leadership conferences/networks intentionally train church leaders on how to implement culture and solutions.

A young person	A local church	The national church
• Knowing that a romantic, intimate relationship is not the answer to loneliness. • Confidently handling growing self-awareness, self-acceptance and sexuality. **Dating & Relationships** • Able to think theologically about dating/relationships/sex and for that to affect conversations, feelings, motivation, behaviour. • Knowing there isn't a set way of doing things, or a silver bullet, but their imagination has been captured by an alternative vision of teenage relationships. • Able to talk about why Jesus' way is better. • Understanding healthy boundaries, why these are helpful, and how to put them in place, including around abstinence. • Realistic understanding of healthy Christian dating, relationships and marriage. • Being selfless in dating/relationships. • Flourishing in dating relationships through recognising each other's gifts. • Intentionally discipled by very honest, healthy married couples (ideally would be parents). • Around married adults who are continuing to grow in faith and model this. • Free from taking on and acting out adult anxieties around relationships.	• Teaching transparently talks about real life. • All teaching has practical, positive next steps – a proactive focus. • All church leaders have mentoring/discipleship support from someone who isn't their line manager, who addresses issues around dating/relationships/sex/marriage. **Dating & Relationships** • Training for adults about how to talk about issues around dating/relationships from a biblical perspective, so they are confident to do this. • Frequent teaching from the front stage about relationships/dating/sex so it's obvious that the issues are addressed, intentionally planned and integrated into teaching. • Adults clearly live out healthy, honest Christian marriage. • Adults of all ages are modelling discussion around dating/relationship issues. • Adults intentionally help young people to think through the nitty gritty of theological teaching around dating/relationships.	• All denominational leaders and national network leaders are aware of resources that are available to support them. **Conferences** • National conferences all have seminars for young people addressing issues around relationships, masturbation, dating, sex, same-sex attraction. • Panel Q & A. • Seminars for church leaders around how to teach issues around the above, based on biblical, theological teaching. • Seminars for parents on how to address the above.

A young person	A local church	The national church
• Free from the sexual prosperity gospel. • Free from addictive behaviours. • Free from legalism. • Free from society's obsession about relationships.		

CHAPTER 12

Next steps

Nathan Blackaby

Congratulations, we made it together to the end of the book and it is fair to say we've covered quite a lot!

We've shown the reasons why we need more men in church to address the gender imbalance, for the sake of men, women, children and young people. And we've looked at how we can do this.

We have explained the intergenerational crisis effect that the decreased number of men and lack of relevant teaching is having on healthy Christian singleness, dating and relationships, marriage and parenting. We have also shared solutions to address the problems.

So, in the light of what we now know, it feels right to come in to land by reflecting again on The Great Commission. Jesus said, "Go and make disciples of all nations, baptising them in the name of the Father and of the Son and of the Holy Spirit, and teaching them to obey everything I have commanded you" (Matthew 28:19-20). Can you imagine if the church across our nation was baptising an increasing and equal number of men and women, boys and girls? That we could see, in our time, the church landscape change in this way for God's glory? We can significantly impact how effective we are in making disciples and in teaching them to follow Jesus dynamically. This will also greatly impact on the issues of singleness, dating, relationships and marriage for each generation.

Paula Pridham noted in her chapter on parenting that change isn't going to be achieved by taking on another project or programme, and she is right. That's not an effective approach, and it's not what most people want anyway. What we need is systemic culture change, and we have shown what this can look like for the national church, local churches and individuals. 'What it would look like if things were working well' is that the issues we've covered will be 'main stage issues' (both literally and metaphorically) not just 'side issues'.

Our hope is that this book will be a spark in your church community that ignites vision, passion and action. Here are a few next steps that we'd recommend:

1. Share a copy of this book with your leadership or staff team and pray together about what you've read.

2. Use the key actions at the end of the chapters and the consultation vision grids to create a specific action plan. The vision grids and a simple planning template can be downloaded from our website www.engage-mcmp.org.uk.

3. Put things in place, then if you have stories about how the subjects covered in this book are working well in your church community, we'd love to collect and share them, so do use our website to get in touch.

Let's create a church culture that engages both men and women effectively, where safe and supportive friendships mean 'it's OK to talk about things in depth,' where it's normal for the whole church to have regular teaching on all the issues we've discussed, and where Christian marriage is possible. In other words, to conclude with our vision again, let's make:

> *"singleness or marriage a genuine choice for all Christian women and men, through a church which is gender balanced and teaches about healthy Christian singleness, dating and marriage."*

Endnotes

CHAPTER 1
What is The Engage Network and why is it needed?

1   YouGov (2014). *Men practising Christian worship.* Christian Vision for Men and Single Christians Ltd.

2   Pullinger, D.J. (2014). *Singleness in the UK Church.* https://www.singlefriendlychurch.co.uk (accessed May 5, 2018).

3   Evangelical Alliance (2012). *How's the family?*

4   http://www.engage-mcmp.org.uk/about1-c17u (accessed May 5, 2018).

5   YouGov (2014). *Men practising Christian worship.* Christian Vision for Men and Single Christians Ltd.

6   Evangelical Alliance (2012). *How's the family?*

7   YouGov (2014). *Men practising Christian worship.* Christian Vision for Men and Single Christians Ltd.

8   Pullinger, D.J. (2014). *Singleness in the UK Church.* https://www.singlefriendlychurch.co.uk (accessed May 5, 2018).

9   Evangelical Alliance (2012). *How's the family?*

10   Clarke, A. (2018). *How do single Christian women feel about not having children?* The Engage Network. http://www.engage-mcmp.org.uk (accessed 1 September, 2018).

11   https://gateway-women.com (accessed May 5, 2018).

12   http://saltwaterandhoney.org (accessed May 5, 2018).

13   Pullinger, D.J. (2014). *Singleness in the UK Church.* https://www.singlefriendlychurch.com/gender-imbalance-in-church/gender-imbalance-in-church (accessed May 5, 2018).

14   Verbi, S. (2017). http://www.eidoresearch.com/wp-content/uploads/2018/03/Not-enough-men-White-Paper.pdf. See also https://www.premierchristianity.com/Blog/70-per-cent-of-single-women-want-Christian-men-to-man-upand-ask-them-out (accessed May 5, 2018).

15   Personal communication.

16   Pullinger, D.J. (2014). *Singleness in the UK Church.* https://www.singlefriendlychurch.co.uk (accessed May 5, 2018).

17   Harris, J. (1997). *I Kissed Dating Goodbye.* Multnomah Books.

18   Evangelical Alliance (2012). *How's the family?*

19   Evangelical Alliance (2012). *How's the family?*

20   Bronfenbrenner, U. (1979). *The Ecology of Human Development:*

Experiments by nature and design. Cambridge, MA: Harvard University Press. Also, Bronfenbrenner, U. (2005). *Making Human Beings Human: Bioecological perspectives on human development.* Sage.

CHAPTER 2
Theological foundations

1   English Benedictine Congregation. *The Oblate Life* (Kindle Locations 4983-4984). Hymns Ancient and Modern Ltd. Kindle Edition.

CHAPTER 3
The wider context: current marriage trends

1   Genesis 2:18.

2   This data comes from my own analysis of Table 2 in Office for National Statistics (2017) *Population estimates by marital status and living arrangements, England and Wales,* 2002-2016.

3   1 Corinthians 7:8 and 7:38.

4   DeRose, L., Lyons-Amos, M., Wilcox, W., & Huarcaya, G. (2017). *The cohabitation go-round: Cohabitation and family instability across the globe.* New York: Social Trends Institute.

5   Benson, H. (2013, May). *The myth of "long-term stable relationships" outside marriage.* Cambridge: Marriage Foundation.

6   Benson, H. (2015). *Get married BEFORE you have children.* Cambridge: Marriage Foundation.

7   Benson, H. (2013, February). *What is the divorce rate?* Cambridge: Marriage Foundation.

8   Matthew 19:8.

9   Benson, H. & McKay, S. (2015). *The marriage gap: The rich get married and stay together; the poor don't.* Cambridge: Marriage Foundation.

10   Benson, H. (2015). *Get married BEFORE you have children.* Cambridge: Marriage Foundation.

11   Office for National Statistics (various) Birth summary tables. Also in Ermisch, J. (2006). *An economic history of bastardy in England and Wales,* ISER Working Paper, 2006-15.

12   Benson, H. & McKay, S. (2017). *Family breakdown and teenage mental health.* Cambridge: Marriage Foundation.

13   This study is the foundation stone for modern commitment theory.

It's well worth reading the whole thing. Search online and you will find a pdf download. Stanley, S., Kline, G., & Markman, H. (2006). Sliding vs. deciding: Inertia and the premarital cohabitation effect. *Family Relations,* 55, 499-509.

14   Genesis 2:24.

15   Stanley, S., Kline, G., & Markman, H. (2006) Sliding vs. deciding: Inertia and the premarital cohabitation effect. *Family Relations,* 55, 499-509.

16   Benson, H. (2010). *Family breakdown in the UK: it's NOT about divorce.* Bristol Community Family Trust, and Benson, H. (2013). *Unmarried parents account for one fifth of couples but half of all family breakdown.* Cambridge: Marriage Foundation.

17   Benson, H. (2015). *Happy families: Men behaving better.* Cambridge: Marriage Foundation.

18   Benson, H. (2015). *Get married BEFORE you have children.* Cambridge: Marriage Foundation.

19   Benson, H. & McKay, S. (2016). *Does religion help couples stay together?* Cambridge: Marriage Foundation.

20   Studies have shown mixed results for whether living together before marriage is always bad news. Galena Rhoades (writing in her maiden name Kline) and Scott Stanley cleared up a lot of the issues with their 2004 study "Timing is everything". Kline, G. H., Stanley, S. M., Markman, H. J., Olmos-Gallo, P. A., St. Peters, M., Whitton, S. W. & Prado, L. M. (2004). Timing is everything: Pre-engagement cohabitation and increased risk for poor marital outcomes. *Journal of Family Psychology,* 18(2), 311–318. They looked at living together before engagement. This makes more sense as it's when the decision to commit happens. They found that men who cohabited before engagement had consistently lower quality marriages over the first five years compared to men who moved in afterwards. There were no differences for women. This study has since been replicated with other samples and provides strong evidence that men's commitment in particular is based on decision.

21   Rhoades, G., Stanley, S., & Markman, H. (2009). Couples' reasons for cohabitation: Associations with individual wellbeing and relationship quality. *Journal of Family Issues,* 30, 233-258.

22   For example, a 2017 survey by the Centre for Social Justice showed eight out of ten 14-17 year olds say they want to get married later in life. Only 4% say it's not part of their plans. 78% say a lasting adult relationship is as important or more important than their career plan. Family Stability Network & Centre for Social Justice (2018),

Relationships and Sex Education.
https://www.centreforsocialjustice.org.uk/core/wpcontent/
uploads/2018/02/Survation_Report.pdf (accessed 12 May, 2018).

23   Benson, H. (2014). *Who's still getting married these days?* Cambridge: Marriage Foundation.

24   Whitton, S., Stanley, S., & Markman, H. (2007). If I help my partner, will it hurt me? Perceptions of sacrifice in romantic relationships. *Journal of Social and Clinical Psychology, 26,* 64.

25   Rhoades, G., Stanley, S., & Markman, H. (2009). The pre-engagement cohabitation effect: A replication and extension of previous findings. *Journal of Family Psychology, 23,* 107.

26   Proverbs 21:9, 21:19 and 25:24.

CHAPTER 4
Men and church: the 'What?' questions

1   Office for National Statistics website 1991-2016, quoted in Brierley, P. (2017). *UK Church Statistics No 3: 2018 Edition.* Tonbridge: ADBC Publishers. Figures rounded to the nearest whole number.

2   https://www.ons.gov.uk/census/2011census (accessed April 28, 2018).

3   Aisthorpe, S. (2016). *The Invisible Church: Learning from the experiences of churchless Christians.* Edinburgh: St Andrew Press.

4   Brierley, P. (2006). *Pulling Out of the Nosedive.* London: Christian Research.

5   Brierley, P. (2017). *UK Church Statistics No 3: 2018 Edition.* Tonbridge: ADBC Publishers.

6   www.brin.ac.uk/2014/changes-in-attendance-at-religious-services-in-britain (accessed April 28, 2018).

7   http://www.pewforum.org/2016/03/22/the-gender-gap-in-religion-around-the-world (accessed April 28, 2018).

8   https://www.ons.gov.uk/census/2011census (accessed April 28, 2018).

9   http://www.scotlandscensus.gov.uk (accessed April 28, 2018).

10   https://www.ons.gov.uk/census/2011census (accessed April 28, 2018).

11   Brierley, P. (2014). *UK Church Statistics No 2: 2010-2020.* Tonbridge: ADBC Publishers.

12   Brierley, P. (2017). *UK Church Statistics No 3: 2018 Edition.* Tonbridge: ADBC Publishers.

13   Brierley, P. (2017). *UK Church Statistics No 3: 2018 Edition.* Tonbridge: ADBC Publishers.

14 Farthing, J. A. (2007). *Churchgoing in the UK*. Tearfund.

15 YouGov (2014). *Men practising Christian worship*. Christian Vision for Men and Single Christians Ltd.

16 https://www.ons.gov.uk/census/2011census (accessed April 28, 2018).

17 http://www.scotlandscensus.gov.uk (accessed April 28, 2018).

18 https://www.ons.gov.uk/census/2001censusandearlier (accessed April 28, 2018).

19 Brierley, P. (2017). *UK Church Statistics No 3: 2018 Edition*. Tonbridge: ADBC Publishers.

20 Brierley, P. (2017). *Growth Amidst Decline*. Tonbridge: ADBC Publishers.

21 England data from Brierley, P. (2017). *UK Church Statistics No 3: 2018 Edition*. Tonbridge: ADBC Publishers. Scotland data from Brierley, P. (2017). *Growth Amidst Decline*. Tonbridge: ADBC Publishers.

22 Brierley, P. (2017). *UK Church Statistics No 3: 2018 Edition*. Tonbridge: ADBC Publishers.

23 Brierley, P. (2017). *Growth Amidst Decline*. Tonbridge: ADBC Publishers.

24 YouGov (2014). *Men practising Christian worship*. Christian Vision for Men and Single Christians Ltd.

25 Evangelical Alliance (2012). *How's the family?*

26 YouGov (2014). *Men practising Christian worship*. Christian Vision for Men and Single Christians Ltd.

27 Brierley, P. (2006). *UK Christian Handbook*. Religious Trends 6. Christian Research.

28 Brierley, P. (2017). *UK Church Statistics No 3: 2018 Edition*. Tonbridge: ADBC Publishers.

29 Brierley, P. (2006). *Pulling Out of the Nosedive*. London: Christian Research.

30 English Church Census, 2005. Brierley Consultancy Report (September 2017).

31 English Church Census 2005 data in Brierley, P. (2017). *UK Church Statistics No 3: 2018 Edition*. Tonbridge: ADBC Publishers.

32 English Church Census 2005 data in Brierley, P. (2006). *Pulling Out of the Nosedive*. London: Christian Research.

33 Brierley, P. (2017). *UK Church Statistics No 3: 2018 Edition*. Tonbridge: ADBC Publishers.

34 Brierley, P. (2017). *UK Church Statistics No 3: 2018 Edition*. Tonbridge: ADBC Publishers.

35 English Church Census data in Brierley, P. (2006). *UK Christian*

Handbook. Religious Trends 6. Christian Research.

36 Not 0% because this figure includes not just Roman Catholics, but also some who are other denominations, such as Anglican Catholics and Methodists.

37 Brierley, P. (2017). *UK Church Statistics No 3: 2018 Edition.* Tonbridge: ADBC Publishers.

38 English Church Census data 2005 in Brierley, P. (2006). *UK Christian Handbook. Religious Trends 6.* Christian Research.

CHAPTER 5
Men and church: the 'Why?' questions

1 http://www.engage-mcmp.org.uk/about1-cxda (accessed April 28, 2018).

2 Jarrett, C. (2015). *Great Myths of the Brain.* Chichester: Wiley-Blackwell.

3 Gray, J. (2013). *Why Mars and Venus Collide: Improve your relationships by understanding how men and women cope differently with stress.* London: Harper Element.

4 Honey, P. and Mumford, A. (1992), *The Manual of Learning Styles.* Maidenhead. Peter Honey Publications.

5 http://dera.ioe.ac.uk/14118/1/learning_styles.pdf (accessed April 28, 2018). Also https://digest.bps.org.uk/2018/04/03/another-nail-in-the-coffin-for-learning-styles-students-did-not-benefit-from-studying-according-to-their-supposed-learning-style (accessed April 28, 2018).

6 Gray, J. (2015). *Men are from Mars, Women are from Venus.* London: HarperThorsons.

7 Byrnes, J., Miller, D., & Schafer, W. (1999). Gender differences in risk taking: A meta-analysis. *Psychological Bulletin,* 125(3), 367-383.

8 Nelson, J. (2014). The power of stereotyping and confirmation bias to overwhelm accurate assessment: the case of economics, gender, and risk aversion. *Journal of Economic Methodology,* 21(3), 211-231.

9 Su, R., Rounds, J., & Armstrong, P. (2009). Men and things, women and people: A meta-analysis of sex differences in interests. *Psychological Bulletin,* 135(6), 859-884.

10 Schwartz, S. H., & Rubel, T. (2005). Sex differences in value priorities: Cross-cultural and multimethod studies. *Journal of Personality and Social Psychology,* 89(6), 1010-1028.

11 Petersen, J. L., & Hyde, J. S. (2010). A meta-analytic review of research

on gender differences in sexuality, 1993–2007. *Psychological Bulletin,* 136(1), 21-38.

12 Archer, J. (2004). Sex differences in aggression in real-world settings: A meta-analytic review. *Review of General Psychology,* 8(4), 291-322.

13 Hyde, J. S. (2005). *The gender similarities hypothesis.* American Psychologist, 60(6), 581-592. Also Hyde, J. S. (2014). Gender similarities and differences. *Annual Review of Psychology,* 65, 373-398.

14 Fine, C. (2011). *Delusions of Gender: The real science behind sex differences.* London. Icon Books. Page 150.

15 Fine, C. (2011). *Delusions of Gender: The real science behind sex differences.* London. Icon Books. Page 32.

16 Lucado, M. (2012). *Just like Jesus.* Thomas Nelson.

17 Dweck, C. S. (2012). *Mindset: The new psychology of success.* Constable & Robinson Limited.

18 Dweck, C. S. (2000). *Self Theories: Their role in motivation, personality, and development.* New York, NY: Taylor & Francis Group.

19 Hattie, J. (2009). *Visible Learning: A synthesis of over 800 meta-analyses relating to achievement.* Abingdon. Routledge. Page 56.

20 Seager, M., Barry, J. & Liddon, L. (June 2018). Overlapping interests in a complex and ambiguous world. *The Psychologist.* The British Psychological Society.

21 YouGov (2014). *Men practising Christian worship.* Christian Vision for Men and Single Christians Ltd.

22 Costa P. T., Terracciano, A. & McCrae, R. R. (2001). Gender differences in personality traits across cultures: Robust and surprising findings. *Journal of Personality and Social Psychology,* 81(2), 322-331.

23 Vianello, M., Schnabel, K., Sriram, N. & Nosek, B. (2013) Gender differences in implicit and explicit personality traits. *Personality and Individual Differences,* 55(8), 994-999.

24 http://www.bbc.com/future/story/20161011-do-men-and-women-really-have-different-personalities (accessed April 28, 2018).

25 Penny, G., Francis, L.J. & Robbins, M. (2015). Why are women more religious than men? Testing the explanatory power of personality theory among undergraduate students in Wales. *Mental Health, Religion & Culture,* 18(6), 492-502. Permanent Warwick Research Archive Portal URL: http://wrap.warwick.ac.uk/81722 (accessed April 28, 2018).

26 Robbins, M., Littler, K. & Francis, L. J., (2001). The personality characteristics of Anglican clergymen and clergywomen: The search for sex differences. *Pastoral Psychology,* 60(6), 877.

27 Robbins, M., Francis, L. J. & Kay, W. K. (2001). The personality characteristics of Methodist ministers: Feminine men and masculine women? *Journal for the Scientific Study of Religion,* 40(1), 123-128.

28 https://www.churchtimes.co.uk/articles/2016/8-july/features/features/planting-a-range-of-personalities (accessed April 28, 2018).

29 https://en.wikipedia.org/wiki/Myers%E2%80%93Briggs_Type_Indicator and https://www.psychologytoday.com/us/blog/cutting-edge-leadership/201402/the-truth-about-myers-briggs-types (accessed April 28, 2018).

30 Brierley, P. (2017). *UK Church Statistics No 3: 2018 Edition.* Tonbridge: ADBC Publishers.

31 http://www.ministrydevelopment.org.uk/UserFiles/File/Research_Consult/Living_Ministry_Panel_Survey_Wave_1_Report.pdf (accessed April 28, 2018).

32 Murrow, D. (2011). *Why Men Hate Going to Church.* Nashville. Thomas Nelson.

33 Pullinger, D.J. (2014). *Singleness in the UK Church.* https://www.singlefriendlychurch.co.uk (accessed April 28, 2018).

34 Peter Brierley, personal communication, May 2018.

CHAPTER 6
Men's ministry: what would it look like if things were working well in the church?

1 For example, YouGov (2014). *Men practising Christian worship.* Christian Vision for Men and Single Christians Ltd. https://www.cvm.org.uk/downloads/YouGov-CVMreport.pdf (accessed May 28, 2018).

2 The '10/40 Window' is a term coined by Christian missionary strategist and Partners International CEO Luis Bush in 1990 to refer to those regions of the eastern hemisphere, plus the European and African part of the western hemisphere, located between 10 and 40 degrees north of the equator.

CHAPTER 7

Singleness: what would it look like if things were working well in the church?

1   YouGov (2014). *The numbers of single adults practising Christian worship.* Christian Vision for Men and Single Christians Ltd. https://www.singlefriendlychurch.com/research/yougov (accessed April 28, 2018).

2   Evangelical Alliance (2012). *How's the Family?*

3   2011 Population Census for England and Wales. Office for National Statistics. http://webarchive.nationalarchives.gov.uk/20160105222341/ http://www.ons.gov.uk/ons/rel/census/2011-censusanalysis/how-have-living-arrangements-and-marital-status-in-england-and-wales-changed-since-2001-/summary.html (accessed April 28, 2018).

4   John 10:10b, Jesus says, "I have come that they may have life, and have it to the full."

5   1 Corinthians 6:19.

6   https://www.singlefriendlychurch.com/for-churches/singleness-in-the-church-an-introduction-for-leaders (accessed April 28, 2018).

7   Kate Wharton (2013). *Single Minded: Being single, whole, and living life to the full.* Monarch.

8   Genesis 2:18.

9   Matthew 22:30.

10   1 Corinthians 7:7.

11   Al Hsu (1997). *The Single Issue.* IVP.

12   https://www.singlefriendlychurch.com/for-churches/singleness-in-the-church-an-introduction-for-leaders (accessed April 28, 2018).

13   http://www.eauk.org/culture/statistics/how-lonely-are-we.cfm (accessed April 28, 2018).

CHAPTER 8

Dating and relationships: what would it look like if things were working well in the church?

1   Pullinger, D.J. (2014). *Singleness in the UK Church.* https://www.singlefriendlychurch.co.uk (accessed April 28, 2018).

2   Keller, T. with Keller, K. (2011). *The Meaning of Marriage.* Hodder and Stoughton.

3   Cloud, H. & Townsend, J. (2017). *Boundaries.* Zondervan.

4   For more on this, see https://blog.christianconnection.com/give-up-

the-ghost (accessed May 28, 2018).

5   Van Abbema, A. (2017). *Dare to Date*. SPCK.

6   https://blog.christianconnection.com/the-science-of-online-dating (accessed May 28, 2018).

7   http://www.engage-mcmp.org.uk/adultschristian-dating--relationships (accessed May 28, 2018).

8   Cloud, H. & Townsend, J. (2009). *Boundaries in Dating: How healthy choices grow healthy relationships*. Zondervan.

9   Lee, N. & Lee, S. (2017). *The Marriage Preparation Course*. Alpha International.

10   Gardner, R. & Adefope, A. (2013). *The Dating Dilemma: A romance revolution*. IVP.

11   Pullinger, D.J. (2014). *Singleness in the UK Church*. https://www.singlefriendlychurch.co.uk (accessed April 28, 2018).

CHAPTER 9
Marriage: what would it look like if things were working well in the church?

1   Bonhoeffer, D. (2017). *Letters and Papers from Prison*. SCM Press.

2   Benson, H. (2010). *Let's Stick Together: The relationship book for new parents*. Lion Hudson.

CHAPTER 10
Parenting and discipleship around young people's dating and relationships: what would it look like if things were working well in the church?

1   Girlguiding (2017). *Annual Girls' Attitude Survey*.

2   NSPCC (2016). *"I wasn't sure it was normal to watch it": The impact of online pornography on the values, attitudes, beliefs and behaviours of children*.

3   Family Stability Network & Centre for Social Justice (2018). *Relationships and Sex Education*.

4   Youth for Christ (2017). *Gen Z: Rethinking Culture*. https://yfc.co.uk/rethinkingculture (accessed May 26, 2018).

5   Young Minds. A leading charity providing mental health information and support for young people, parents and professionals.

https://www.youngminds.org.uk (accessed May 26, 2018).

6   https://www.careforthefamily.org.uk/family-life/parent-support/ everyday-parenting/setting-the-boundaries (accessed May 28, 2018).

7   Chapman, G. & Campbell, R. (2016). *The Five Love Languages of Children.* Moody Publishing.

CHAPTER 11
Youth work and discipleship around young people's dating and relationships: what would it look like if things were working well in the church?

1   Youth for Christ (2017) *Gen Z: Rethinking Culture.* https://yfc.co.uk/rethinkingculture (accessed May 26, 2018).

2   For example, Weinschenk, S. (2012). *Why we're all addicted to texts, Twitter and Google.* https://www.psychologytoday.com/intl/blog/ brain-wise/201209/why-were-all-addicted-texts-twitter-and-google (accessed May 26, 2018).

3   Stonard, K., Bowen, E., Lawrence, T. and Price, S. A. (2014). The relevance of technology to the nature, prevalence and impact of adolescent dating violence and abuse: A research synthesis. *Aggression and Violent Behavior,* 19 (4), 390–417. http://www.safelives.org.uk/practice_blog/violence-young-people%E2%80%99s-relationships-%E2%80%93-reflections-two-serious-case-reviews (accessed May 26, 2018).

4   Powell, K., Griffin, B. & Crawford, C. (2011). *Sticky Faith: Youth worker edition.* Zondervan.

34033889R00125

Printed in Poland
by Amazon Fulfillment
Poland Sp. z o.o., Wrocław